The
Breaking Point Killing

And Other True Cases of Murder and Malice

"Dr. Wyatt does an outstanding job of seamlessly working in psychological fundamentals into the legal process in this book. He details how psychologists can play a crucial role in forensic cases and what exactly forensic psychology entails. Very interesting cases, assessment procedures, and outcomes."
— *Dr. Jennifer Tiano,*
Assistant Professor of Psychology, Marshall University.

"In *The Breaking Point Killing*, Dr. Joseph Wyatt, a forensic psychologist, takes the reader through cases he has worked on. With him, we experience the severing of once affectionate bonds connecting people; friendship, even love, turned to hatred, affection ending in murder.

"A talented writer, Wyatt's perspective gives us a dramatic and first-hand view of the underside of lives gone awry, turned inside out; lives ended in violence. Through courtroom testimony and forensic clinical opinions, Wyatt helps us understand how these tragedies occurred; why they happened.

"*The Breaking Point Killing* is a book of high intensity human tragedies. While alternately wrenching, fascinating and enjoyable, it is one I recommend the reader sample slowly."
—*Dwight Harshbarger,*
Author of Witness at Hawks Nest *and* Valley at Risk

"This book offers an authentic, close-up view of intriguing cases wherein the art and science of forensic psychology was brought to bear. I hope you will find, as I did, that the text is evocative, educational and even inspiring."
—*from the foreword by Bob Wilkinson,*
Public Defender, Cabell County, West Virginia

The
Breaking Point Killing

And Other True Cases of Murder and Malice

W. Joseph Wyatt

MID-ATLANTIC HIGHLANDS

Mid-Atlantic Highlands
Huntington, West Virginia

Cover Design: Erika Bias
Cover Image: Debbie Richardson
Interior Design: Erika Bias
Interior Art: Debbie Richardson
Interior Photos: As credited.
If uncredited, photos by W. Joseph Wyatt.

10 9 8 7 6 5 4 3 2 1

Printed in the United States of America

ISBN: 978-0-986-4267-3-5

Mid-Atlantic Highlands
An Imprint of Publishers Place, Inc.
821 Fourth Avenue, Suite 201
Huntington, West Virginia 25701

www.publishersplace.org

This book is dedicated to my son, Sgt. Daniel Wyatt of the St. Albans, West Virginia Police Department. It also is dedicated to all the other law enforcement officers, emergency workers, mental health professionals, attorneys judges and magistrates who deal thoughtfully, humanely and forthrightly with the mentally and behaviorally disordered.

A note on sources:

All information in this book is within the public domain, taken from Dr. Wyatt's written reports that were submitted as exhibits to the courts, from his testimony, from statements by others in court, media accounts and other public documents.

CONTENTS

ONE: The Breaking Point Killing   1

TWO: He Murdered His Gay Partner   20

THREE: Caught Faking a Mental Illness   43

FOUR: Death in Room 127   60

FIVE: The Kid Who Killed With a Sword   74

SIX: She Killed Her Abuser   87

SEVEN: He Hammered His Stepfather to Death   105

EIGHT: Counterfeit Kingpin, Or King of Pranks?   120

NINE: Wrongly Convicted   134

TEN: A Case of Child Sexual Abuse?   150

ELEVEN: What Must We Do When a Child

     Alleges Sexual Abuse?   171

TWELVE: A Flash of Cash   184

THIRTEEN: More About Forensic Psychology   201

REFERENCES   217

INDEX   218

Foreword

WITH TWO MILLION INDIVIDUALS incarcerated in the United States —almost all of whom have family and friends "on the outside—plus the communities of police officers, social workers, officers of the courts and anyone who has ever served on jury duty, the readership for *The Breaking Point Killing* would seem vast.

What readers will get here is the perspective of a highly qualified forensic psychologist who has served as an expert witness in well over 200 criminal cases. Eleven of those cases are highlighted in Dr. Joe Wyatt's book, mostly high-profile homicides.

The book covers many complex and controversial aspects of criminal justice, among them: What happens to someone who commits a crime but who has been suffering from a mental illness? How should the court establish whether the individual was under the influence of the mental illness at the time the crime was committed?

Both the prosecution and the defense are prone to hire expert witnesses to help prove their case. Thus, oftentimes, expert witness testimonies will conflict.

In this regard it's important to understand that the best expert witnesses struggle to maintain their independence--their impartiality--even though one side of the case is footing their bill.

Dr. Joe Wyatt has been outstanding as to his quest for objectivity, in my experience of working with him over 20 years of cases. As I like to put it, he starts with "a clean slate." He does not begin with a presumption of either innocence or guilt, or with an understanding of the side that has hired him as having the strongest case.

Whereas he may be paid by the Defense (and occasionally by the Prosecution) Wyatt always works only to see that the hard facts are privileged and that "the truth," as so often is alleged, does not become "the first casualty in the courtroom."

Expert witnesses most often break down into one of two kinds: One kind researches case histories, the legal literature, and comes into the courtroom armed with references to precedents and psychological and medical theories. Frequently this kind of witness considers himself (or herself) to be "part of the team" of whichever side hired them.

The second kind of expert witness puts in the hard work of examining all the facts available in the case, as well as reviewing the legal literature, and interviewing the defendant, the victim(s) and any others associated with the episode to determine just where the chips actually fall. That's the kind Joe Wyatt is.

I once had a bench trial involving charges of child sexual abuse, with Dr. Wyatt as my expert witness. After describing the literature used by professional psychologists and then applying it to his interview with the child, Dr. Wyatt said he thought the account the child gave was believable. An opposing witness was called by the prosecution, and testified that in his estimation the interviews Wyatt had conducted were not valid. However he based his analysis purely upon articles he himself had written, not recognized by his peers in foresenic psychology.

Wyatt's opinion was admitted by the court, the other witness's testimony was rejected.

It is not uncommon for people facing charges of criminal violence to have a history of mental health treatment. In those cases where a recognized mental condition is suspected, the court invites expert testimony from both the prosecution and the defense. The experts' analysis, credentials and past testimony are then used by both sides to argue either for or against a finding of mitigation based on mental illness.

Experts must be able to translate specialized phrases and jargon used in their field into terms a jury can understand. Those experts must also be able to withstand challenges to their presentations during cross examination.

I recall well a 1994 case my office had with Dr. Wyatt as our expert witness. The case involved a murder charge against a woman named Betty Riley. In this case Ms. Riley's boyfriend had extensive histories of mental health issues. The two had met in a treatment facility and had decided to move in together after their discharge.

Betty Riley ended up killing her boyfriend after alleging she had suffered serial episodes of physical abuse. At that time the State of West Virginia had recognized battered woman's syndrome as a plausible defense, but there were few precedents for how to define it or how a court was supposed to take it into account.

Dr. Wyatt's testimony became the centerpiece of our defense, and, thanks to his expertise, the public defender's office prevailed against the prosecutors and won exoneration of Ms. Riley.

This book offers an authentic, close-up view of intriguing cases wherein the art and science of forensic psychology was brought to bear. I hope you will find, as I did, that the text is evocative, educational and even inspiring.

Bob Wilkinson
    Chief Public Defender
    Cabell County Public Defender Services
    Huntington, WV
    July 4, 2015

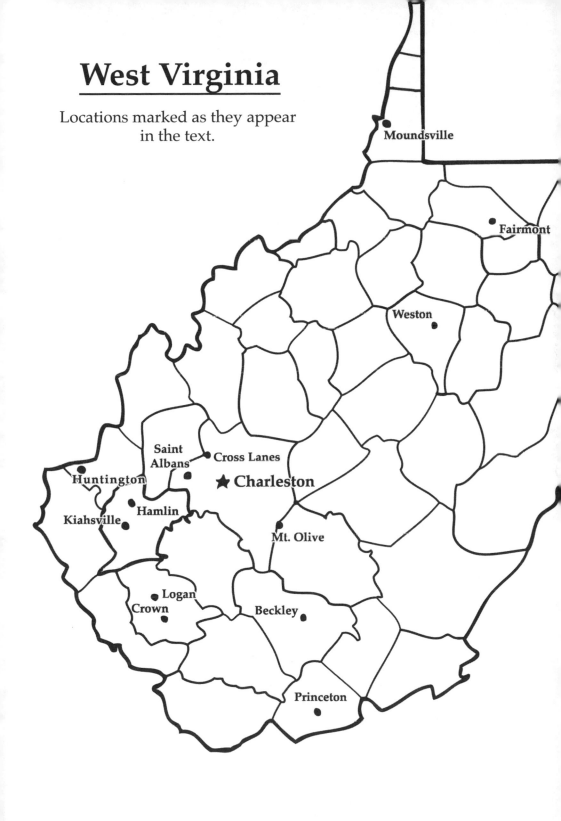

West Virginia

Locations marked as they appear in the text.

Moundsville

Fairmont

Weston

Saint Albans

Cross Lanes

★ Charleston

Huntington

Hamlin

Kiahsville

Mt. Olive

Logan

Crown

Beckley

Princeton

One
The Breaking Point Killing

A N ANTSY EARL MCCOY STEPPED into his front yard,
paused and listened intently for vehicle sounds as he eyed the
Wayne County, West Virginia, two-lane that ran past his home. The
silence provided Earl with a temporary rest from his unrelenting
worry about what Emmett Brooks would do next. Brooks had bullied Earl for six years, with little letup.

Earl stood there a while longer as he listened to the comfort
of silence along his stretch of State Route 37, a strip of blacktop
that meandered along the valley floor in either direction before
him, low among steep hills in the community called Kiahsville.

It was late summer. The oak, sycamore and maple stood in
defiance of the coming fall's polite request that they shed their
summer garb, even as each tree understood that autumn soon
would dispose of good manners and insist that her preferred
tints of gold, red and brown must replace September's deep
green. Along with the turn of the trees, a bizarre phenomenon
would paint a new color onto the pallid canvas that was Earl
McCoy's life.

The day September 28, 2002 had begun badly for the slightly built, 26-year-old McCoy. After a frustrating morning of
work on his ailing truck, he had walked the road's berm to the
home of a neighbor in hopes he could catch a ride to an auto
parts store. Disappointed at finding the neighbor not there, he

began the trek home.

He had walked for a few minutes, then paused, listening, then hurried his pace as he perceived the approach of a vehicle. Someone in the vehicle shouted at him. Tires screeched and gravel flew up like a startled quail as the vehicle swerved, lost control and slid into a ditch. Earl McCoy saw Emmett Brooks get out. Brooks' emergence sent Earl's nerves to the same plane of fear that had haunted him for years. Evidently uninjured, Emmett Brooks eyed Earl and walked to the vehicle's trunk. Was Brooks reaching for a gun? Earl escaped into the woods and made his way home.

* * * * * * * *

Earl McCoy and Emmett Brooks had known each other since their grade school days. They had been neither close nor perpetually at odds. Around the sixth grade, Emmett Brooks had moved away. Later, when Brooks returned to Kiahsville around age eighteen, he weighed nearly two hundred pounds, dwarfing the short, rail-thin Earl McCoy whose frame nudged the scale to register a mere hundred and thirty-five pounds. The two became friends. They got along. Earl occasionally provided Brooks with a lift and once in a while worked on his vehicles.

But something soured. On a morning in early March, 1996, the two newly acquainted pals met up as Brooks asked Earl to give him a ride on some now forgotten errand. That done, the two parted, although the relationship between the two men had taken a very bad turn. That afternoon their paths crossed again in an incident that remains a mystery to those – the police, family members, attorneys and to me, in my role much later as a forensic psychologist – who would attempt to piece together the scene that played out.

This much is known. A few hours following their parting, Earl, with his wife Kristie and Earl's father, Earl McCoy, Sr., sat in Earl's truck in front of Emmett Brooks' home where Earl talked with Brooks. For reasons never disclosed, talk turned ugly, then threatening. As Earl described it to me later, the encounter escalated until Brooks became so agitated that Earl sped away in fear for his life and the lives of his wife and father. Brooks, with a high-powered assault rifle in hand, followed them a few paces, stopped and opened fire at the fleeing truck in an attack that riddled the truck with bullets. Several pierced the seatback, narrowly missing Kristie and Earl, Sr. Two rounds hit Earl in the back, another grazed his head. Earl McCoy's truck slid off the road and came to a stop.

The era was pre-cellphone and Earl was twenty miles from a hospital. Fortunately, a neighbor had heard the disturbance, knew it was bad and called for help. Earl was airlifted to St. Mary's Hospital in Huntington, West Virginia. By a combination of luck and medical expertise, Earl survived, although surgeons had to remove sections of his large intestines, small intestines and colon. Nine days later he was released with a slug still in his belly.

Earl's healing process was beyond arduous. At home, both Kristie and Earl's mother, Julia McCoy, nursed him constantly. Several times each day they packed the hole in his back with gauze, pushing it into the wound and then soaking it with a saline solution. An infection sprang up and set back the recovery process.

What could have transformed the two men's relationship from friendship to hate? Only Earl, his wife and father knew details of the dispute for certain, and they weren't talking. It is possible that neither Kristie nor Earl, Sr. fully understood the roiling soup of enmity that erupted in gunfire that day. And, although it was unlikely, Earl's physical trauma may have compromised his memory of salient events.

Brooks was apprehended and soon struck a deal with the Wayne County prosecutor. Initially, he was charged with one count of malicious wounding, three counts of wanton endangerment and one count of shooting from the center of the road. In a strange twist, the charge of shooting Earl McCoy was dismissed. Brooks was allowed to plead guilty to two counts of wanton endangerment, one on Kristie McCoy and one on Earl's father, neither of whom had been hit.

When a perpetrator appears before the court for sentencing, it is not unusual that his victim is in attendance. But in this case, family passions ran high. Prior to Brooks' plea hearing an official met Earl, by then healed sufficiently to be up and about, and Kristie at the courthouse door. The man advised Earl to remain outside. Wisely, Earl agreed, while Kristie entered the building and attended the proceedings. When Kristie emerged she described Brooks' sentence to Earl. Brooks would spend two years on home confinement, to be followed by probation and no jail time. That was it.

However, despite his assault on Earl McCoy, Emmett Brooks was not content to lay low and abide by the court's instructions. Instead, Brooks amped up his overt animosity toward Earl.

Seven months had elapsed since the shooting when, in November, 1996, during a chance meeting on the road, Brooks intentionally had rammed Earl's truck, immobilizing both vehicles. Petrified, Earl McCoy hunkered in his truck while Brooks first smashed the vehicle's window, then reached for a two-by-four. Earl raced to a neighbor's home and called the West Virginia State Police. Later, both Earl and his farther complained to the East Lynn Sheriff's office. When the two were told that nothing could be done, Earl, Sr. became so agitated that he was arrested and spent the remainder of the day in jail for his own protection. No charges were filed against Brooks.

Later, in my role as forensic psychologist, Earl told me that in the years after the shooting he had simply been attempting to stay out of Brooks' way. This was a difficult task in a small community where chance encounters were likely. Despite his efforts to avoid Brooks, there were more encounters. As weeks and months trudged by Earl's anxiety grew to full-blown maturity. Sleep deserted him. He became hypervigilent, constantly scanning the landscape when away from home. Even his home felt less secure.

As the weeks rolled by following Brooks' release from home confinement, "It became an everyday thing...harassing me..." Earl told me. Brooks frequently drove by Earl's home, shouting, tossing beer cans into the yard, escalating the animus. On one occasion Earl photographed Brooks and took the picture to the Wayne County probation office, which was still responsible for Brooks. Instead of finding relief, Earl was accused of following Brooks, despite the fact that the photograph had been taken at Earl and Kristie's home. Little wonder that Earl and Kristie soon lost faith in the authorities. Increasingly unable to sleep, Earl's found his nerves breaking. He moved several miles away to the community of Branchland where his father lived, with the result that Earl and Kristie's lives improved — temporarily. At Branchland Earl felt more at home, more relaxed. Sleep was less a stranger. He began work at the IGA grocery store, then took a second job at the Wal-Mart on Rt. 60 in Huntington, a town of fifty thousand. Should the worst happen, Huntington meant shorter police response time, usually just two or three minutes, as compared to the forlorn isolation of rural Wayne County where it often took law enforcement 30 minutes or more to reach the scene of a disturbance. By March, 1998, two years had elapsed since the shooting. Earl had worked at both jobs for about six months and things were improving for him and Kristie.

It was then that Emmett Brooks, still on probation, re-emerged into Earl's life. On the job at the Wal-Mart store that day, Earl inched backward as he pulled a large skid of dog food. He moved carefully through the store as he edged closer to the pet aisle where he would unload the merchandise. The skid was stacked head high so that Earl could not see the area behind the skid as he pulled it forward. Without warning, suddenly the skid began to move rapidly toward Earl, much faster than Earl pulled it, as if an unseen person on its other side entertained visions of either overrunning Earl or pushing some of the one-ton skid's weight onto him. As Earl darted to avoid being run over, he saw behind it, pushing hard, the forms of Emmett Brooks and Brooks' uncle, Doug Porter.

Earl ran. A co-worker had seen the two men push the skid dangerously close to Earl and had called the store's security. Brooks and Porter flew for the exit but were detained by store security until Huntington city police arrived. The two men were carted away by the officers. Earl remained on the job for another ninety minutes but, with his nerves frayed to the breaking point, went home. Brooks was charged with battery and convicted, but he remained on the loose, sentenced only to additional probation.

Earl began to drink heavily. Alcohol very shortly became his only means to feel relaxed or gain sleep. With steady deterioration in his nerves, the months that followed found Earl unable to shake the thought that Emmett Brooks might appear at the store at any moment. In psychological terms, Earl had undergone a classically conditioned aversive reaction to the sight of his place of employment. Now Earl worked in constant fear of what Brooks might do next. Psychologically, Earl's thoughts and feelings paralleled those of the abused woman who enters her workplace every day asking herself whether this would be the day the abuser took his act "over the top."

When not at work, Earl remained at home, petrified with worry about what Brooks was capable of. His nerves frayed. He took a leave of absence from Wal-Mart. Finally, his anxiety and drinking had advanced to the point that he needed help. And he knew it. He went to the emergency room at St. Mary's Hospital in Huntington. The doctor referred him to a local substance abuse center, Parkwest, which operated a thirty-day treatment program. In a Catch-22, Earl was unable to work, which meant his Wal-Mart health insurance was dropped. Earl was discharged from Parkwest after three days, although the staff arranged an appointment for an out-patient visit at the Prestera Behavioral Health Center. Earl never followed up.

Over the next couple of years things failed to improve for Earl McCoy. In June, 2001, Kristie McCoy came home shaken following her shopping at the local Save-A-Lot. She described how Emmett Brooks and another man had shadowed her and called her names as she shopped. Much later, when I examined Earl, I asked why no police report had been filed regarding that incident. He replied simply that any lingering grain of faith he'd had in the authorities' capacity to rein in Brooks had dissolved.

Brooks' intimidation had taken another turn. Now, late at night, it had become the man's habit to sit in his car in front of Earl's home as if to say, "I am here. I am watching you." And when that occurred, the anxiety in Earl McCoy crept closer to the red line. Earl had become nightmarishly nervous, awash with the sort of distress felt by a combat soldier. Earl's fear had ripened to a level that made him dangerous. He began to carry a gun.

Another year passed until a pleasant June day in 2002 when Earl's look-alike brother, Luther McCoy, and another man encountered Emmett Brooks on a back road. Brooks peered into the truck and mistaking Luther for his brother, pulled Luther from the truck and shouted, "I'm going to kill you, Earl!" Brooks called for a buddy to get his gun which, as a convicted felon, it was illegal for Brooks to either own or possess. Terrified, Luther escaped into the woods, arriving home covered with scrapes and cuts from barbed wire and brambles. The last thing Luther had seen was Brooks retrieving a gun.

For Earl, that summer crept by like a thief that was determined to rob him of all hope for relief from fear. His trips out of the house grew less frequent. His hypervigilance and tension continued unabated. June turned to July, and then summer in southern West Virginia slid into the dog days of August. These were the days when the heat and humidity went to sweat lodge intensity. Standing still in the shade took effort. Thirty minutes in the sun soaked a man's clothes to drenching wet.

It was on such a day that a friend, Tony Mayberry, asked Earl for a small favor. Mayberry explained that he and his girlfriend, Teresa Ramey, had split up. Some of Mayberry's belongings remained at Ramey's home and he asked Earl to help him retrieve the items. In sight of Ramey's home, Tony Mayberry suddenly told Earl they should turn back. They could come back another time, Tony said. Teresa Ramey had begun dating Emmett Brooks and Tony could tell that Brooks was in the house. Mayberry knew of the harassment, the years of intimidation, the shooting, and had heard Brooks threaten to kill Earl. Wisely, the two men withdrew.

Days later, Mayberry confided something else to Earl. He had learned from Teresa Ramey that Brooks had seen the men's approach and sudden departure. Brooks had told Teresa that he would kill them both. Aware of that, Earl and Tony discussed whether to call the police. Earl advised against it. History suggested that the police were unlikely to be helpful. Moreover,

Earl reasoned, any visit to Brooks by the authorities would accomplish little more than to further infuriate the volatile bully.

August turned to September with a slight break in the weather in the month's third week. Earl continued to drink heavily. He became increasingly sick to his stomach due to the one-two punch of alcohol and raging anxiety. By now, however, the drinking didn't help much when it came to Earl's need for sleep. He kept watch day and night, looking for the presence of Emmett Brooks. Sometimes Brooks was there, out front. And even when Brooks wasn't there, Earl's mind imagined him lurking there.

* * * * * * * * *

September 28, 2002 — the day that would alter forever the meager existences of both Earl and Emmett had arrived. This was the day that Earl had watched as Emmett Brooks' vehicle slid off the road, the day that Emmett, cursing at Earl, had reached for something in the trunk, the day that Earl had escaped into the woods and made it safely home. That afternoon Earl sat on the porch, watching. Was Brooks coming? He drank several beers. His mind was stoked with a clutter of fears, fluttering bats that had haunted him for six years. Three-quarters of an hour elapsed. Brooks had not appeared. Earl tried to relax. Maybe he was safe...

Cautiously, Earl walked to the home of a friend, Bobby Napier. Would Napier give him a ride to his grandmother's home? Maybe Earl's Uncle Larry was there and would help Earl work on the truck. Napier couldn't help him. Earl inquired similarly of several other people in Napier's neighborhood. Still, no success. Disappointed, he walked home.

Kristie would soon be home from work. He would take her car and get the part for his truck. In the meantime, Earl would wait for Kristie, and sip a couple more beers. Maybe his tension would ease off and the day would turn out OK after all. Upon Kristie's return, Earl left the house in her vehicle, not knowing that the next time he would see her, his life would be turned on its head. He drove along the two-lane, constantly scanning, on edge, in hopes that he would not encounter Emmett Brooks.

* * * * * * * * *

Earl McCoy's perambulation had taken him just across the county line, from Wayne County into Lincoln County, when he saw people ahead at the edge of the road. It was not unusual to see a laid back crowd "partying," drinking beer, at a wide spot in a country back road. Earl slowed, then halted the vehicle so as not to hit the one man among the partyers who was in the center of the road. Emmett Brooks leaned forward and peered into Earl's windshield. Recognizing Earl, Brooks bolted for his vehicle a few strides away in which two loaded shotguns lay on the seat.

Earl's panic exploded. Should he fly straight ahead, again to expose his back? Would Brooks be given another chance to shoot him as he fled? Brooks approached his truck. Earl raised his gun to the window, aimed at Brooks and fired. Brooks fell and Earl drove away. Brooks' father Bobby Swimm was present, and would testify later that he was able to tell his son that he loved him, a moment before Emmett Brooks drew his final breath.

Profound shock gripped Earl. He drove to the home of his grandmother and sat frozen in his car, his mind a blank. Earl's memory of what happened next was vague, jumbled. The sound of his uncle's fists as they pounded the car's window brought Earl to himself. News had travelled fast. Police arrived and arrested Earl and jailed him. Later he told me that he had only the vaguest memories of the incident, but based on statements of witnesses, he had no doubt that he had shot and killed Emmett Brooks.

Brooks' death had occurred just across the line into Lincoln County. Thus, his trial would take place in the county seat of Hamlin, a close knit hamlet whose best known export had been Brigadier General Charles "Chuck" Yeager. Yeager had left town for the military soon after high school and in 1947 had become the first person to fly faster than sound. As the next decades eased by, Yeager returned mostly for quickie visits as he buzzed the occasional "Howdy" over the home of his folks.

Such little places as Hamlin are integral threads in the fabric of America. They are the towns where everybody knows everybody and tribalism reigns. Earl's trial on the charge of first degree murder was set and, with family animosities at a boil, authorities dared to hope that there would be no courtroom outbursts. They wanted no incidents that approached the volatility of an episode of a few years prior when a woman had given testimony about the grisly rape and murder of her granddaughter. At the conclusion of her testimony, the grieving grandmother stepped from the witness box, reached into her purse and produced a pistol with which she opened fire at the defendant as he sat with his attorney. In an irony not lost on bystanders, the defendant was saved by ducking behind a stack of law books, one of which took the slug. A courthouse wag postulated that perhaps this had been the only occasion that the injured tome had been of any perceptible help to a defendant.

Earl McCoy's appointed lawyers were two highly capable men, James Spurlock and Vic Navy. Spurlock practiced in Huntington but had been raised in Lincoln County, where the shooting had occurred. He knew the culture. Navy, like Spurlock, was a native West Virginian. He too understood the enmeshed nature of the rural landscape. The two lawyers considered the facets of the case and concluded the obvious – they would argue that, having endured years of bullying, assault and general terrorism, and with two loaded guns on the seat of Brooks' truck, Earl had killed in self-defense.

However, to the stunned chagrin of both Spurlock and Navy, trial judge Jay M. Hoke refused to allow a plea of self-defense. Judge Hoke had reasoned that because he had not actually seen the guns lying on the seat of Brooks' vehicle, Earl could not claim self-defense. With that, Earl McCoy's primary defense evaporated.

Attorneys Spurlock and Navy suspected that the judge had made an errant decision, one serious enough that a higher court well might overturn any conviction. The lawyers knew that in order to make a successful claim of self-defense, West Virginia law required only that an individual feel that he or she was in imminent danger of coming to serious harm. Such a defense had been used successfully on many occasions.

Despite having been dealt a severe judicial blow to Earl's chances, the lawyers pushed on with their next line of defense – that Earl McCoy had suffered a mental illness, perhaps post-traumatic stress disorder, brought on by years of abuse by the deceased. If Earl had suffered PTSD or another disorder so severe that he had been unable to conform his actions to the requirements of the law, an expert witness in the mental health field would need to describe that to the jury. Thus, Spurlock and Navy asked me to examine Earl, to determine whether their argument had merit.

My examination of Earl took place on March 4, 2004. As is my practice, prior to the examination I sifted through numerous documents. They included the statements of seventeen witnesses who could confirm the history of bullying. Two other witnesses who had been at the scene of the homicide, Terry Dean and April Ramey, had seen Emmett Brooks illegally handling shotguns prior to the shooting. Their testimony would, I thought, be compelling evidence of Brooks' general disregard for the law. I reviewed Brooks' criminal records, which confirmed the 1996 shooting as Earl, his dad and Kristie attempted to flee in Earl's truck. They also confirmed the Wal-Mart incident and other episodes of Brooks' relentless terrorism of Earl. The toxicology and autopsy report showed Brooks' blood alcohol level was 0.15 when he died, far above the state's legal limit.

I reviewed a report co-authored by psychologist Andrew Riffle and psychiatrist Teodoro Sablay, who had examined Earl McCoy in spring, 2003, eight months after Brooks' death. They had concluded that Earl's mental functioning was consistent with post-traumatic stress disorder. But they equivocated on whether the disorder had played a significant role in Earl's actions at the moment he took aim at Emmett Brooks. Perhaps it had, perhaps not, they concluded.

Additionally, Riffle and Sablay had administered to Earl the

Minnesota Multi-Phasic Personality Inventory (2nd ed.), probably the most widely used of the objective tests of psychological disorders. Their interpretation of Earl's responses showed that Earl exhibited excessive concerns about his physical well-being, that he was somewhat depressed, quite anxious and suffered low self-esteem, among other issues. But those findings failed to reveal whether Earl had been that way all his life, or only since the bullying had begun, or only since the killing.

Equally important were the MMPI's validity scales that showed that Earl was not faking his symptoms. Riffle and Sablay concluded, in part, that Earl "may have been experiencing symptoms of post-traumatic stress disorder" at the time of the shooting. But they demurred on whether PTSD thus would be a suitable defense. They said it was about equally likely that Earl either experienced a flashback or was acting "of his own volition" when he shot Emmett Brooks.

Having reviewed all of that, and as with the case in any forensic examination, I advised Earl that I would examine him and would send my report to his lawyers. I said further that anything he told me might find its way into my written report or into my testimony at his trial. Once he knew that, Earl agreed to undergo my forensic examination.

Earl told me about his history with Emmett Brooks, from their nondescript childhoods to the events that surrounded the shooting. He left me with the impression that he was an individual who would avoid trouble rather than seek it. He was non-assertive and constantly wrung his hands. I asked myself, was his anxiety the result of years of bullying by Brooks, or had it been brought on in anticipation of his trial and the possibility of life in prison? As well, I had to consider the possibility that Earl had been that way since his childhood or adolescence. That is, I had to consider the possibility, however unlikely, that Emmett Brooks' activities had no causal role in Earl's PTSD, which I diagnosed.

Earl described how, following the 1996 shooting and his painful recovery, he had become increasingly anxious. He couldn't sleep, at least not without drinking. The possibility that Brooks would kill him gnawed at his thoughts like a hungry rat. When able to sleep, his nights were consumed with dreams about Brooks. In his daytime hours he had become jumpy, always watchful. Sometimes he cried. His appetite was nil and concentration had become difficult. Mostly, the full-blown fear of Emmett Brooks had become a cancer with little hope for a cure. To calibrate his nervousness I administered the well-known Beck Anxiety Inventory. Earl's score was 21, another clear indication of extreme anxiety.

As a forensic psychologist, I am routinely wary of the possibility that an accused individual such as Earl McCoy, who is faced with the possibility of life in prison, may feign mental illness. I thought that was unlikely given Earl's well documented history of abuse at the hands of Emmett Brooks and in light of the examination by Riffle and Sablay that had shown Earl was not pretending. However, to be certain I administered two additional tests that are designed to catch those who fake a mental illness. Both showed that Earl was not malingering. His debilitated mental status was real.

It also is common that a forensic psychologist will interview other individuals beyond the defendant, as part of the overall examination. This strategy may allow for crosschecking numerous events described by the defendant. Thus, I discussed Earl's behaviors with his wife Kristie, all the while alert to any effort she might make to manipulate the interview process with stories rehearsed or unnatural.

Kristie and Earl had married about five months after Earl was shot, but had lived together for a year before that. Thus, Kristie was in a position to note any changes in Earl that followed the initial and continuing series of assaults and intimidation by Brooks. Her husband had gone from easy going and fun loving to irritable and tense, she said. She told me how an exhausted Earl fell asleep only to awake and get up fearful. She had looked on as he peeped out the windows, evidently hopeless as his thoughts tumbled over and over, consumed with worry about where Brooks might be and what he might do next.

Although Emmett Brooks was dead now, Earl's worries had

transferred to Brooks' family members. His anxiety grew in proportion to the proximity of the next court appearance as he worried whether the dead man's family would be there, Kristie said. He had become convinced that they might attempt a reprisal on him for having ended Emmett's life, as if Brooks' family members were somehow unaware of the role that Brooks himself had played in his own demise. She recalled the Save-A-Lot incident in which Brooks followed her through the store, cursing and calling her a bitch. She summed up Earl's mental status; "It's an awful way to live your life."

I concluded my examination, dictated my report and sent it to Jim Spurlock and Vic Navy. I wrote, in part, of Earl's state of mind at the moment he pulled the trigger:

In my opinion, Earl experienced a flashback to one or more of the previous incidents with Emmett Brooks, and it was triggered by seeing Brooks in the road and Brooks' moving toward his car...Earl exhibits the classic history and signs and symptoms of post-traumatic stress disorder....Earl McCoy, Jr. experienced a substantial diminished capacity to either appreciate his actions or to conform his actions to the requirements of the law on September 28, 2002, at which time he shot and killed Emmett Brooks....

I added that Earl was not responsible for his actions due to post-traumatic disorder and a flashback episode. I concluded my written report with a caution. Although a psychological diagnosis such as PTSD is not necessarily causal in any given individual's criminal act,

...that is not such a case as we have here. Rather we have a tight connection between the events that gave rise to the post-traumatic stress disorder and the subsequent shooting of Emmett Brooks.

* * * * * * * * *

Earl McCoy, Jr. stood trial for first degree murder. Numerous members of the Brooks family attended each day, as did several members of the McCoy family. Earl, Kristie and Earl, Sr. testified, as did I and the first psychologist to have examined Earl, Andrew Riffle. In their testimony, Earl and Kristie described for the jury the litany of events from the time Earl had been shot by Brooks in 1996, up to the day six years later when Earl killed Brooks. Psychologist Andrew Riffle's testimony was equivocal as to Earl's mental state at the time of the shooting. He would not state definitively that Earl's deadly actions were linked to PTSD.

My testimony paralleled my written report and I was more certain than the other mental health expert. I described how Earl indeed suffered from post-traumatic stress disorder and that the disorder had been caused by the actions of Emmett Brooks. I added my conclusion that Earl's history with Brooks had brought about a PTSD-related dissociative reaction. When he had seen Brooks quickly stride toward his vehicle, Earl had been unable to discern right from wrong. All he knew at that moment was cascading fear for his life, a fear brought on by six years of Brooks' relentless efforts to kill him. Under such a burden Earl had collapsed emotionally and cognitively, a man for whom the law could not have had meaning. If causing Earl such anguish had been Brooks' goal, he had succeeded, but only at the cost of his own life.

I then underwent lengthy cross-examination by prosecutor Jack Stevens. I saw Brooks' family members, their gazes fixed on me as I sat in the witness box. As Stevens peppered me with questions, I wondered whether any among the Brooks family ever had quietly engaged Brooks in a "Dutch uncle" conversation, whether they had counseled Emmett that he was playing a dangerous game, whether any among them had suggested to Emmett that Earl McCoy might break and become dangerous. I concluded my testimony with this: "Emmett Brooks didn't know it, but every time he bullied Earl McCoy, he was driving another nail into his own coffin."

The testimony was done. There were no additional witnesses. I walked out of the courthouse and drove home, asking myself what the jurors might have thought as they listened to the lawyers' summations.

The jury was rightly skeptical of the validity of testimony by Earl, Kristie and Earl's father. After all, Earl was facing a charge of first degree murder and may have concocted a fictional story of bullying and terrorism. Moreover, jury box skepticism probably bled over to my own testimony, given that I had based my opinions in part on events as Earl and Kristie had described them to me. How was a jury to know whether Brooks had shot Earl in 1996, or attacked him at Wal-Mart, or threatened to kill Earl's brother (thinking it was Earl himself), or whether Brooks had bluntly told Tony Mayberry's former girlfriend, Teresa Ramey, that he would kill Earl?

In a curious second ruling, Judge Hoke had refused to allow testimony from any of the more than a dozen additional individuals who would have confirmed the history of assault, intimidation and bullying. To my thinking, as well as to that of Spurlock and Navy, there was no reasonable justification for a judge to bar witnesses who could verify the defendant's side of the story.

Had the judge not prohibited them from doing so, Jim Spurlock and Vic Navy would have produced witness after witness to verify Brooks' history of terroristic bullying toward Earl McCoy. The importance of such witnesses could not be overestimated. Judge Jay Hoke, himself a Lincoln County native, had deprived the jury of its only means to erase their concerns.

Among the potential witnesses to whom the judge refused entry into the witness box were doctors who would have described the extent of Earl's injuries and treatment as a result of the 1996 shooting; members of the Wayne County Deputy Sheriff's Department who could have verified that it was Emmett Brooks who had perpetrated that near-fatal shooting, as well as the incident in which Brooks rammed McCoy's truck; witnesses who could have described how Brooks had stood in the road and, on recognizing Earl, had gone for his shotguns; those who would have told jurors that Brooks had shotgun shells in his pocket when he died and had been handling guns prior to the shooting and that those guns were only a few steps from Brooks' reach. Nor was Wal-Mart manager Brent Hagen permitted to describe Brooks' attempted assault on Earl. Nor would Teresa Ramey be permitted to tell the jury that she had listened as Emmett Brooks bluntly told her that he planned to kill Earl.

Without witnesses who would have removed jurors' doubts about the scope of Brooks' assaults, harassment, threats and intimidation, it came as no surprise that prosecutor W. Jack "Jackie" Stevens hammered away to convince the jury that Earl could not be trusted to tell the truth. Stevens asked Earl on cross-examination, "You only remember things that benefit you in this trial, don't you?"

Following the trial, *Lincoln County Journal* writer Lee Arnold wrote of Earl's testimony:

McCoy repeatedly claimed that Brooks, along with his friends, harassed him and threatened him up until the day of the fatal shooting…McCoy claimed Brooks attacked him on one occasion at his job at Wal-Mart, and also at various other times in public places.

Unfortunately, Earl's attorneys were not permitted to call witnesses who would have verified the awful history for the reporter and, more importantly, for the jury.

The testimony concluded and the lawyers gave their summations. The jury deliberated and found Earl guilty of first degree murder, with a recommendation of mercy. Earl would spend a minimum of fifteen years in prison and, most likely, several additional years beyond. Strangely, in the sentencing phase of the case Judge Hoke had reversed field and allowed testimony by several of the corroborating witnesses, a factor that likely accounted for the jury's recommendation of mercy. What motivated the judge's change of heart remains unknown.

* * * * * * * * *

When it was over, I came away with the uneasy feeling that justice had not been served. An appeal to the West Virginia Supreme Court might succeed. Earl's lawyers had not been allowed to call witnesses who easily would have verified the years of bullying, assault and intimidation and, thus, would have bolstered his testimony as well as my own. Also, I was nagged by the thought that it was improper for Judge Hoke to have denied Earl the opportunity to claim self-defense. I had been around the court system long enough to understand that a jury, rather than a judge, ought to decide whether a defendant had acted in self-defense.

Jim Spurlock and Vic Navy also believed that the Judge had erred. They appealed Earl's conviction to the West Virginia Supreme Court of Appeals, which agreed to hear the case. Spurlock was invited to appear before the state's highest court and he invited me to observe the session. It remains the only time I ever sat in as an attorney argued a case before the state's highest court. As Spurlock laid out the facts of the case, the five justices took on quizzical looks, as if they were having difficulty grasping the reality that Judge Hoke had ruled as Jim Spurlock described. They questioned Spurlock for clarification after clarification. Some of the black-robed jurists grew wide-eyed, leaned forward and peered down at Spurlock as one asked, in essence, "Are you saying the trial judge disallowed a plea of self-defense, even though the deceased had repeatedly threatened, even had shot the defendant?" Astonished glances went up and down the huge oak-paneled bench as Spurlock replied, "That's correct." As I listened, it became clear to me that the members of the West Virginia Supreme Court were about to decide that Judge Hoke had made a reversible error.

And that is precisely what happened. Ultimately, the jurists also concluded that Judge Hoke's decision to bar corroborating witnesses had been equally improper. Although Earl by then had been imprisoned for nearly two years, the West Virginia Supreme Court rendered an overwhelming decision. Judge Hoke's errors were substantial. By a five to nothing margin, Earl McCoy's conviction of first degree murder was overturned.

The practical implications of the reversal of Earl's murder conviction were clear. If prosecutor Jack Stevens wished to re-try Earl McCoy, he would be faced with a new jury that would be permitted to consider both whether Earl McCoy had acted in self-defense, and the testimony of witness after witness who would describe six years of assaults, threats and intimidation. And a new jury would consider whether all of that had driven Earl McCoy over the edge.

Each side now had a decision to make. The bar would be set much higher for prosecutor Jack Stevens to get a conviction. Earl's chances for acquittal now rose, should he insist on a re-trial. But as Jim Spurlock and Vic Navy knew, a trial always involved a roll of the dice.

What would be Earl's most favorable course of action? What would be Jack Stevens' best direction? Would either risk a re-trial, or ought they make the best possible plea deal?

Following negotiations among Spurlock, Navy and Stevens, Earl pleaded guilty to second degree murder with the understanding that he would not go back to prison. Rather, he would be placed on probation and would return to his home. It was finished. A few months following the start of Earl's probation, Judge Jay Hoke released Earl from it. Earl now is employed in his home county of Wayne. He and Kristie are now parents of a daughter.

Two

He Murdered His Gay Partner

I F, IN THE PANTHEON, there existed a god of cruel tricks, surely that deity paused to congratulate himself on the irony of his timing, given that it was Halloween, October 31, 2002. On that autumn afternoon a chain of circumstances began for Princeton, West Virginia, realtor James Constantino that would end in a drama of insanity and blood-soaked murder.

Constantino stepped to the fax machine and read the letter that had settled into the tray. The sender was a man who signed his name Oliver Umbezie. He described himself as an employee of the South African Ministry of Energy and Mineral Resources. James Constantino, Mr. Umbezie advised, had inherited $15.95 million from a distant relative named David Constintino. The money was being held in trust at the South African Ministry, the fax stated. Although James Constantino had never heard of such a relative, and though the message reeked of a scam, James rose to the bait. Mr. "Umbezie" added that he and his associates would help James recover his inheritance, for a commission of sixty percent of the inherited amount.

* * * * * * * * *

James Constantino had lived his entire fifty-six years in southern West Virginia. Growing up in a respected family, he had attended McDowell County schools and graduated from

Concord College, now Concord University, in Athens. He had taught physical education to thousands of elementary students for most of the years from 1971 to 2001. During those decades his interests had diverged. He had become an adjunct faculty member at Concord College, then for about three years in the 1980s, worked as its full-time director of student services and director of its Upward Bound program. Upward Bound is a national program that helps at-risk high school students further their education. The program enables students to tour a college, chat with students and faculty members and, with luck, form a bond. The program director then continues to motivate the students with contacts and invitations to events on campus, in hopes of leading each to enroll in higher education. Upward Bound achieves remarkable results, as evidenced by its best known graduate — Oprah Winfrey.

Also in the 1980s James had embarked on part-time realty sales. Finding that he had a knack for selling property, in 1992 James purchased a local realty company, Century 21 Four Seasons Properties, and left his education-related professions. He built a solid reputation as both a businessman and member of the community. He was upstanding. He never ran afoul of realty regulations or the law. In fact, he was never accused of misconduct in all his years as a teacher and a realtor. As a gay man in conservative southern West Virginia, James kept a low profile when not tending to his business activities. He did his work each day, then went home to his long-time partner, Pat Brougham.

* * * * * * * * *

Over the next ten months, following receipt of the inheritance fax, James corresponded with the alleged South African and his associates, whom Umbezie claimed had offices in the Netherlands and Canada, regarding procedures to finalize James' receipt of his portion of the inheritance. Step one took place a week after he received the Halloween fax, in early November, 2002, when James flew to the Netherlands — at his own expense — to meet one of the "associates." James delivered $5,000 in cash to the man, to cover various fees related to transfer of the cash. That was the tip of an iceberg.

By July, 2003, James had transferred more than $120,000 from his personal bank account at First Community Bank in Princeton to Umbezie and his partners, all necessary the scammers told him, to accomplish the transfer of his inheritance. At that point James' immediately available cash was tapped out. He could send no additional funds. He suggested that Umbezie take any additional fees as credits against the sum to be inherited. Umbezie, perhaps convinced that his fish was about to wriggle off the hook, set phase two of the scam in place. A still gullible James Constantino fell for every bit of it.

Umbezie put James in touch with an individual who called himself David Ochese who oozed sympathetic understanding of James' frustrations. There was a way to work it out, "Ochese" told him, although it would involve some money shuffling. Ochese would arrange several loans for James from individuals who would take a small cut of the inheritance for their efforts. This would cost James almost nothing. Ochese told James to expect to receive the loans in the form of checks to James as payee, with instructions to deposit them into his personal account in Princeton and then immediately wire various prescribed amounts by Western Union to a corporation in Tokyo and to several individuals. Now that he was no longer spending his own money, James dutifully did as he was told.

In mid-July Ochese sent James a check in the amount of $75,700. On August 7, James received another, this time in the amount of $64,500. A third check arrived on August 22, in the amount of $101,200. All three checks from Ochese had been drawn on the Provident Bank account of Felician College, a small Jesuit school in Lodi, New Jersey. The checks were forgeries. James, unawares, thus participated in an effort to steal $241,000 from Felician College. It had been money in, money out, laundered by an unsuspecting James Constantino, more than two hundred thousand dollars to the criminals who had devised the scheme.

As former teacher James Constantino was about to learn, he had paid an outrageous tuition in order to be schooled in the ways of Scam 101. In late August, 2003, Provident Bank notified James that he was being sued for having cashed forged checks on the bank's Felician College account. With that certified letter, James' ugly epiphany shifted into high gear. Harsh reality now delivered several tons of its cargo to the realtor: James became aware he had thrown away $120,000 of his own money. The First Community Bank in Princeton soon charged James' savings account an additional $101,000 as partial restitution for the $241,000 in forged checks drawn on the Felician College account.

Another crushing blow followed: New Jersey authorities charged James with theft by deception and uttering of fraudulent checks totaling $241,000, crimes that could get him locked up for years.

All that was bad, but there was more. The once respected former teacher and successful businessman now had a very different persona around Princeton, West Virginia. Police authorities obtained a warrant for his arrest as a fugitive from justice. Everything he had ever believed about himself and his place in the community was shattered. His existence had become a broken statue, its tiny pieces scattered in the yard, with no glue strong enough to restore James' former self.

James Constantino cooperated fully with the police. He was arraigned on September 3, 2003, waived his privilege of self-incrimination and voluntarily met with Princeton Police Detective Charles Poe, Assistant U. S. Attorney Stephanie Ojeda and a representative of the United States Secret Service who had been contacted by the Bergen County, New Jersey, state prosecutor. James "did the right thing." He told them everything, going back to receipt of the initial fax from Mr. "Umbezie."

By mid-December, 2003, James had entered into an agreement to repay the New Jersey bank the entire amount of the funds that had been pilfered from it. Also that fall, his long-standing good reputation in the community had proved an invaluable asset as several individuals wrote to West Virginia's Governor, Robert Wise, in a successful effort to forestall New Jersey's extradition request. State Senator Shirley Love wrote, "He is a respected retired school teacher ...community members hold Jim in high esteem." James even received an endorsement from the Executive Vice

President of his bank. Gary R. Mills wrote, "In his personal and professional dealings with First Community Bank, Mr. Constantino has always conducted himself with the utmost integrity...and enjoys a fine reputation for honesty in his business as a realtor."

State Editor of the Bluefield Daily Telegraph, Barbara Hawkins, wrote to Governor Wise as well, "Mr. Constantino enjoys an excellent reputation...He is respected and trusted by people in all walks of life in our community." And Rev. Father Manuel T. Gelido advised the governor that "Jim Constantino is an active and faithful member of our parish...very well liked in our church community...He was a victim of a scam..." As a result of his years of good citizenship, James was not extradited to New Jersey.

A few months slid by as authorities sorted out the details. By mid-2004 they concluded that James had not participated in the scheme to defraud either the college or his bank, much less the bank in New Jersey. Rather, there was agreement all around that, as Fr. Gelido put it, James had been a victim, not a perpetrator. If having been putty in the hands of slick operators was a criminal act, James would have faced a lengthy stretch in prison. But kind and thoughtful heads had prevailed.

Much of the credit went to James' attorney,, Michael F. Gibson, who had done yeoman work in his representation of James. Although James suffered financial losses and humiliation in roughly equal proportions, Gibson saw to it that James avoided prison. He could go on with his life, wiser and perhaps somewhat bitter at himself for not having seen past the shiny millions that the scammers had dangled in front of him. As December 2003 drew to its conclusion, things were looking up. Within six months, the books on his legal problems would close.

* * * * * * * * *

Unfortunately, James Constantino's life was in a downward spiral that was obvious only to his closest associates and family. As the inheritance scam and charges against James played out, his nerves had collapsed. His ability to think rationally began to fade. His partner, Pat Brougham, had urged James to get help for the obvious deterioration in his functioning, as had both James' mother and his brother, Frank Constantino.

In an effort to provide his family with reassurance that he was looking after himself psychologically, James had seen psychiatrist Nusrath Hasan. At the initial visit on September 29, 2003, the doctor had prescribed medications, scheduled a return visit and referred James to a licensed professional counselor named Neil Jackson. Dr. Hasan had diagnosed anxiety and depression but concluded that James was not suffering from psychosis. Counselor Jackson saw James twice in October, once again in November and finally on December 18, 2003, the same week that the letters of support for James were being received in the governor's office. Therapist Jackson wrote in his notes that James continued to suffer from elevated anxiety, poor sleep and poor concentration. James saw Dr. Hasan for a dozen additional visits, the last on August 2, 2004, at which time James was "Doing well on medication but feels anxious," according to the doctor's notes.

But months earlier, even as Attorney Gibson expertly had guided the case to its successful resolution, family members remained skeptical that James was doing well. A disinterested observer well might have concluded that the dawn of 2004, a new year that would drop the final curtain on his legal difficulties, would have brought an upturn in James' mental status. But such an upturn was not to be. As attorney Gibson negotiated the end to James' legal problems, James' mother, eighty-year-old Nellie Constantino, increasingly felt the gravity of James' disturbing behaviors. Although she was coping with the burdens of her husband's dementia, she paused to write a letter to Dr. Hasan on January 14, 2004. As she looked back over the past few months of treatment by Hasan and counselor Jackson, her four-page letter communicated a mother's growing fears about incidents that had continued to gather like storm clouds over the lives of James and those who loved him:

Dear Dr. Hasan,

I am very concerned about Jimmy...on a daily basis he cannot function or perform the simplest tasks. For example, his bills are piling up because he can't seem to fill out the bill, write the check and then address, stamp and mail it... He won't even let his accountant do his bills for him or even Pat help him...

When Jimmy comes to my house for dinner, he'll walk in and out of every room just wringing his hands, shaking his head, mumbling to himself, and then he'll just sit, blink his eyes numerous times and stare out into space. Nothing at the office is completed and when Sue (Williams, office manager – parentheses mine, WJW) asks advice on certain matters, Jimmy just stares at her...

Pat told me that at night he hears Jimmy pacing the floor talking to himself. When they are out in public, Jimmy is always looking over his shoulder to see if someone is following or if someone knows him and is talking about him...

His brother Frank is a very successful businessman in Atlanta. He has tried to help Jimmy in numerous ways...However, Jimmy became very paranoid and thought his brother was trying to take (the real estate business, parentheses again are mine, WJW) from him...

Jimmy's younger brother, Nicky, said he would help in any way that he could. Jimmy is now paranoid that Nicky is after his furniture...

Jimmy cannot even coherently talk in his own defense concerning his criminal and civil cases. He has to go to New Jersey for a preliminary hearing...We've tried to ask questions that we thought they may ask, and Jimmy just rambles on with no understanding of what he was asked...

...he is in serious danger of total bankruptcy...Now, he won't return a phone call or show a property, so clients are going elsewhere...

It is my thought that you may not be aware of all these facts. I doubt if Jimmy is forthright with his counselor or you although he says he is. I don't even think he is taking his medication as prescribed.

...I'm truly at my wit's end...and I hate to see such a successful person lose everything and possibly go to prison for not being able to function properly or communicate coherently. How can we help him?...

Sincerely,
Nellie Constantino

* * * * * * * * *

How, indeed? By the time Nellie Constantino wrote her letter, her son had seen Dr. Hasan on six occasions, with an additional visit scheduled for the next day, and another six visits to follow, the final one on August 2, 2004. James' mental health was not getting better. Instead, his paranoia was growing steadily. He failed to conduct business at the Century 21 office. Throughout 2004 his deteriorated functioning brought his once successful business dangerously close to a halt. And as of early 2005, his relationship with partner Pat Brougham had reached a new low. Now Pat was threatening to leave the relationship if James' functioning did not improve. Like others in the family, more than once Pat had talked to James about the need for more intensive treatment – including treatment as an inpatient. Their talk was in vain.

In a last ditch effort to convince Pat that he would get better, James made an appointment with another psychiatrist, Dr. Philip B. Robertson. The appointment took place on March 11, 2005. As with his visits to Dr. Hasan and therapist Jackson, James concealed the worst of his symptoms, probably out of concern that he would undergo involuntary commitment to a psychiatric hospital if he told the doctor about his belief in family conspiracies to take his business, his furniture and more. It is one of the curiosities of paranoid psychosis that the individual is able to think in a faux-coherent manner, provided his thinking remains within the complex web of his delusions of persecution. If someone actually had been plotting against him, James' thinking and actions would have been completely understandable. Unfortunately, when paranoid delusions are challenged directly, the individual interprets such challenges as part of the plot against him. What typically follows is a spiral of self-fulfilling false beliefs in which the individual's irrational behavior worsens. This then leads to greater efforts at intervention, which the patient interprets as additional evidence that the plots against him are real. His delusions deepen, and it all spirals downward to dark and dangerous depths.

To those who moved in James' sphere, it was clear that he had become filled with the demons of his delusions and was now actively psychotic. In contrast, Dr. Robertson, like Dr. Hasan before him, concluded that James exhibited no psychotic symptoms during the visit. Rather, the doctor found James to be mildly depressed and nervous, and to be having difficulty with sleep, irritability and poor concentration. Nothing more. Dr. Robertson diagnosed him as undergoing an adjustment disorder, terminology that implies a relatively mild level of distress with no distortions of reality. He prescribed Lexapro and suggested psychotherapy for stress management. But James' life extended well beyond his doctor visits, to the world outside the therapy room. There life lasted more than a few minutes, there he was unable to keep up his role-play of rationality, as he had so often done during brief visits with mental health professionals. Having fooled another doctor, James went home. He never saw Dr. Robertson again.

It is the nature of the psychotically paranoid individual to reject loved ones' encouragement to get therapy. The subject interprets expressions of concern as little more than evidence of cabals designed to undo him. Thus, the genuineness of family entreaties were lost on James. Rather, he believed that their pleas for him to get help were evidence of a grand conspiracy to take everything from him. When he overheard pieces of conversation just out of earshot, benign chats became evidence that people were talking about him. If he noticed a routine piece of unopened mail on a table at his mother's home, he believed it contained a message about the family's plan to take his property. On it went, beyond the visit with Dr. Robertson and throughout the remainder of March, 2005. James' raging paranoia had acquired a life of its own. It strengthened daily, as one mundane event after another took on special significance. These phenomena are termed "ideas of reference" in mental health jargon – everyday happenings that the delusional paranoiac believes have persecutory meaning for him alone. As dusk turned to dark on March 31, 2005, the black thunderheads over James' mind smothered the final rays of hope that things would improve.

If Halloween 2002 had been unkind to James Constantino,

the dawn of Friday, April 1, 2005, would bring about a disaster neither his mother nor anyone else could have anticipated. April Fool's broke with Pat still asleep. James got up around 7:30 and ate some cereal in the living room. He entertained thoughts of going to work, but dismissed them. Other, more fearful, cogitations intruded. The possibility that Pat would leave him buzzed in his head like the sound of a thousand bees. All rationality had fled. James opened a drawer and grasped the pistol he had surreptitiously taken from his parents' home a few weeks earlier. He walked upstairs to the bedroom where Pat still slept and gently laid down beside his partner. Later, when I examined James, I asked him to describe his thoughts and feelings at that moment. Haltingly, he said, "I probably kept thinking about money and *et cetera*." He didn't remember why he had gotten the gun from the closet. Following a lengthy pause he said, "I can remember, but I don't think I was going to hurt myself or someone else. But why would I have a gun?" He asked me that rather blankly, as if I might have an answer. He leaned forward and told me, "Possibly I was going to do murder/suicide."

James got out of bed. His thoughts were racing — money, the scam, whether Pat would leave him. A moment later he abruptly stood over Pat, aimed the gun at Pat's head and pulled the trigger. Pat rose up, shouted and fell back. Immediately, James aimed and fired again. Pat Brougham died instantly. James said he didn't remember firing the second shot, but recalled that he thought about killing himself, then for reasons he later could not fathom, decided against it.

My examination of James took place twenty-five days later at River Park Hospital in Huntington, West Virginia, where he described the bloody events. He said that throughout the remainder of that Friday he had paced the house, sometimes going to the bedroom, viewing the crimson scene with distress while shouting at Pat's body to get up. The day had dragged on like that. Night fell like a curtain on the house where Pat lay dead. James wandered the rooms and hallways, restlessly. He slept in fits. James was up and down in the dark. Saturday's dawn found him still in the house, where he remained most of the day. In the afternoon he made phone calls related to his realty business. He visited his parents briefly. His distorted demeanor appeared to his mother as it had for months. He went home and stayed in that night, as Pat's body remained in the bed. James rested on the couch at times, and spent another night up and down. Again he visited the bedroom frequently. In a bizarre flight from reality, he entertained the notion that there might be a way to undo what he had done.

The morning of Sunday, April 3, 2005, arrived. James had been in the house with Pat's body for nearly all of the previous forty-eight hours. Finally, he picked up the phone and dialed 911:

Operator:	911.
James:	Hello, is this not the emergency line?
Operator:	This is 911, do you have an emergency?
James:	Huh?
Operator:	Do you have an emergency?
James:	Yeah, yeah.
Operator:	Well, what is it then?
James:	Huh?
Operator:	What's the problem?
James:	Uh, there, uh, couple of days ago there was, uh, someone like, shot in the head.
Operator:	Where was this?
James:	And I need them to come up.
Operator:	What's your name?
James:	Okay, my name's Jim Constantino and it's up here on Unity Road.
Operator:	Where on Unity Road?
James:	Uh, 1458. Do you know where Unity is?
Operator:	Yes.
James:	Yeah, there's a sign.
Operator:	Has this been reported before?
James:	Do what, now?
Operator:	Has this been reported before? Or
James:	No, nuh uh.
Operator:	Did this just take place?
James:	No, no, no, no…It happened like, uh, let's see it

was, uh, Friday I think, Friday morning.

Operator: Well what do you need to talk to the police about it for now?

James: Huh?

Operator: What do you need the police for now?

James: Well because he sh, he was like shot, like a wound.

Operator: Where is he now?

James: He's here at the house.

Operator: Is he alive?

James: Uh, I don't think…that's why I was calling, ya know.

Operator: Who shot him, you?

James: Do what?

Operator: Who shot him?

James: No, nuh uh.

Operator: Okay, what kind, uh, describe the house to me.

James: Okay, it's a long driveway and you come down it and it's like, uh, 2-3 story, uh, cedar looking house.

Operator: Is there a mailbox out front saying that?

James: No, but there's a sign that says Jim Constantino and Pat Brougham.

Operator: Who's the person that got shot?

James: Un, Pat Brougham.

Operator: Where's the gun?

James: Um, it's a, here, it's here, uh, like in a drawer… yeah.

Operator: Is Pat Brougham male?

James: Yeah, he's a male.

Operator: And when did this take place?

James: Uh, Friday morning…today's what, Saturday, Sunday, yeah.

Operator: Sunday.

James: Yeah, yeah.

Operator: What's your phone number? 952-6551?

James: That's my cell phone.
Operator: Okay, do you have a house phone too?
James: Uh, 384-9365.
Operator: 9365.
James: Uh huh.
Operator: Okay. Alright, we'll have an officer give you a
call and get him out there to you.
James: Ok, thanks.
Operator: OK.

End

Police arrived quickly and soon concluded that the physical evidence against James was overwhelming. James volunteered a statement to the police. The investigation into Pat's death was brief and decisive, with a single additional revelation. Investigator Lt. A. D. Beasley talked to a woman named Tina Powers, an official at a local cemetery. She told Beasley that on the day prior to the shooting she had received a call from James. They had discussed cemetery property and arrangements. It had been her impression that James wanted to be certain that funeral and cemetery costs had been covered, and that he and Pat would be together forever.

* * * * * * * * *

When I examined James a little over three weeks later, he had been at River Park Hospital in Huntington for 13 days, transferred there from jail as a result of his bizarre behavior that had become evident to both the jail personnel and to his lawyer, Michael Gibson. Jail staff had reported conversations with James in which he asserted a number of suspicions including that his family, and later the jail personnel themselves, were in a conspiracy to steal his house. Attorney Gibson contacted me and asked that I examine James and answer three questions. First, was James competent to stand trial? To be competent, a defendant must understand the charges against him, including the consequences if he is found guilty, or not guilty.

He must be able to assist his attorney in his defense, a difficult task for an individual whose thinking has strayed from reality. Generally speaking, a defendant must be able to understand the legal process, the roles of his attorney , the prosecutor, the judge and jury.

Second, Attorney Gibson asked whether, at the time of the killing, James had suffered a mental illness that would have made it impossible for him to act lawfully. That is, was he possessed of delusions, hallucinations or some other aberrant mental health process that had rendered him unable to appreciate the wrongfulness of what he was doing. Had he functioned in the grip of a disorder that rendered him unable to conform his actions to what the law requires? Last, Michael Gibson was concerned that James had given an extensive statement to the police. Gibson asked me to determine whether James' statement to the police on the day of his arrest was entirely voluntary. Was it possible that the combination of James' delusional functioning, stress, fatigue, medications or any other factor had left him willing to assent to anything the authorities suggested?

When admitted to River Park Hospital James had told admitting physician Dr. Jacqueline Cole that the jail guards had devised plans to murder him. His attending physician, Dr. Andrea Vidal, listened as he described how people in New Jersey also were plotting to murder him. Both doctors were convinced that James was psychotic at the time of his admission to the hospital. It then fell to me to answer attorney Gibson's questions.

By the time I examined James I was glad to discover that his psychosis had abated somewhat, a factor that would make my examination proceed more smoothly. He was able to tell me how, in the days leading up to the shooting, various people had urged him to get psychological help. He admitted that he had ignored his realty business, had failed to go to work, avoided appearances to show homes and forgotten about appointments. He described the South African scam, how it had triggered his mental deterioration, how his family and Pat had urged him to get help. He demonstrated some insight as he admitted, "I just couldn't function." He related how he had sold some of his belongings in order to make repayments to the New Jersey bank, although he had become increasingly concerned about "holding things together financially." I found it particularly interesting that James had gained a measure of self-awareness about the decline in his functioning.

It was especially difficult for James to describe the shooting. Halting frequently as he spoke, he denied that he and Pat had been fighting, although he felt that Pat had been contemplating "plan B" — calling an end to their relationship. During the evening prior to the shooting they had talked, watched some TV and gone to bed. Then James described the shooting, his forty-eight hours in the house with Pat's body, his visit to his parents' home and his call to 911. He spoke quietly, frequently starting his sentences with the curious phrase, " I probably..." (did this or that).

It is important that a forensic psychologist take note of a patient's verbal style. That James began many of his responses to my questions with, "I probably did..." told me that he was making an effort to reconstruct some of what he had done, perhaps based in part on what he had been told about the shooting, rather than on direct memory of the events. I asked myself whether he had been out of touch with reality to the extent that he had only partial memory of the shooting. When I pointed out his unusual, self-questioning style, James was chagrined, as if he had been unaware of it, and thereafter he attempted to correct the way that he related what had occurred. But I wanted to know whether he possessed direct memory of the tragic episode or instead was engaged in a pattern that involved combining the information he remembered with what he had been told by his lawyer and the authorities. Was he extrapolating "probable" scenarios that would fill in his memory gaps, so as to answer my questions? I never determined to my satisfaction which phenomenon it was.

Initially, James told me he had never considered murder/ suicide, primarily because his Catholic faith prevented him from doing so. However, later in the interview he recalled that he had carried the gun upstairs to where Pat was asleep and that he had contemplated suicide. He recalled lying on the bed, gun in hand, as his thoughts sped with concerns about money, the scam and the possibility that Pat would leave him. He said, "Possibly I was going to do murder/suicide." He remembered only the initial shot and that Pat had raised up and shouted, nothing more. He then described the events of the next two days, up to the 911 call. He told me that he had shown the police the gun, which he had replaced in its drawer. Police discovered Pat's body, unmoved. James recalled that his thoughts and feelings were like "a dream or an unconscious" experience. He could not believe it was all real, he said haltingly. As our discussion continued, he frequently became vague, although it was not my impression that he was attempting to dissemble. I concluded the interview with uncertainties still lingering in my thinking. As I would later write in my report of the examination, "Perhaps most interesting, I formed the impression that he wanted to tell me all the details of what had happened, but because he could not remember them, he used the verbal device, 'I probably did (this or that)'."

In my work as a forensic psychologist I often interview others who may shed light on the patient's functioning. My examination of James was no exception. I spoke with his brother Frank Constantino who confirmed the deterioration in James' thinking that had played out during and following the scam. Frank had noticed a worsening in a period when James' behavior and thinking ought to have been on the upswing, after Michael Gibson had worked out the difficulties with both the banks and law enforcement authorities in West Virginia and New Jersey. James' mental status had worsened to the point that in August, 2003, Frank had obtained a durable power of attorney over James, including medical and legal powers of attorney .

Although Frank resided in Atlanta, as fallout from the scam played out, he had visited James a number of times and had maintained frequent contact with their mother, as well as with Pat Brougham and Sue Williams, the Century 21 office manager. Frank described how James had shopped at Wal-Mart, hugging the shelves because he thought people were talking about him. James had begun to stay in the house for two weeks at a time, Frank told me, and he frequently failed to follow up on home sale leads. His neglect was causing his realty business, which earlier had been responsible for almost fifty percent of the sales in Mercer County, to go "from top to bottom."

Frank had learned that James once accused their mother of attempts to take his home. And on one occasion family members had found James hiding from imaginary evildoers in the car in his garage. Another particularly revealing episode had occurred at Christmas in their parents' home. James had followed family members around the house listening at doorways, fearful of their "plots" against him.

Frank had visited his brother at River Park Hospital a few days prior to my examination. James had told Frank of his belief that there had been a public demonstration about him in the street outside the hospital, which was preposterous. He also "disclosed" to Frank that, at a memorial service for Pat, five hundred people had showed up and that jail guards had forced James to attend. There was not a grain of truth to any of it.

Even after the scam and its attendant legal issues had been settled, Frank described how James continued to believe that New Jersey authorities were coming after him. He had refused to pay his taxes, telling Frank, "It's coming down. It's coming down." As Frank put it, James was, "…180 degrees from where he was before." At a court hearing relative to the scam, James had told the judge that their other brother, Nicky, had sold his house. In fact, his house and car had to be sold to pay his legal debts. Finally, Frank added that everyone knew James was gay but that James thought he had covered it up. And in a chilling hint of what would come, Frank had learned of the gun that James had taken from their parents' home. When Frank confronted him, James justified his possession of the gun. "I thought I might need it for myself," James had told him.

Following my conversation with Frank Constantino, I called Sue Williams. She had worked for years in James' Century 21 office. With observations that paralleled Frank's, Sue believed James' mental deterioration began around September, 2003, and was triggered by the scam that had begun on Halloween, 2002. At the start of his part-time realty work, James had been a dynamo. She said that he taught school until 2:30, then sold real estate.

After the scam he had begun to believe that people were talking about him and he was constantly afraid of lawsuits. By Thanksgiving, 2004, his decision-making had fallen off to the point that he often had trouble deciding what to wear. He became frozen, Sue Williams told me, paralyzed with fear that he would make a mistake, unable to do things that he previously had done routinely.

Sue remembered that when James came to the office, which was almost never during the final year, there were times that he was badly distracted. So much so, she said, that as he talked to a customer on the phone, she would listen in and write notes to him which he then would repeat to the customer. At other times she would place checks in front of him and would have to gently tell him, "Sign your name." At times his face became contorted with twitches (Note: perhaps a side effect of medication). He walked around the office, picked up papers, but did not know what he should do with them. He failed to shave and became unkempt. Sue became frightened of his driving when they went to a home to conduct business. He asked her the same questions repeatedly. He had become, "Like a little baby or a puppy dog," Sue Williams told me.

In early 2005 James hit his lowest point. His aunt sued him for repayment of a $150,000 loan. Sue guessed that his aunt had sued because James had not paid much attention to her, as he found himself in an ever tightening vise of circumstances that outmatched his coping systems.

At one point on a Friday in late March 2005, she and Frank had visited James and Pat at their home. They spent three hours with him. Frank, Sue and Pat each emphasized their concerns to James. They broached the suggestion that hospitalization could be helpful. James was "nice," she said, but insisted he didn't need help. Exactly one week later Pat would be shot dead.

Early on April 1, 2005, Sue Williams was already at the Century 21 office when the phone rang. It was James. He asked whether she would go to a real estate listing around 11:00. A bit later, around 8:30, as the body of Pat Brougham now lay dead upstairs, he called to ask again whether she would be there.

* * * * * * * * *

My conversations with Frank Constantino and Sue Williams fit with all that I had discovered up to then. However, it was important to consider, as I do in every case, whether James, now faced with life in prison, had somehow fabricated an elaborate ruse of mental illness. I knew it was improbable, given that his well-documented mental deterioration had become obvious more than a year prior to the homicide. But to be certain I administered several psychological assessment devices. The Miller Assessment of Symptoms Test (M-FAST) revealed that James was not pretending to be mentally ill. The same was the case for the Sixteen Items Test which assesses memory. The Beck Anxiety Inventory and the Beck Depression Inventory resulted in scores of 27 and 40, respectively. These were clear indications of severe anxiety and depression. The Minnesota Multiphasic Personality Inventory, which is among the handful of most frequently employed tests of psychological functioning, confirmed what already was clear — James saw himself as functioning extremely poorly. He admitted to many bizarre thoughts, feelings and behaviors.

I had concluded my examination. I was in possession of the information I needed in order to answer attorney Michael Gibson's questions. It was time to formulate my opinions.

* * * * * * * * *

I concluded that James was actively psychotic prior to, during and immediately after he shot Pat Brougham. His paranoid psychotic process had rendered him unable to stay within the bounds of the law. The people closest to him had noticed his suspiciousness, his feeling that others were attempting to undo him, his worries that law enforcement officials including the FBI were watching him, even after the South African scam charges had been resolved. It was clear to me that James, as is typical of paranoid individuals, had been in denial about the seriousness of his decline. This explains why he had denied to Dr. Robertson that he had previously undergone psychiatric treatment. So much in denial was he that he had refused to consider the efforts of his brother Frank and office manager Sue Williams that he seek additional treatment, just a week before the killing.

A number of individuals, including two physicians at River Park Hospital, corroborated his psychosis. His history, combined with my testing, eliminated the possibility that he had cleverly created a mental illness, after the killing, to beat the charges he faced. Lastly, as I sat face-to-face with James, as I probed each aspect of the events that had led him to fall for the scam, then to kill Pat, I had come to know James well, perhaps better than anyone else. I saw him as a study in pathos, a broken man who once had been successful and well-functioning. I concluded my report, in part:

It is my opinion, to a reasonable degree of psychological certainty, that at the time of the shooting of Pat Brougham, James suffered from a psychotic process which caused him to lack the capacity to appreciate the wrongfulness of his conduct or to conform his conduct to the requirements of the law. There is ample evidence to support this, from what I have learned.

Many times during my work with James and lawyer Gibson, I had asked myself an obvious question: Following the scam, why had he not taken his lumps and moved on? Certainly it had been a colossal embarrassment. He had been duped by people of reprehensible ethics and character. His financial losses were enormous. But other people had been similarly victimized and had shown great resilience. Wherein lay the difference between James Constantino and other victims of scam artists? What had led James to fall apart? The answer, I concluded, was that James lacked a valuable cognitive skill, an ability that is central to human happiness — the ability to acknowledge a foolish error in judgment, cut one's losses and move on a great deal wiser. Each of us, if we are to thrive, must be able to exhale and say "I blew it." But such a coping skill was not part of James' behavioral repertoire.

An equal partner in James' collapse, oddly enough, was that he had been successful at nearly everything he had attempted to do. He had little history of coping with forces of the sort that ultimately crushed him. It had befallen him to be faced simultaneously with a huge financial loss, the possible loss of his business, the selloff of his home, the possibility (however remote) that Pat would leave him, his loss of esteem and reputation in the community and that his sexual orientation would be revealed. He had long borne within him the unfortunate assumption that whatever he touched would turn to gold, even a South African "inheritance."

An important question, one generally raised by prosecutors, is this: How is it possible that an individual is out of touch with reality, yet engages in careful planning of a horrible act such as homicide? The answer is straightforward. Psychosis does not preclude planning, provided the details of the plan fit neatly within the individual's delusional system. Consider the case of John Hinckley, the man who shot President Ronald Reagan. Hinckley had fallen in love with actress Jodie Foster, although he had no connection with her. Over time, he had come to believe that she would return his love if he assassinated the president. Clearly, he was functioning well outside the bounds of reality. He was psychotic. Yet he carefully planned the shooting. He purchased the gun, flew across the country to Washington DC, studied how best to find an opportunity to shadow the president, waited until the crucial moment, and fired. To repeat, psychosis does not preclude planning.

Another of Lawyer Michael Gibson's questions to me was whether James now was competent to stand trial. I concluded that he was indeed competent. He had answered my questions about the charges against him and the legal process correctly. He would be able to assist his attorney in his defense, given that he had been hospitalized and his thought processes essentially had normalized. He could go to trial.

Gibson's final question concerned whether, on the day of the shooting, James' statement to the police had been voluntarily given. That was a more difficult question than one of competency because it was possible James was shocked into reality by the stark violence of his own actions. He had called 911. At some level, he knew what he had done and that it was wrong, or at a minimum he had concluded that Pat's death was irreversible and he had caused it.

I reviewed the transcript of his interview with Lt. A. D. Beasley and Deputy S. J. Cary, both of the Mercer County Sheriff's Office. James was able to describe the shooting to them in reasonably good detail. There was no evidence that the officers had used any coercion, threats, promises, inducements or the like in their interview with James. They had conducted themselves properly. Yet James clearly had been psychotic at the time of the shooting and during much of the forty-eight hours he had spent in the home with Pat's body, as evidenced by the fact that he shouted at the body to get up and thought there might be a way to make things better, to somehow undo what could never be undone. Additionally, it was likely that he continued to experience some level of shock and confusion as he talked to the officers. Thus, I concluded that I was unable to determine whether the statement he had given had been entirely voluntary, or not.

* * * * * * * * *

I concluded my examination and sent my report to Michael Gibson. During the year that followed, James was examined by two other local mental health professionals, each of whom concluded that James had suffered from severe mental illness, although they disagreed slightly on the proper diagnosis.

James never went to trial. On May 11, 2006, James pled guilty to second degree murder, which carries a penalty of one to 40 years. James' placement became a concern. Michael Gibson contacted me on August 21, 2006, to ask my opinion in regard to whether James ought to be placed in the state's prison or at one of its two forensic hospitals. I recommended the latter:

...(Placement at) Sharp Psychiatric Hospital will be more beneficial to Mr. Constantino and to society, than would incarceration (even on the mental health unit) at Mt. Olive State Prison. It stands to reason that the staff at Sharp Hospital, which has but a single specialty (forensic

mental health), is in a better position to provide treatment than is Mt. Olive where mental health treatment is not the primary focus.

In the end, James was placed within the prison system. At the time this book was published, he remained housed at the McDowell County Correctional Center, rather than Mt. Olive State Prison, with a projected release date of December 2015.

Three

Caught Faking a Mental Illness

FOR MORE THAN TWENTY YEARS Rhuann Cabral had lived across Gil-Bob Street from the James Mauro family in their upscale Fairmont, West Virginia, neighborhood. At 1:50 on the afternoon of July 21, 1992, she noticed Mauro standing in his driveway and a man in gray pants and white shirt walking up. A moment later, Cabral heard what sounded like firecrackers. She saw her neighbor fall into the arms of the man in the white shirt. As James Mauro fell, the other man grabbed him by the shoulders and pulled him into the garage. Rhuann Cabral heard the man in the white shirt say, "I told you, Jimmy, don't mess with me!" Moments later the garage door closed. Cabral then heard two more bangs.

The man in the white shirt was James Mauro's brother, Nicholas "Nick" Mauro, 48. Over the next several hours, Rhuann saw nothing more of her neighbor. Instead, she saw Nick Mauro leave the house and return several times in James' blue Pontiac. She continued watching until, an hour or two later, during one of Nick Mauro's return trips to the house, James Mauro's wife Frances arrived and entered. Immediately Rhuann Cabral heard the sharp sounds of what she again thought might be firecrackers. Moments later, James and Frances Mauro's grown son Jeff arrived at the home and walked through the front door. Rhuann Cabral heard more bangs.

Rhuann's husband Jim had seen and heard some of the curious activities too. "As soon as she (Frances) got in the door, it was bang, bang," he said. "(Jeff) went in and it was bang, bang again. I thought the boys were playing around." Neither Rhuann Cabral nor her husband called police. "I wasn't thinking murder because out there where we live, it's a nice community," she said later.

Nick Mauro had shot four people to death. They were his brother James Mauro Sr., 51, James' wife Frances, 48 and their two grown sons, James II, 26 and Jeff, 22. In the garage, two bodies lay under a car cover. Two others were in the living room, hidden beneath a second car cover. The four had been shot sixteen times over a couple of hours. Other neighbors besides the Cabrals also had heard "firecracker" sounds. Finally, one of them called police, around 9 p.m.

James Mauro was a law school graduate who had become a businessman. He operated a successful pharmacy in Kingwood, West Virginia. His wife, Frances, ran a card shop in nearby Bridge-port. Their older son, James II, managed a convenience store his parents owned. His wedding was to have taken place the following week. Younger son Jeff Mauro was a recent honors graduate who was to attend law school at West Virginia University in the fall. "They were a very industrious, hard-working family that was extremely successful," Police Chief Ted Offutt said. He might have added that the man who had murdered them was anything but.

Nicholas Mauro quickly became a suspect. Police found the car he had been driving parked near the grisly death scene. It was a vehicle he had borrowed from his mother because his own car was undergoing repairs. Following the shootings, Nick drove his brother's Pontiac twenty miles to the Econo Lodge Motel in the town of Westover, where he and his wife Sandy, along with their three-year-old son and her eleven-year-old daughter, had lived for several weeks. At 2:30 a.m. police spotted the Pontiac. Made aware by management that Nick was not alone in the room, police waited in the darkness and considered their options. Cautiously, they asked themselves whether Nick's killing spree might extend to his wife and the children, if they, the police, should fail to exercise the greatest care in apprehending the gunman. With

Sandy and the children inside, they could not risk charging into the room. At 5:30 a.m., they dialed the Mauros' room number. Sandy answered. They asked her to turn on the television. Horrified, she watched breaking news of the quadruple slayings. As morning light streaked the sky, Sandy Mauro experienced a dawning realization of her own. If Nick had done this, might he be capable of killing her and the children, and then himself?

Police knew their single best hope for resolution lay in maintaining communication with the couple, and Sandy sensed the same. Looking back, if there was a hero that day, it was Sandy Mauro. She continued talking to the police and to Nick. She calmed the children. The hours crept by until noon with no resolution. Outside, the summer's heat continued to climb. Inside, fatigue and tension mounted in equal measures. Two o'clock came and went, with no progress. Then, at 3:30, Nick gave up. Sandy and the kids walked safely out of the motel room. Moments later, Nick surrendered.

* * * * * * * * *

The evidence against Nick Mauro was overwhelming. At 5:11 p.m. during one of his trips away from the death scene, Nick had cashed a $6,000 check, forged on his dead brother's account. Bank teller Tina Yost gave him the cash in $100 and $50 bills. Later in the evening, Econo Lodge clerk Carrie Austin noticed that Nick's shirt was dirty and he was sweating heavily as he handed her six $100 bills, payment toward the more than $1,000 that he owed. Nick had visited his mother Bertha that evening. He had given her $2,000 in cash to repay a loan.

Among Nick's things in the motel room, police found another forged check, uncashed, in the amount of $4,000, written on the business account of James Mauro Jr. Also in the room they discovered James Mauro's wallet and a loaded .38-caliber handgun in the pocket of a bloody jacket. Ballistics tests showed the gun had fired the fatal shots. When authorities inspected the dead man's car, they discovered items that hinted at Nick's eerie plan to dispose of the bodies. In the car's trunk were four sleeping bags and a pair of five-gallon gas cans. Nick Mauro had purchased them at K-Mart during one of his trips away from the death house.

Immediately following the shootings, neither Rhuann nor her husband was able to identify Nicholas "Nick" Mauro as the man in the white shirt. In contrast, more than a year later Mrs. Cabral named Nick Mauro as the shooter. Asked about the discrepancy in her statements she said, "I saw the man's face...I know who I saw."

* * * * * * * * *

Nick and Sandy Mauro had wed in 1988. At the Econo Lodge, Nick had registered under an assumed name. Sandy explained that Nick said the deception was necessary to help them avoid an irrational ex-wife who had been stalking him.

On the morning of the shootings Sandy had looked forward to dinner out that evening to celebrate their son's third birthday. Nick left the room between 7 a.m. and 8 a.m. after telling Sandy that whatever plans she made for the birthday would be OK with him. "He kissed our son on the forehead...then kissed me and left," she said. Nick called her around 5 p.m. from his mother's home to say he would be back at the motel shortly, although he didn't arrive until around 8 p.m. Not recognizing the vehicle he drove, Sandy innocently concluded Nick had obtained a rental while their vehicle continued to be in the shop. She suspected nothing to be amiss.

Nick had convinced Sandy that the family had no money troubles. But there was a dark side to her husband that she had yet to suspect. Acquaintances described Nick as perpetually in pursuit of big business deals that seemed never to materialize. He fancied himself a wheeler-dealer, a high roller, they said. He made junkets to Las Vegas and Atlantic City and had gambling debts, according to a man who knew him. In 1991 he and his mother were sued for defaulting on a $14,000 loan. He had been taken to court a number of other times over money problems. Moreover, he had a tendency toward violence. At the time of the shootings, police held two outstanding battery and assault warrants as well as several bad check warrants against him which, more than likely, explained his use of an assumed name at the motel. Perhaps a tipping point had occurred when Nick learned that he had been cut out of his late father's $400,000 will. Although it never will be known for a certainty, it is likely that Nick and his brother had argued over money on the day of the killings. Perhaps Nick again had sought to borrow cash. Perhaps his brother at last had said, "Enough!"

Sandy was Nick's fourth wife. His first marriage had split up after nine years. He had a daughter, by this time twenty-four years of age, from that union. His second marriage dissolved after eleven years. It had produced a son, now fifteen, and a daughter, now twelve. A third marriage lasted only ten months. He and Sandy had been married for four years.

Sandy Mauro probably was unaware of another troubling side to her husband – his history of a mental health breakdown. Six years before the shootings, Nick had become psychotic. His 1984 hospitalization had been at the West Virginia University School of Medicine's Department of Behavioral Medicine and Psychiatry. He was admitted following an auto wreck, thought by some of his treatment team members to have been intentional. Hospital staff learned that Nick was suffering both business difficulties and family problems. He and his second wife had been separated for five months. He had lost weight and had trouble sleeping. The admitting physician wrote that Nick was "absolutely at a loss when trying to make decisions or engage in any sustained, goal-directed thinking."

During his hospitalization, staff saw an ebb and flow in Nick's contact with reality as well as in his moods. However, there was concern that Nick might have been manipulative with his therapists. At one point he told his attending physician that his major reason for coming to the hospital was "so my wife would drop breaking and entering charges." Sometimes he expressed excessive concern for material things, his doctor reported. He was worried about possibly going to jail. The doctor noted, "Does not seem sincere in plea for help."

At other times, Nick exhibited signs of psychosis. There were indications that he feared he was being watched by the Internal

Revenue Service, although it was not clear whether his concern was real or delusional. The day after his admission, the attending physician noticed that Nick was talking in *non-sequiturs*. When asked for the date he was unable to respond. He gave no response when asked to repeat a series of numbers. By the next day, he was unable to respond to questions and was so indecisive and confused that he could not remove his contact lenses.

He was convinced that the people who administered an EEG had drilled holes in his head and continued to believe that even after the staff had helped him inspect his scalp in a mirror. As the next few days passed, Nick's condition improved. His mood lightened. He was smiling and joking. By the tenth day of his hospital stay there were no indications of psychosis. His delusional thinking had abated. He remained hospitalized until November 16, 1984, when he was discharged after seventeen days, with a diagnosis of major depressive disorder with melancholia. Nick was given a follow-up appointment at the local community mental health center. Whether he ever kept it is unknown.

* * * * * * * * *

Defense attorneys Patrick Wilson and James Shields knew that they faced an uphill battle. There was essentially no dispute that Nick Mauro had committed four homicides. But Nick's more than two weeks of treatment as a psychiatric inpatient caught their attention. Wilson and Shields asked themselves whether it was possible Nick had lapsed into psychosis on the day he killed his brother's family. To explore that possibility, they asked me to conduct a forensic examination. Had Nick become psychotic at the time of the killings? Was he competent to stand trial?

From mid-August to late September 1992, I met with Nick Mauro on five occasions. Our discussions took place in a small room in the Marion County courthouse next to the jail. Nick entered each day clad in inmate clothing and shackles, escorted by a deputy. Because I wanted him to feel as comfortable as possible and because he would need to complete some psychological testing, I asked that the shackles be removed during each meeting. Additionally, good practice dictates that no outsiders be in earshot. I asked the deputy to leave the room. He did, however, wait just outside the door of the examination room. Consistent with my usual practice, I made it clear to Nick that anything he told me might go into my written report or into my testimony at his trial. He agreed to proceed with the examination.

During our first meeting, Nick said he recalled going to his brother's home, but said he did not remember shooting anyone. He recalled his return to the Econo Lodge feeling he wanted to be with his family, and thinking about his son's birthday celebration. He said that the first he knew anything was wrong was when police called the motel room. He added that, with the exception of Sandy, everybody in Fairmont hated him, including his remaining family members. He even felt the eyes of his dead relatives looking down at him in disapproval.

Given that he faced possible life in prison, Nick exhibited a surprising characteristic – jail life irritated him. He felt he was intellectually superior to other inmates. Actually, this may have been true, given that Nick was a graduate of West Virginia University with a degree in biology and had taught seventh and eighth grade science for five years. He complained about jail restrictions, such as being allowed to shave just twice a week. He found it unacceptable that inmates were permitted to play their televisions at all hours and that there was no one with whom to have intelligent conversations. "They live like animals," he said. "They use words like 'chow,' rather than saying breakfast, lunch and dinner." He discussed the possibility that he would be sent to the state's prison, then located in the northern panhandle town of Moundsville. He asked, rhetorically, "Is there one intelligent person up there?" He had ended the lives of four unoffending individuals, yet he felt it was reasonable to complain about the inconveniences of life in lock-up. I got the impression that, in Nick's convoluted thinking, the permanent loss of his liberty was no big deal provided he could keep on thinking of himself as superior.

Nick was interested in my potential findings, as well as in the findings of any other mental health professionals who might be hired by the county prosecutor to examine him. He brought up the possibility that, instead of going to Moundsville, he might eventually be confined in the state's forensic mental hospital in Weston, perhaps in hopes that I would recommend he be placed there.

Although I was learning a good deal about Nick, throughout the first meeting he tended to ramble. He also seemed preoccupied and distant. He frequently avoided direct answers and shifted from topic to topic, although he generally was lucid. I was forming an impression of Nick Mauro – that he was feeling me out, attempting to determine whether he might manipulate the examination process to his advantage. It didn't take long to discover that my suspicion was well founded.

On the morning of our second day together, Nick entered the room minus his glasses, and with a bandanna wrapped around his head. He seemed confused. He said little when I greeted him, except to respond with the word, "Jerry." Otherwise, for more than ten minutes he remained silent, as he furtively scanned the room. Finally, he broke his silence with a request for his glasses. The deputy accompanied him back to the jail. He returned with the glasses which, rather than wearing, he laid on the table that separated us. To my suggestion that he appeared to be unsettled, he gave no response.

Soon the deputy knocked on the door. He informed me that Sandy Mauro had arrived at the courthouse and was waiting in the corridor. I had asked her to meet with me so that I could learn her perspective on Nick's behavior on the day of the shootings. Nick, on hearing that she was nearby, asked to go to the restroom. He removed the do-rag and left it on the table. He put on his glasses, then stepped into the hallway. Quietly, I advised the deputy that I wanted to observe Nick as he talked with Sandy. I was not able hear their conversation, but the conversation appeared thoughtful. Except for the bright orange jail jumpsuit, their chat would have appeared normal to a disinterested onlooker. Was Nick indeed in touch with reality? It appeared so.

That afternoon we met again. Nick was more talkative and thoughtful, at least initially. Then I began to discuss his memory of the events on the day of the shootings. His talk suddenly became bizarre. He said, "I didn't go, did I?" Then he asked, "Was it before Christmas?" I clarified that it had occurred in July and that his brother had been shot and killed, upon which he looked shocked and asked, "My brother is dead!?!"

I began a series of questions to assess his orientation. Did he know who he was? Where he was? Could he identify the time frame? He responded that he presently lived at 1660 Clifton Road in Fairmont with his wife Rosetta. I knew, however, that they had been divorced many years prior. He said they had a daughter about six years of age. Again, not true. I asked him why he had worn handcuffs when he was led into the room. He answered that he felt someone was playing games with him. He said that the courthouse was City National Bank and he was there to apply for a loan to purchase a washer and dryer. He addressed me as if I were a loan officer. I asked him the present date. June 6, 1974, he said. He was off by eighteen years. The date was actually August 18, 1992.

I sensed that Nick was the one who was playing games — that he was attempting to feign a dissociative disorder. Such disorders usually arise when there is a history of sustained, severe childhood abuse. Dissociative identity disorder (historically termed multiple personality disorder) results when a child's means of adaptation to severe, sustained stress in childhood continues into adulthood, where it becomes maladaptive. Such a child may invent an imaginary friend to take some of his or her abuse. Doubtless, such a coping strategy helps the child deal with pain. Because it is helpful to the child, the imaginary friend tends to be employed as long as the abuse continues. But for successful adult functioning, this coping mechanism must come to an end. However, when it continues, dissociative identity disorder may result as the adult may invoke an imaginary other person to bear some of his burdens, in times of extreme stress. The behavioral pattern may be psychologically helpful in easing pain for the child, but later leads to lapses in functioning with regard to identity, when he or she is grown up. In behavioral science terms, it is important to avoid the lure of a cinema version of the disorder. The notion that the patient's odd behaviors are caused by multiple "personalities" that lurk within the psyche, ready to fight with each other for dominance, is not much removed from the notion of demonic possession, and is equally useless as an explanation of the disorder.

I tested whether Nick might be pretending to be disoriented, whether he was faking a dissociative reaction. First I asked his age, which I knew to be fifty-one. He responded that he was "thirty or thirty-one," then added, obtusely, "Is this necessary for the application?" Next I asked him to name the president and the governor. He replied, "Nixon, he should be in jail...(and) Hewlett C. Smith." Nick was correct about Nixon who indeed was president on June 6, 1974, but would resign two months later. However, Hewlett C. Smith had been the state's governor from 1965 to 1969. Nick's guess was off by five years. Quickly, I had confirmed that Nick was engaging in a crude attempt to fake a dissociative disorder. He had presented me with a Hollywood version of mental illness.

I stopped the examination and asked the deputy to take Nick back to the jail. I left the courthouse and walked to the office of attorneys Patrick Wilson and Charles Shields. I went straight to the point — their client had engaged in a poorly done imitation of a person having a psychotic episode. They appreciated that I was frank with them. I added that, given his hospitalization history, it was possible that he actually had been psychotic on the day he ended the lives of four relatives. Thus, I suggested that Wilson and Shields meet with Nick and push him to be honest with me. They agreed. A few days later Patrick Wilson called. Their meeting with Nick had gone well enough. Nick admitted to them that he had pretended to be mentally ill.

I returned to Fairmont and continued the examination. It was my fifth meeting with Nick. He apologized for his earlier effort to dissimulate. He described going to his brother's home three times on the day of the shootings. He said he had partial memory of the events. He had arrived to discuss a potential business associate whom his brother may not have known. He maintained that in the beginning there had been no conflict. After some discussion with James, Nick left, went to McDonald's, then returned to James' home. It was then that the two began to argue. Their dispute involved money, and James brought up Nick's business losses in the 1970s. Nick recalled having a gun in his pocket, only because his mother had asked him to sell it for her, telling him it didn't work. As the argument escalated, his brother attempted to shut the door. The next thing Nick recalled was the gun firing, he said.

He told me he had been unable to maneuver his brother into the car, so he laid him in the garage. He claimed not to remember what happened during the next few minutes. Evidently Nick's nephew, hearing the initial shots, had rushed to the garage where he then was murdered. The next thing Nick remembered was his nephew's briefcase lying in the yard. He picked it up, put it in his brother's car and left. He added, "The papers say I cashed a check at the bank." He denied any memory of seeing either his second nephew or his sister-in-law, both of whom he killed during the next couple of hours.

I learned more about Nick's history. I noticed his interest in impressing me with the fact that everybody in the family was successful and intelligent. The family was thought of as important in the community. An uncle was chairman of the board of a local bank, he said. Nick added one additional important insight. In the past year he had become involved in "too many businesses, too scattered and unfocused."

He, Sandy and the children had lived in a rented townhouse and paid $1,100 a month, he claimed. They were forced to move when the owner decided to sell, Nick said. They were looking for a home to purchase but decided to live in the Econo Lodge temporarily, so that Sandy's daughter could finish out the school year. As my final meeting with Nick drew to a close, I had learned a great deal about him, and much of it wasn't good.

On the same day that Nick had pretended to lose his grip on reality, I interviewed Sandy Mauro. The day of the shootings began routinely, she said. After a kiss good bye, Nick left the room. However, he seemed not to be himself when he phoned her around 5 p.m. to say that he would be home soon. He did not return until around 8:00. "He wasn't like he usually was... he was stressed...he didn't look right," she said. They went to Shoney's restaurant to celebrate their son's birthday. Nick didn't eat much. Rather, "He moved food around on his plate." By 11:30 that evening Nick was pacing up and down, which was unlike him. Sometime in the middle of the night he took her hand and said, "I love you. I don't always show you."

Around 5:30 in the morning the police called their room, told her about the shooting and asked her to turn on the television. As the news reported the shootings, she noticed a strange look on her husband's face. He looked like a different person, she said. As the standoff dragged on through the morning and into the early afternoon, Sandy stayed on the phone with the authorities. Occasionally she hugged Nick. At times she read stories to the children to keep them occupied. Sometimes she prayed.

Eventually, Nick talked to the police. He took some medication they left by the motel room door. Nick asked to speak to a priest. If she and the children left the room safely, police told her, they would arrange it. Nick told Sandy that he was feeling that his spirit would always remain in the motel room. She felt he was becoming convinced he would die there. Sandy had a decision to make. Should she remain in the room in hopes she could save him? Or should she leave with the children if an opportunity arose?

Around 3:30 in the afternoon, the ordeal was about to end. Sandy finally convinced Nick that he should surrender. He told the police that he would do so after a few minutes alone with his family. He hugged each of them and said that he loved them. Then Nick walked across the hall to where police waited. Sandy's efforts had worked. She and the kids were alive, as was Nick. She rode with Nick to the police station. They scarcely talked during the brief ride. Her abiding memory was of "the haunting look on his face...I see it every time I close my eyes," she whispered.

Sandy told me that she never had seen Nick as she had observed him that night. In fact, she had never noticed any behavior that she considered bizarre. She recalled the routine things of their relationship. They played tennis in the mornings, although he had lost interest in the game in the past couple of weeks. She knew little of their finances. The name Jerry meant nothing to her. She knew of no bad blood between Nick and his brother. There had been no history of violence as long as she had known Nick. She frequently talked to his second wife, who also never mentioned any violent tendencies.

She had visited with James Mauro and his family only five times in four years. She recalled twice that they met in restaurants to celebrate the birthday of the brothers' grandmother. Another time she had chatted with her sister-in-law, Frances Mauro, at a Mother's Day church event to which both had been invited by Nick's mother Bertha. Once they stopped briefly at James Mauro's drug store. And they had attended a party in honor of James Mauro's fiftieth birthday on July 20, 1991. None of those present at the celebration could have suspected that James Mauro and his family would be dead just a year and a day later.

There is a cold, professional side to forensic psychology. Our training helps us to be dispassionate. Yet, although it sounds trite, most of us enter the field of psychology because we care about people. I felt for Sandy Mauro, as I did for the James Mauro family and, in some sense, for Nick himself. Sandy was sincere, open and overwhelmed. I recommended that she seek supportive counseling. She needed someone to lean on while the legal system meandered its way to a conclusion of Nick's case. In her disappointment, disillusionment and in her sadness, it was her case too.

We talked a while longer, until it was time for her to visit Nick at the jail. When she stood up to go, I handed her the bandanna Nick had left on the table. Eying it, she turned it over and over in her hands. Then she said, "This isn't Nick."

* * * * * * * * *

The charges were four counts of premeditated murder. In light of the Fairmont area's extensive pre-trial publicity and the community's esteem for the James Mauro family, Patrick Wilson and Charles Shields requested and were awarded a change of venue. The trial began on August 29, 1994, almost 150 miles south of Fairmont, at the courthouse in Beckley, West Virginia.

It was my conclusion that Nick had not visited his brother with the intention of killing him. Rather, it had been the heat of the moment combined with his anger and the availability of the gun that had led to the initial shooting. I testified that I did not consider Nick to have been psychotic during the first shooting, and possibly not during the second. By the time he killed Frances Mauro and the second of his nephews, however, rationality was gone. I felt that he had suffered a brief psychotic reaction. His actions had been inconsistent with rational thinking. In my report to Wilson and Shields I wrote, "Had Mr. Mauro not been psychotic he would not have left his car at the scene, would not have driven his brother's car home, would not have cashed a check on his brother's account and simply returned home." While some of his actions (purchase of the sleeping bags and gas cans) could well have been rational, the totality of Nick's functioning, put together with his history of hospitalization and paranoia, supported my conclusion that at some point he had lapsed into psychosis.

At the trial I repeated my opinion. Regarding premeditation, I testified, "If he was going to plan a crime, he would have done a better job than this." I added, "I don't think he went to his brother's house with the intention to kill him that day." I told the jury that Mauro had attempted to convince me that he was insane, but that he later admitted he had been faking. However, I also reminded them of Nick's stay in the psychiatric unit of the West Virginia University hospital six years previously, and that while there he had become convinced that a staff member had bored holes in his head. "This is not a case of a person who's making up a mental illness defense now, out of the blue," I testified. "I believe as the day wore on, the fog was lifting from his brain…and he began to understand that something terrible had happened and he could potentially be in a lot of trouble."

Assistant Marion County Prosecutor James Hearst described Mauro's activities of the day and noted that Nick had to reload the pistol three times. "Does that not seem to be a premeditated, calculated set of circumstances?" Hearst asked. In reply, I reminded the jury that the ability to plan is not inconsistent with psychosis.

"The fact that he could do that does not mean he was sane," I said.

A second defense expert was Dr. Jonas Rappaport, whose former patients included John Hinckley Jr., the man who shot President Ronald Reagan. Rappaport agreed with another of my findings, that Nick suffered a narcissistic personality disorder. That disturbance, which is marked by powerful feelings of self-importance, had combined with his business losses, gambling debts, marriage failures and his inability to approach the successes of his brother to set the stage for an episode of psychosis.

The prosecutor also called mental health experts who testified that Nick was sane at the time of each of the four killings. Dr. Thomas Adamski, deputy medical director at William R. Sharp Hospital, and Dr. William Fremouw, a faculty member at West Virginia University's Department of Psychology, each rejected the notion that Nick had been insane at some point. Interestingly, Fremouw had been one of my professors. When Patrick Wilson asked Adamski to consider Nick's history of depression and psychosis during his stay in the hospital six years earlier, the doctor seemed to focus only on the depression. He replied, in part, "I would not have offered the opinion that he was insane at the time… He suffered from an affliction that affects millions of people."

Dr. William Fremouw and I had come to Morgantown in 1975, he as a young faculty member and I as an advanced graduate student. Several times we have found ourselves on opposite sides of forensic cases. I am proud to have been his student and pleased that he and I have had no hard feelings even though our opinions have differed at times. He taught me a great deal, and I trust that he appreciates that I have attempted to build on all of it. Fremouw testified that a psychotic person, "…would not be able to go to a bank, cash a check and talk to a teller." I disagreed.

* * * * * * * * *

There were other moments during the trial that I found compelling. If any witness deserved compassion, it was Sandy Mauro. Life as she had come to live it had been pierced through its heart. Given that it was Sandy whose efforts had been the lynchpin to a bloodless resolution at the motel, I found it somewhat surprising that assistant prosecutor Hearst attacked her over some inconsistencies in her statements to police. "You lied to protect him, didn't you?" Hearst asked. "I'm not lying," she replied. Hearst hammered at Sandy's assertion that often she was unaware of Nick's activities during the day, and that she tended to be in the dark as to his whereabouts when he disappeared for a day or two. "That was pretty convenient for him wasn't it?" Hearst asked. If Hearst was suggesting that Sandy Mauro somehow was involved in Nick's murderous activities, he was dead wrong.

One of Bertha Mauro's sons had killed the other. Shaken and tearful, she told the jury that Nick had suffered from seizures as a teen. "He wasn't a bad person," she said. "You just couldn't talk to him at times." She testified about a time in his adult years when he had become afraid to leave the family's skating rink at night. "He was afraid someone was coming after him." And maybe someone was. Bertha's testimony concluded. She was helped from the courtroom by Sandy Mauro. The two walked out of the courthouse. One had lost her husband. The other would have to live on minus her sons, grandsons and her other daughter-in-law.

* * * * * * * * *

The jury listened to the evidence and undertook its deliberations. As it did so, Patrick Wilson and Charles Shields, along with Nick and Assistant Prosecutor Hearst, met in the judge's chambers to discuss a Jury question regarding premeditation. Suddenly, without warning and before either Wilson or Shields could stop him, Nick bolted and leapt from the second story courthouse window. He fell twenty feet, seriously injuring his foot. Beckley resident Charles Stack was walking nearby. "He said, 'Help me away from here,'" Stack said. Deputies quickly caught up with the injured defendant. Fortunately, the jurors hadn't heard the fracas. An hour after Nick's leap the verdict was returned. Nick Mauro was found guilty of second degree murder in the death of his brother James. Thus, jurors concurred with my opinion that he had not visited his brother with a premeditated plan to kill. But they rejected the idea that Nick, at any time, had suffered a mental illness. He was found guilty on three counts of first degree murder. Frances Mauro's three sisters wept as the verdict was read. James Mauro Jr.'s former fiancée Judy Warren said, "It's a relief...We're just glad it's over. It was a long time coming." The jury did not recommend mercy, which meant that Nick Mauro would live out his days with no hope of parole.

Fifteen years later, Nick rested in his cell at the Mt. Olive state penitentiary, gravely ill. Staff transported him to a Charleston hospital where, a few days later, he passed away quietly. He was sixty-seven years old.

Four

Death in Room 127

LATE ON OCTOBER 4, 2003, stripper Misty Cabral ended her shift at JB's Club. The teenager walked east along the berm of U.S. Rt. 60. She and boyfriend Keith "Bobby" Lowe lived a quarter-mile from the club, in room 127 at the seedy Rustic Motel in the town of Jefferson, West Virginia.

Jefferson is a three-mile strip of highway between St. Albans and South Charleston, sometimes termed the "badlands." Its residents incorporated the town following the growth of the area's sex industry. Porn shops and gentlemen's clubs like JB's had proliferated in recent years. Following incorporation, the citizens established limits on new sex businesses, but JB's and several others remained because they pre-existed the city's regulations.

Misty and Bobby had come to Jefferson from Louisa, Kentucky. Misty had grown up there. Bobby had arrived in Louisa to reconnect with his mother, Hope Good, following a dishonorable discharge (he had gone AWOL) after sixteen months in the Army, as well as a stay in a hospital during which he had become psychotic. Misty and Bobby hoped to save enough money from her work and his job building modular garages to purchase a trailer and get out of Jefferson.

Although Misty's shift at JB's was over, her night's work was not. Also headed toward room 127 was her personal client, fifty-five-year-old Roy Loyd, who had come for both a private dance and for sex with Misty. Loyd, a resident of the Braxton County town of Flatwoods, was a regular who routinely paid hundreds of dollars for sex. He also possessed an interesting quirk: He compulsively recorded the most intimate details of his and his partner's sexual activities in a diary.

Misty arrived at the Rustic and told Bobby that Roy Loyd was coming. As Bobby had done on other such occasions, he made himself scarce. There was unease in Bobby's mood that evening. He vacillated between his desire to trust Misty and his growing suspicion that Misty was prostituting herself, despite the young woman's reassurances to the contrary. She was earning more money from the private "dances" than seemed reasonable, or so Bobby thought.

Bobby's uncertainty had heightened a week ago. Misty had told Bobby, and her mother, Deborah Cabral, who was visiting from Louisa, that recently Roy had refused to pay for a private dance because she wouldn't provide sex. Outraged, Bobby might have harmed Roy then, but the man had already left. Deborah and Misty listened as Bobby said, "Well, I know what I'm going to have to do with him. I'm going to have his head." But Bobby calmed down in a couple of days and told Misty she could see Roy, provided it was clear to Roy that it was only for private dances, not sex. Even so, Bobby wondered whether Misty might have had sex with Roy and pocketed the cash to purchase crack cocaine, and then later concocted the story of Roy's non-payment.

From Bobby's perspective another recent development had entered the equation – Misty and Bobby learned that she was pregnant with his baby. Bobby Lowe was elated at the news. As a child of abuse and neglect, Bobby Lowe would now have a real family. With the child's arrival, he would feel the closeness and stability that had eluded him as he grew up.

* * * * * * * * *

Roy Loyd arrived at the Rustic motel and entered room 127 where Misty waited. Bobby, though still suspicious, had left the room to the couple. As he waited, Bobby's worries churned.

This was the third or fourth time that Misty had provided Roy with a private dance. Each time Bobby had gone to a friend's home to wait it out. Once while he was there, his host's girlfriend told Bobby that there was more than dancing going on.

Bobby's thoughts drifted back to his childhood and the abuse at the hands of his alcoholic father. Images of Misty and Roy in the room sent his anxiety soaring dangerously close to its boiling point. Were Misty and Roy doing something that could harm his unborn child? Unable to bear it, Bobby quietly walked to the door of room 127 and peered in through a hole in the blind. Misty and Roy were having sex.

When I examined him at the request of Kanawha County Deputy Public Defenders Gail I. Michelson and Zoe Shavers, Bobby described what happened next. Instantly, his naïve trust in Misty vanished. He burst into the room feeling as if his "head was on fire." He grabbed a hammer that lay just inside the door and began to hit Roy over and over — he could not remember how many times. Minutes later, Roy expired. Bobby and Misty sat on the bed and cried. They said nothing, except for Misty's plea to Bobby that he forgive her and not harm her. "My main thought was that he was hurting my baby…I wouldn't have flipped out except for the baby… the baby was why I went so far overboard," he told me. Bobby said that he never would have harmed Misty, although he was consumed with intense feelings of anger because she had betrayed him.

He told Misty to go to another room in the motel while he dealt with the bloody scene in room 127. He brought in a large trash can and a roll of duct tape. He stuffed Roy's body into the can, taped it shut, dragged it to the riverbank behind the motel and rolled it to the edge of the dark waters of the Kanawha River. Bobby returned to the room and scrubbed it clean. A man chasing a groundhog discovered the corpse several days later.

Authorities quickly identified the body. That led them to Roy's diary which, in turn, pointed the police to Misty, and from Misty there was a straight line to Bobby and room 127. Soon police developed their theory of the homicide. Bobby had killed Roy Loyd and Misty had been involved, either luring him to the hotel or, at least helping him cover up the killing. Perhaps she had done both.

Police and prosecutors considered the two theories of the killing. Had Bobby killed the victim in a moment of passionate outrage, or had he and Misty lured Roy to the motel with a plan to rob him? The latter scenario seemed improbable, given that Roy had become a cash cow for the couple. But when the case went to trial, Misty told the jury that she and Bobby had planned to rob the victim all along. However, Misty's version of events was unsatisfying to Bobby's attorneys. Michelson and Shavers felt that it made little sense that Bobby and Misty would have conspired to slay a man who had quickly become an ongoing source of easy income to the couple. Instead, Bobby's attorneys proposed an alternate reason to explain Misty's story of premeditated murder — Police investigators had suggested the story to her during an interrogation, in hopes her testimony would accomplish dual ends: Prosecutors would convict Bobby of first degree murder, and Misty could receive leniency if she helped them do it. For Michelson and Shavers the distinction was crucial. Premeditation carried a life sentence for Bobby. In contrast, a crime of the moment might give their 30-year-old client a chance to be released from prison after a decade or so.

* * * * * * * * *

While Michaelson and Shavers grappled with the divergence of Misty's and Bobby's descriptions of the brutal murder, they sensed another issue that might be crucial to Bobby's defense. Aware that he had a history of mental health treatment, the attorneys asked me to conduct a forensic examination to determine whether Bobby suffered from a mental illness that might have weakened his capacity to follow the law at the moment of the homicide. The "diminished capacity" defense would not absolve him of the crime, but it might bolster Bobby's contention that the killing had not been planned in advance. If he suffered diminished capacity, a jury could find him guilty of a lesser crime, such as second degree murder. With the attorneys' legal question in mind,

I examined Bobby at the South Central Regional Jail in Charleston.

As with every individual I examine, I took an extensive history. Bobby described his childhood years in Columbus, Ohio, as rife with abuse at the hands of his alcoholic father. His dad ran bars in which Bobby and his older brother, Michael, spent most of their time. Their father was violent and their mother was an alcoholic, often too drunk to protect her boys from their father's abuse. When Bobby was three and Michael was seven, they were made wards of the state because of the home's alcoholism and abuse. Bobby added that his awful childhood caused him to feel especially protective of his unborn baby. The sight of Roy and Misty having sex had triggered a feeling that the baby inside Misty was being harmed.

For a time, Bobby and his brother shuffled among the homes of two of his aunts, several foster homes and a facility called Buckeye Village. He never completed a full year in any one school. By age eleven he was doing drugs, including crack cocaine. By twelve or thirteen he was selling drugs on the street to support his growing habit. At one point he was arrested and spent six months in a juvenile facility. On his release, he continued using and selling drugs. In time, he graduated to stealing cars.

When he was eight, his father took custody for a while. Bobby described his father as "inhuman." His dad abused the boys with severe beatings, and by having them perform oral sex on each other. He described his dad as sometimes "sly" about the abuse, giving them treats to get them to perform. At other times his father was brutally violent. Bobby remembered an incident when he was so filled with fear during a vicious spanking that he urinated on his father's lap. Their dad, Harry, used cords to whip them and, if they cried, would tell them to be quiet or he would whip them more. An outcome of their madhouse of a childhood was an important lesson: There was safety in silence. It was always wise to suppress their emotions, to avoid further punishment.

Bobby's father was verbally abusive as well. He called Bobby worthless and said he would never amount to anything. The abuse never ceased. Their dad treated his boys the same way he treated unruly bar customers — He threw them into the street. His father was arrested more than twenty times for assault, and bragged about it. Bobby had a theory about his father's brutality – "Because granddad was the same way toward him."

As part of my examination, I sought further information from Bobby's brother. Michael confirmed their abusive childhoods, but refused to testify in court. Michelson and Shavers stressed to Michael that his testimony could be helpful to Bobby's case. If Michael confirmed the years of abuse, Bobby's descriptions would bear more credibility with the jury. But Michael said that he had been successful in life and wanted to keep the pain of his child hood in the past. During my conversation with Michael, he revealed that the degradation and physical violence of their childhoods was even worse than Bobby had described it. At one point the brothers were with sitter Grace Betts for two or three years, Michael said. Michael was certain that Bobby had been sexually molested there, although Michael had not been. The boys bounced from one place to another. "You were never sure what was home, who was your mom, who was your dad…," Michael said.

In 1985, when Michael was fourteen and Bobby was eleven, the boys again were living with their father and grandmother, Harry's mother, when their mom, Hope, returned to Columbus with a new husband. She had mostly remained out of their lives for the past seven years. Michael soon ran from their father's abuse to live with his mom, and the trio moved to Oswego, New York, leaving Bobby with his dad and grandmother. "My brother would call me begging me to come home. I was more of a parent to him than mom or dad," Michael said.

When Michael was seventeen he returned to Columbus and began living with a girl who worked for an escort service. He visited Bobby, who by then had been moved to a Methodist home because their father had decided that Bobby was incorrigible. Michael asked Bobby to move in with him and his girlfriend. The home was a mire of cocaine, strange visitors and his girlfriend's prostitution. Unable to take the chaos any longer, Michael left the house, but encouraged Bobby to remain, believing that the girl would look after Bobby for a while. In six months, Bobby was on the street. In a while, both boys reunited back at their mother's home in Columbus. Mostly, however, they lived on the streets, Michael said. They even left Columbus for a while, hitching to South Carolina where a Baptist minister helped them for a few weeks before they returned to the Ohio capital.

Around that time, Bobby met Lori, a woman about forty, and moved in with her. During their eight years together the much older woman brought Bobby's feelings of self-worth up somewhat, Bobby told me. Also, he remained fairly clean from drugs, was in far less legal difficulty and earned a living by driving a truck, while under Lori's influence. However, at some point he began to use drugs heavily again and the couple broke up.

The brothers' paths had begun to diverge several years earlier. Michael married, and the couple had lived in South Carolina ever since. As life improved for Michael, the years crawled by for his brother. "Bobby feels I deserted him," Michael added. For a while, "I put him in an apartment and paid for it," the older brother said. "Bobby got a job but soon was on drugs...In a while he went to Kentucky to be with our mom." And that is where he met Misty Cabral. Bobby never matured beyond the age of twelve or thirteen, Michael added.

I asked Michael several questions that I felt would help me to better understand his brother. What were the differences between him and Bobby? Michael said he had fared better because he was older and had found a good woman.

I asked Michael about details of the abuse by their dad and he reported, "It was nothing for my father to smack us around, throw us down. We had many sitters while mom and dad drank....Our mother, her sisters, Harry and his brother-in-law, all constantly were drinking and smoking pot. Once Harry put mom in the hospital. Another time she stabbed Harry. The men would fight. They did all of this in the house." Michael never understood why the women stayed with the abusive men. During the fighting, Michael and Bobby would hide in their room until the brawling stopped. Michael described a period in which his parents "were stealing us from each other." He said, "They used us to fight with each other. Once, our dad hid us in a dumpster out back when mom came to get us."

While Bobby had told me about sexual abuse at the hands of their dad, Michael went further. He described fondling and oral sex done to both of them by older boys, while living with their grandmother and Harry. Once a man molested them and was caught by police and went to prison. Their mother had shown them a clipping about it. I formed the impression that Michael considered the instability to have been the worst facet of their deplorable childhoods. Nothing was permanent. The boys had no sense of place, no person to consistently nurture them, no close emotional relationship with another human being. Michael poignantly told me how, when Bobby's dog died, his little brother wrapped his arms around the pet and refused to let go for two hours.

Would he describe their terrifying childhood at Bobby's trial? "I'm not going to start over (by attending the trial)," he said. Michael feared that his testimony might somehow hurt Bobby's chances. And perhaps the conversations with Bobby, his lawyers and with me, already had taken Michael too close to the decay of the childhood he had fled. We had transported Michael to the boundary of something terrible, something no longer part of his life that he had safely walled off. I understood that Michael felt as though he had been re-born in his twenties and that the childhood he described had almost faded out of perspective, only now to re-emerge into clear focus. Michael was adamant that he would not testify, and he didn't.

* * * * * * * * *

I also spoke with Bobby's mother, Hope Good. She confirmed the abuse and neglect of her boys and herself. Harry beat her two or three times a week. "The police were called a thousand times. His mother would pay my rent to get me to drop the charges. The boys were there and sometimes would try to jump on Harry. They cried and screamed. I wasn't a very good mother. I got plastered before Harry got out of jail each time, because it was easier," Hope added. Harry called her and the boys, "sons of a bitch, bastard, and screamed we were no fucking good."

For a time, she took the boys to Texas with a new man, Jim, who also was abusive. She and Jim drank a lot. On one occasion Jim beat her savagely, putting her in the hospital. Upon her release, she moved in with her sister and her sister's husband, who also was abusive, so she and the boys moved out. When Bobby was about twelve, she sent the boys back to Columbus, back to the sitters, back to Harry, back to abuse and molestation. When Bobby was in his mid-twenties, he told her about the sexual abuse, including "fondling and probably the whole nine yards," Hope said. The people in one abusive sitter's home were "dopers, filthy, dirty, nasty people," she told me. Bobby had told her how Harry had forced the boys to perform oral sex on each other. In a while, Bobby ran away from Columbus, from Harry, from the sitters and the abuse and returned to Hope, in Texas. Her memory of that era was dim, she said, because she drank heavily then.

Like Michael, Hope refused to testify. Although corroboration of Bobby's abusive, chaotic childhood might have proven vital to Bobby's defense, Hope was terrified of testifying. She had panic attacks and other nerve problems, she said, and she feared prosecutors would twist her testimony in ways that would hurt Bobby. Either that or, like Michael, she could not bear to relive her own awful part in Bobby's history.

* * * * * * * * *

Bobby told me about his psychiatric problems. He heard voices that told him he was ugly and he was reluctant to look in a mirror, although I found his physical appearance to be normal. The voices also told him he was worthless, and that he should hurt people. In Charleston's South Central Regional Jail, he heard people having conversations and he thought they were talking about him, saying they hated him. Sometimes he grew angry enough that he confronted those people. It wasn't the first time Bobby had lost his grip on what was real, as I learned when I reviewed his medical records.

Well before the killing, he had undergone several courses of mental health treatment. One occurred while Bobby was jailed for four months in Florida for stealing a truck, after his discharge from the Army. His mental status deteriorated and the jail's doctor was consulted. The doctor prescribed several psychotropic medications including Zoloft, Lithium and Seroquel. That combination of drugs meant the doctor viewed Bobby as depressed and suffering from either bi-polar disorder or schizophrenia, or some combination of the two.

When Bobby left jail, he travelled to Kentucky to be with his mother. He was far from psychologically stable. A few days after his arrival in Louisa, on December 28, 2002, he sought admission to Three Rivers Hospital. The doctor quickly determined that Bobby was out of touch with reality. He was paranoid, hearing voices that said he was ugly and that people hated him, and saying he should hurt people. The physician also noted that Bobby had a history of "physical, sexual, emotional and mental abuse" at the hands of his father. The doctor started Bobby on a course of drug treatment including more of the anti-psychotic Seroquel as well as Paxil, which commonly is prescribed for both depression and anxiety disorders. Unfortunately, the long-term treatment he obviously needed did not take place. Bobby was discharged from Three Rivers Hospital on January 2, 2003, just five days after his admission. The physician's discharge summary gave me the impression that the doctor believed more help was needed. The hospital's physician wrote that Bobby continued to suffer in a world detached from reality. Bobby's discharge diagnoses were "psychotic disorder," and "post-traumatic stress disorder." Ten months later, Roy Loyd would be dead.

Something else occurred in Louisa. Bobby met Misty Cabral and the two became a couple. Misty's sister had been a stripper and when Misty couldn't find work, she entered the profession and found herself at JB's in Jefferson. Bobby came with her and the couple moved into the Rustic motel.

For a while at Charleston's South Central Regional Jail,

Bobby had taken the anti-psychotic Risperdal, which helped him to be less irritable, he said. However, Risperdal was discontinued after about two weeks and replaced with the anti-depressant Prozac. Prozac seemed to help him somewhat, although he reported still hearing voices frequently.

During my examination, Bobby was cooperative and thoughtful. He showed no active hallucinations and heard no voices, as long as I was with him. He expressed a great deal of regret about the killing, and never attempted to deny it. He wasn't psychotic, although he was somewhat depressed and anxious. Those feelings were appropriate for a person facing charges that could send him to prison for life. My testing revealed mainly that Bobby admitted to a history of many bizarre thoughts, feelings and behaviors, and suggested he experienced episodes of paranoid schizophrenia, which I diagnosed. My assessment of whether he might be malingering suggested that it was unlikely.

Bobby told me another chilling fact: He was obsessed by the smell of the dead man's blood. I doubt that Bobby had ever read Shakespeare, but his haunting olfactory hallucination paralleled the visions of Lady Macbeth: "Yet here's a spot… Out, damn spot…Who would have thought the old man to have had so much blood in him?" (Macbeth, Act 5, Scene 1).

* * * * * * * *

I concluded that Bobby was competent to stand trial, and that his paranoid schizophrenia had caused a degree of diminished capacity at the moment he killed Roy Loyd. In my report to his lawyers I wrote, "He did not arrive at room 127 with the thought of killing the victim. Rather, on seeing his girlfriend, Misty Cabral, prostituting herself while pregnant with his baby, Bobby's schizophrenic process caused him to suffer a diminished capacity to form the specific intent to harm the deceased. His actions were without thought, without malice, without an evil or a wicked heart." The words I chose were a stilted mix of clinical psychology and necessary legalese. The terminology was cold and clinical. Such words are necessary, but they put almost no flesh on the bones of Bobby's chaotic life.

* * * * * * * *

To save herself, Misty Cabral made a deal with prosecutors. During her negotiations, for each inch of ground she gained, Bobby lost a foot. She pled guilty and spun out a story of a planned robbery that had gone bad. Prosecutors dismissed her charge of first-degree murder in exchange for her testimony that she and Bobby had planned to rob Roy all along. She said that she lured the victim to the motel with the robbery plan in mind. Originally charged with first degree murder, had she not made the deal, she would have faced life in prison. Even though she hadn't killed Roy, she faced charges of felony murder – an illegal act in which someone dies. Her cooperation and plea to second degree murder meant she would serve no more than ten years.

As Bobby's trial date grew near, he decided that his attorneys were not pursuing his case properly. He requested a change in representation and that was done, so that Kanawha Public Defender Ronnie Sheets represented him at his trial. With Misty's statements against him, and with the fact that he had killed Roy Loyd, attorney Sheets was faced with the same set of issues as Bobby's previous counsel. He was found guilty of first degree murder, notwithstanding his well-established history of psychosis. He was sentenced to life in prison. Of the dead man's family, Kanawha County Prosecutor Bill Charnock said, "Obviously, I think they would suggest that justice has been served." Possibly it was.

Today, Bobby remains in West Virginia's state penitentiary at Mt. Olive. Misty Cabral's whereabouts are unknown.

* * * * * * * *

Author note: On July 17, 2012, at 11:30 p.m., correctional officers at Mt. Olive prison discovered a discrepancy in their head count.

Bobby Lowe and inmates Daniel Smith and Stephen Wilson, who were serving life sentences for the murder of Huntington Rev. (pastor) Mark McCalla, were missing. "They really weren't there," state Corrections Commissioner Jim Rubenstein told a West Virginia House-Senate oversight committee. "The official investigation will indicate exactly what happened...But it's obvious there was some human error somewhere within all of this," Rubenstein added.

Although the trio cleared at least one interior fence during their escape attempt, they were captured while still within the eighty-two acre complex. Their capture occurred within about fifteen minutes, once they were discovered missing. They appeared to have had no plan to breach the double set of razor-wire, the commissioner told lawmakers. "At no time did they breach any outer security," Rubenstein said, according to a news item by Associated Press writer Lawrence Messina, as published in The Charleston Gazette.

The escape attempt came as the prison, which had dozens of staff vacancies and the next-to-lowest pay rate in the nation, was struggling to keep enough guards employed.

* * * * * * * * *

Author note: Bobby's case is typical of the state of mental health care in the twenty-first century. He needed treatment but instead received only drugs. He was given prescription after prescription, with little or no improvement. The problem is cultural. I have traced it back forty years, when the forces of the pharmaceutical industry aligned with organized psychiatry. Drug makers always are in search of a new market niche. And in the 1970s psychiatry was attempting a retrenchment from its steady loss of patients to professions such as psychology, counseling, and psychiatric social work. Moreover, young physicians were rejecting psychiatry as the specialty of choice. In fact, during the decade of the '70s, the percentage of medical school graduates who opted for psychiatry dropped from eleven percent to just five percent. Many young physicians viewed psychiatry as mired in the confusing non-science of psychoanalysis. Other factors, such as the heightened emphasis on family practice, also cut into psychiatry's recruitment of young doctors. To solve their *twin crises of dwindling patient numbers and lack of interest among new doctors, psychiatry set out to improve its flagging image by becoming more scientific. Psychiatry did so, but the field's "scientific revolution" was accomplished minus any significant scientific breakthroughs. Buoyed by collaboration with the drug industry, psychiatrists soon began to prescribe "wonder drugs" such as many of those that were prescribed to Bobby Lowe. But the blaze of publicity was based on the unproven assumption that the causes of the majority of mental disorders were rooted in human biology – genetic defects, chemical imbalances and other physical difficulties. By the mid-1990s, advertisement of prescription medications directly to consumers was legalized by the U. S. Congress, which compounded the problem. Soon it was not uncommon for patients to self-diagnose, based on nothing more than advertisements and an endless cadre of doctors in the media who reassured listeners that their mental health problems were biologic, "just like diabetes or cancer." It wasn't true. Even non-psychiatrists were swept into the vortex of unsubstantiated belief in biological causation of disorders of mood, nerves and psychosis. For example, it now is common for depressed patients to visit their family doctor and be told that their depression is due to a chemical imbalance in the brain, which an antidepressant will fix. However, such patients seldom are told that this is unfounded speculation. There is no medical test to directly measure such a chemical imbalance in a living person. Nor are they told that such "imbalances" are hypothetical and have never been substantiated by researchers.*

The result of the fusion of the drug industry with psychiatry is that fewer people receive therapy. For the majority, the term "treatment" means nothing but psychotropic drugs. I am convinced that Bobby Lowe is among the victims of this aberration. I have wondered whether his life would have turned out differently, and whether Roy Loyd would have lived, if only Bobby had received therapy that would have helped him deal with the abuse of his childhood, instead of a steady diet of pills. For more on this topic, the reader is referred to an article I and Dr. Donna Midkiff authored for the journal Behavior and Social Issues. *It is available free on-line at: http://journals.uic.edu/ojs/index.php/bsi/article/view/372/295.*

Five

The Kid Who Killed With a Sword

FOR THE PAST TWO MONTHS, seventeen-year-old Timothy "Scott" Skeens had been dealing crack from his seedy apartment at 824 Ninth Avenue in Huntington, West Virginia. With few salable skills, the disaffected, mixed-race dropout had left his home in Point Pleasant for the streets of the city. He soon was picked up by an older dealer known only as "Snoop," who put Scott in the apartment, paid the rent and supplied the drugs to be sold. There were not many rules to follow, although Snoop made one precept very clear to the boy: If any shortages in cash from the sales were discovered, the consequences for Scott would be severe.

One of Scott Skeens' customers was Walter Lee Henry, forty-five, who lived a block away at 908 Ninth Avenue. Henry had a tendency toward aggression, especially when he needed to feed his crack habit. His history of arrests for violent crimes went back fifteen years. Henry had been charged with stealing money and property and, most recently, had been convicted of battery for breaking his victim's jaw. People on the block often saw the large African-American man practicing karate moves on a punching bag in his yard. Henry towered over the slightly built, 130-pound Scott Skeens. Henry was no man to mess with, and Scott knew it. Skeens and Henry met up three times on Thursday, October 13, 2005, beginning in the wee hours and ending as the early morning's rays streaked through the trees, when one of them would die.

When he was broke, it was Walter Henry's habit to trade merchandise for crack. Although Scott Skeens preferred to deal in cash, Henry was sufficiently intimidating that the boy strategically supplied the drugs in exchange for an item of value, to keep Henry from escalating his violence. On one such occasion, Skeens had accepted a "karate sword" from Henry, in exchange for crack. The gleaming weapon had an 18-inch blade. Henry also had given Skeens a cell phone for crack, but a sword and a phone would not impress Snoop, who wanted cash.

Sometime between 1 and 2 a.m. on October 13, an agitated Henry showed up demanding crack. He pounded on the apartment door insisting that he be let in. Sensing that Henry was without cash, Skeens said no. The husky Henry was in no mood to be refused. He kicked down the door, which fell flat on the apartment floor, and entered. Skeens put up a brief argument, then gave the intruder a few crumbs of crack in hopes that Henry would be pacified and depart. Although Skeens' plan worked, as Henry exited he told Skeens, "This will get me hyped up and I'll come back with a hammer and fix the door." Scott Skeens picked up the door and leaned it against the gaping entryway.

Ten minutes later, Walter Henry was back. He demanded that Scott Skeens give him back the cell phone that he had traded for crack on a previous visit. They argued again, and the dispute became more violent. Henry grabbed the boy around the neck in a show of fierce intimidation. Then, perhaps feeling he had made his point, Henry left the apartment without the phone. Skeens' fear of Henry, known around the neighborhood as "karate man," intensified. Several hours elapsed until around 7 a.m. when the cell phone rang. Skeens answered and heard a woman's voice. She said the phone was hers and that Henry had no right to have traded it for drugs. She demanded that Skeens return it. After some discussion, Skeens and the woman reached an agreement. The two would meet in a few minutes at the Speedway convenience store next door, on the corner of 8th Street and 9th Avenue. He would give the phone to her, no questions asked. Scott Skeens hoped that ridding himself of the phone would avoid another confrontation with Walter Henry.

At 7:30 a.m., Skeens walked to the Speedway, phone in hand. The woman was there. And so, unfortunately, was her boyfriend, Walter Henry. Skeens felt as if he had been misled, ambushed, and he was right. Quickly, the pair swarmed Skeens and the boy found himself in a struggle. He dropped the phone, but the angry couple's rage continued unabated. Fearing for his life, Skeens managed to escape, or perhaps the couple released him, believing he now was fearful enough that he would never again refuse a demand by Henry. Arriving back in his apartment, minus its door, he briefly felt safe. But what if they came for him? It was then that Scott Skeens made a fateful decision. He picked up the karate sword and returned to the street. He knew that, physically, he was not a match for the volatile crack addict. But with the sword he hoped to show Walter Henry that the large man's drug-fueled attacks must end. Skeens laid the sword, still in its sheath, in the grass near where he stood, as Henry approached.

Initially, the two stood about ten feet apart and argued. Then, as Henry edged closer, Skeens' fear escalated to the critical point, and he picked up the sword. Henry pounced, rapidly overpowering the boy. The large man immediately maneuvered himself behind Skeens and, with his left arm, placed Skeens in a headlock and began to squeeze. With his right hand Henry pulled a can of mace from his pocket and began spraying Skeens in the face. Scott Skeens maintained his grip on the sword. He held it tightly with both hands, unable to see and having trouble breathing. The mace and Henry's vise-like grip set Skeens' eyes and lungs on fire as he gasped for breath. In seconds he was completely blinded, and was losing his struggle to breathe. Did Walter Henry intend to kill him? Keeping one hand on the sword, with the other he made a final effort to pull the older man's arm from around his neck. He couldn't. He was badly overmatched, he couldn't see and now was starving for oxygen.

Skeens felt the life draining from his body. Henry was indeed attempting to strangle him to death, the boy felt. Again he grasped the sword with both hands and loosened its sheath, which dropped to the ground. Summoning the last measure of his flagging strength, he blindly swung the blade over his left shoulder where it found the chest, and the heart, of Walter Lee Henry. Immediately, Henry released the boy and staggered backward. Skeens, gasping for breath and rubbing his eyes, whirled around and briefly opened his eyes, barely able to make out the image of Walter Henry, with the blade buried deep, and its handle sticking out of the man's chest. "Pull it out! Pull it out!" Henry screamed. Scott ran, first to the apartment, then to the home of some friends. Walter Henry staggered into the Speedway and collapsed. He was rushed to St. Mary's Hospital, where he died an hour later.

Scott Skeens already was known to the city's police. At the time of Henry's death, Scott was on probation for robbing a pop machine. Thus, the authorities quickly found him and soon the teen was charged with murder.

* * * * * * * * *

A few weeks later I received a call from private investigator Greg Cook, who was working for Huntington attorney Jack Laishley. Laishley, along with attorney Crista Conway, had been assigned to defend Scott Skeens against a charge of first degree murder. Cook described the basic events of the homicide and asked for my reaction. "Sounds like self-defense," I answered. Cook said he would ask the attorneys to get in touch with me.

Laishley called and asked me to examine Skeens, to get to know him, to try to understand Skeens' mindset at the time of the killing. Interestingly, Laishley did not ask me to conduct competence and responsibility assessments. Those were not matters of dispute. Rather, the lawyers planned to argue self-defense. Vital to such a defense was Skeens' thinking during the homicide. Laishley and Conway were well aware of the law's requirement that, in order to prove first degree murder, prosecutors would have to convince a jury that the killing was "willful, deliberate and premeditated." For the most part, it could be argued that Walter Henry's death had been the product of Henry's own actions. If Walter Henry had not attacked the boy, the man would still be alive. But there were complications. First, Skeens had escaped and returned to the relative safety of his apartment, minus its door, of course. Then he had returned to the street with a weapon, where he assumed he would find Walter Henry. Laishley and Conway felt confident that the circumstances of the killing – Skeens had killed while undergoing a vicious attack – were essentially consistent with self-defense. But under the law, premeditation may happen in an instant. Intent to kill may be formed in the blink of an eye, even one that burned with Mace. Thus, the defense attorneys and Cabell County Prosecutor Chris Chiles faced the same set of factors, seen in mirror images: For Laishley and Conway the case amounted to self-defense that might be viewed as tainted by Skeens' return to the street with a deadly weapon. For prosecutor Chiles it was the reverse: Skeens had premeditated the killing, but likely wouldn't have done it had Walter Henry not viciously attacked him. A jury would have to determine the truth.

* * * * * * * * *

At Laishley's request, I met with Skeens at the James H. "Tiger" Morton Center in Dunbar, West Virginia, on October 27, 2005, two weeks after the killing. The center is located within Shawnee Regional Park, where local families enjoy outings on languid summer afternoons, scarcely aware that they share the park with a "children's prison." The facility is secure. The juveniles wear orange jumpsuits. Daily activities are strictly regimented. For at least a few of the youths housed there, the structured dehumanization may jolt them toward more favorable life decisions. Others may be less fortunate.

I got to know Scott Skeens well. The smallish boy was quiet and respectful. Initially, we talked about why I was there and I told him his attorneys believed I might learn some things about him that would help his case.

We talked about his years growing up. Scott said he didn't know his father, but had been told that the man had hoped for a professional tennis career. That dream was cut short by an accident. Eventually, Scott's father began to use drugs and now was in prison. That, essentially, was the extent of Scott's knowledge of his father. An uncle was "a mess" and chronically in the court system too, he said. It occurred to me that the boy who sat with me might become victim to a morbid sense of fatalism about his own potential for spending much of his life behind bars. On a more favorable note, Scott described an aunt in North Carolina as "One of my idols...She knows how to talk to me."

Scott's mother, Kim Skeens, worked for an agency attached to Marshall University. Her office was located in a building just five blocks from the scene of the fatal confrontation. From his remarks about his mother, I got the feeling that Scott felt Kim had given up on him. Perhaps she had, because, while growing up in the primarily rural Point Pleasant area as a fatherless bi-racial child had been difficult for Scott, surely his sullen disaffection and his behavior problems had worn on his mother too. When I asked how his mother would describe him, Scott answered, "Smart, doesn't apply himself, a good kid."

At Point Pleasant High School Scott foundered. He liked his science teacher, Mrs. Burris, he said. The basketball coach/behavior disorders teacher, Mr. Blaine, was good too, Scott said. However, after completing the ninth grade, he dropped out. His attempt to earn a GED had failed. He worked at a McDonald's for nine months, then at a Penn Station restaurant for a few weeks. Sometimes he did odd jobs, such as mowing lawns. He had a girlfriend of six months who was pregnant, but the baby wasn't his, he said.

The more we talked, the more Scott relaxed. He began to relate the sequence of events of the morning of October 13, 2005. His account was generally consistent with the way his lawyers and the police had described it, and he would remain consistent in his description of the tragedy throughout two later times that I would meet with him. I was forming my impression of Scott Skeens. He was immature, his judgment was poor and he possessed few of the skills needed for coping with the everyday demands of life, much less life as a crack dealer.

Sensing that Scott may have been somewhat intellectually disadvantaged, I administered the Wechsler Adult Intelligence Scale (3rd edition), which is the most frequently used test of general intellectual functioning in America. The test is well standardized and I felt it would help me better understand his school failure. That was important to me because it is well established by researchers that poor school performance often leads to childhood conduct problems which, in turn, may lead to grown-up conflict with society's norms, standards and laws. Scott's overall IQ score was 79. That placed his intellectual functioning in the lowest eight percent of the population. Interestingly, it was the same score he had obtained when, at age fifteen, he was examined by psychologist Brian Bailey.

I have known Brian Baily for many years and I respect his work. Thus, I carefully reviewed Bailey's report of his examination of Skeens, two years before the homicide. In April 2003, at age fifteen, Scott had been placed on probation for "verbal assault" against a teacher. Then, while the probationary period remained in force, he stole a car and went joy riding. His probation officer asked Bailey to examine Scott in order to provide a diagnosis of any mental health disorder and to recommend treatment that might help.

Brian Bailey had discovered a great deal about Scott Skeens. His mother, Kim Skeens, told Bailey that Scott's problem behavior had become evident around the fourth or fifth grade. He wouldn't comply with school regulations. School personnel had termed Scott "totally unmanageable," his mother said. As his behavior deteriorated, it was decided that he would live with his maternal grandfather during his seventh grade year. The result was a sharp decline in reports of unacceptable behavior. Psychologist Bailey noted that Kim Skeens worked long hours and that Scott suffered from inadequate structure and discipline. Bailey added, "Mrs. Skeens acknowledged that she had been allowing Scott to use alcohol on a limited basis since he was eleven or twelve years of age."

* * * * * * * * *

The next time I saw Scott Skeens was December 12, 2005, six weeks after the killing. I met with him in an anteroom at the Cabell County Courthouse. Scott's courtroom appearance was to determine whether he ought to be tried as an adult.

By that time, Scott had left Tiger Morton and was housed at the Donald R. Kuhn Juvenile Center in Julian, West Virginia, halfway between Charleston and Logan, on U.S. Route 119. The Kuhn center had been an elementary school. It had run out of students as a result of the area's decline in population. Thus, the facility was converted to a juvenile detention center, much like the Tiger Morten Center. Scott had agreed to be transferred to the Kuhn Center after having difficulty with other juveniles at Tiger Morten. He admitted he had been "written up" there several times, though he said it was for infractions such as not folding and putting away his clothing, and for sitting down while waiting to eat his meals, laughing inappropriately and the like. He told me that his mood had been variable and he was having some crying spells. He said his sleep was poor because he couldn't get images of his family and his future out of his head.

I asked Scott many questions, including what he would have done differently. I have never forgotten the absence of insight that was revealed by his answer. He replied he never should have gotten in with the people who robbed the pop machine. He considered that incident, which occurred soon after he arrived in Huntington, as the initial link in a chain that led to the stabbing of Walter Henry. But the pop machine had been a minor event near the end of the chain. The initial link had been forged years earlier.

Circuit Judge Alfred Ferguson announced that justice would be best served by Scott's transfer to adult status. Following the hearing, Laishley spoke to *The Huntington Herald Dispatch's* reporter Curtis Johnson. "The biggest problem," Laishley said, "is communication with children that do not have the worldly experience necessary to make good decisions. We think, with the help of this court, we've put together a team and (Skeens) has been communicating with us, and we've been communicating with him and that's what is important."

Three months later, on March 11, 2006, Scott Skeens turned eighteen. He was transferred to the Western Regional jail in Barboursville, fewer than ten miles from the Cabell County courthouse. That made visits with his attorneys and his family easier. I saw him there the following month. His description of the killing and related events never changed, although he added some peripheral details. For example, he said that "higher people" in his drug sales job had made it clear he would face serious consequences (they would break his hands, he said) if he ever held out money on them. That may have provided an incentive for Scott to push back at Walter Henry. If Henry continued to demand crack for free, or in trade for merchandise, Scott would be unable to balance the books with Snoop. Scott said he had seen Walter Henry man-handling known crack heads, possibly to steal their drugs. He had witnessed Henry pounding away at the punching bag in his yard, and had seen him take a 40-ounce bottle, fill it with water and crush it with one punch. Scott Skeens wasn't alone. I already knew that numerous individuals in the neighborhood had seen Henry do such things. To Scott Skeens, Walter Henry had been a malevolent force of nature that swirled through the block.

* * * * * * * * *

Over the next four months, Laishley, Conway and prosecutor Chris Chiles negotiated the fate of the young man who had killed Walter Henry. Scott Skeens' attorneys asked me to provide them with a list of any factors in Scott's case that also had served as viable arguments for self-defense in other cases. There were many.

I told Laishley and Conway that, of the variables that various defense attorneys had used successfully to argue self-defense, size differential was among the most relevant. Henry outweighed

Skeens by about 100 pounds. There were many cases in which that had been the crucial factor to bring about successful claims of self-defense.

Another variable often seen in other cases was engagement in a hand-to-hand struggle at the moment of the death blow. That factor had led to a successful claim of self-defense in a Martinsburg, West Virginia, case and in cases elsewhere. In other instances, defendants' lawyers had argued self-defense with success when the deceased was well known to be prone to violence. In still other cases of self-defense, clear visibility of a weapon carried by an individual who used it to protect himself had caused juries to acquit. And when jurors believed the defendant was convinced that the deceased was "on a mission" to harm him, they had found "not guilty." Each of those factors appeared to fit their defense of Scott Skeens, I told Jack Laishley.

Another factor in various self-defense cases was whether the defendant had been able to retreat. This cut both ways. Scott Skeens initially had retreated, but then returned, sword in hand, to where he assumed he would find Henry. However, once in the grasp of Henry, escape was not possible. In some cases it had been necessary to ask jurors to consider whether the defendant's response (in this case, the stabbing) was a "reasonable reaction to the circumstances." In some of those cases, that had led to acquittals.

Two additional factors also had led to jury verdicts of not guilty. First, acquittals had occurred when the physical injuries fit a claim of self-defense which, in this case, they did. That is, the smaller Skeens claimed he was held from behind and was being sprayed with mace, at which point he flailed wildly with the sword. The downward arc of the blade into Henry's chest fit the description given by Skeens. And police had discovered a partially spent can of mace at the fight's scene. Last, some cases had been won by defense attorneys when it was shown that the defendant had been bullied by the deceased. That too was a reasonable argument, I told Jack Laishley and Crista Conway.

I had provided the attorneys with a list of details of other cases that matched their case and might argue for a claim of self-defense. Thus, the lawyers used that list in negotiations with prosecutor Chiles. It was their goal that Chiles abandon the notion of taking Scott to trial on charges of first degree murder.

* * * * * * * * *

Ultimately, Laishley and Conway got the offer they wanted for their client. Timothy Scott Skeens was brought to the Cabell County Courthouse on July 18, 2006, where he pleaded guilty to second-degree murder. The plea carried a sentence of ten to forty years. The Prosecutor announced he would seek a maximum sentence of twenty-five years, rather than the forty years that were possible, due to Skeens' age and other factors surrounding the case. "The victim's family very much agrees with the plea and the possible outcome," Chris Chiles told the media. Sentencing was set for October 13, 2006, the one-year anniversary of Walter Henry's death. Jack Laishley and Crista Conway had done well on behalf of their client. With good behavior, Skeens could be out of prison, with much of his life ahead of him.

It was fair to say that neither side had wanted to go to trial. To have done so would have been a roll of the dice that could either have freed Scott Skeens, or left him in prison for the rest of his life. While Chris Chiles would have been hard pressed to convince a jury that Walter Henry had played absolutely no role in his own death, Laishly and Conway would have borne the burden of justifying self-defense, given that Skeens had run to safety, then left his apartment to confront Walter Henry with a deadly weapon.

* * * * * * * * *

The sentencing date was delayed until February 1, 2007. Jack Laishley and Crista Conway approached the date with a single focus – to convince Judge Dan O'Hanlon, to whom the case had been transferred, to send their client anywhere other than to the state's maximum security prison at Mt. Olive where he would be among the most hardened criminals.

At the sentencing hearing, I testified that, given his age and intellect, Scott Skeens functioned at the level of a thirteen-year-old at the time of the homicide, and wasn't much above that at present. There was little hope for Scott Skeens, if he were to be placed at the state's maximum security prison, I told Judge O'Hanlon. I questioned the findings of another psychologist who had examined Skeens just prior to sentencing. That professional, who worked for the correctional system, concluded that Skeens was still violent and was a high risk to re-offend.

There was at least some degree of hope that Scott Skeens would grow and become a law-abiding citizen, I said. During my cross-examination, prosecutor Chiles focused on matters that, essentially, had little relevance to Henry's death. Chiles portrayed Skeens as a long-term violent criminal, even bringing up his verbal assault on a teacher and the joyriding charges from Skeens' early teens. Chiles pushed hard at me. I responded, in part, "...Mr. Chiles, if someone had you or me in a headlock, spraying mace in our faces, we would do whatever we could to survive, too. So it (the stabbing) was an aggressive act (by Skeens) but it was one that had some mitigating circumstances."

On his own behalf, Scott Skeens said, "I think about it every day. My nightmare is seeing him every day and having to live with what happened. I never saw myself ever being up here, standing up here for a murder charge." Few people do.

Walter Henry's sister, Minnie Martin, told O'Hanlon she sympathized with Skeens, but still asked that he be given the maximum. Finally, Judge O'Hanlon spoke to Scott, but he was speaking to the community too. "Mr. Skeens, you can see what you've done to this (Henry's) family. This is terrible...And I'm tired, and I think this community is tired of drug addicts in Cabell County, West Virginia. I want the word to go out that it has to come to an end." Then he sentenced Timothy Scott Skeens to twenty-five years in prison. As this book is being written, the state's Department of Corrections website lists Skeens' projected release date as April 15, 2018. If that date holds, he will be a month past his thirtieth birthday and will have served twelve and a half years.

* * * * * * * * *

In October, 2011, Scott Skeens filed a habeas corpus petition with the West Virginia Supreme Court of Appeals. Skeens based his appeal on five grounds. He claimed that Jack Laishley and Krista Conway had wrongly advised him of the sentence he likely would receive; had not properly advised him of the elements (definition) of second degree murder; had failed to properly develop his self-defense claim; and had failed to appeal his transfer to adult status. Also, Skeens alleged that Detective Chris Sperry had coerced a confession from him, saying he could speak to his mother only after he confessed. An Omnibus Hearing was held on June 5, 2014, at which Skeens, Laishley, Conway, Sperry and original guardian ad leitum Cathy Greiner testified. On August 26, 2014, Cabell County Chief Circuit Judge Paul T. Farrell denied each rationale for the appeal, leaving Scott Skeens to serve out his sentence.

Six

She Killed Her Abuser

JACK BROWN'S PERSONAL HISTORY was filled with crimes. The Huntington resident, fifty-seven, had been charged at least ten times, mostly with offenses like passing worthless checks, being drunk and disorderly, and once with simple assault. Although most of his crimes were non-violent, his relationships with women were a different matter.

His one-time wife, Barbara Mays Poindexter, fed up with his violence and drinking, filed for divorce. The day before her final court appearance, Jack told her he would kill her if she followed through. Her friend, Linda Hobbs, was present and heard the threat. The next day, Barbara Poindexter went through with the divorce, although her attorney arranged for protection from Jack, as she came and went from the court-house.

* * * * * * * *

In early 1993, Jack Brown was hospitalized in the psychiatric unit at St. Mary's Hospital in Huntington, West Virginia. Also there for treatment of her long-standing mental health problems was Betty Riley, fifty-three. Jack noticed Betty, and gave her some attention. The emotionally needy Betty fell for Jack. The two were discharged and Betty moved out of her daughter's home, and into Jack's.

Professionals understand that the relationships of couples who meet as psychiatric inpatients typically end badly. Betty and Jack's were no exception. Soon, Jack refused to pay the rent and Betty took on the obligation. Then Jack began to get rough with Betty. The first time it happened, he shoved her against the refrigerator. He drank day and night. The more he drank the more violent he became. Like many battered women, Betty stayed. She told me that she was "addicted" to people who abused her. She said she loved Jack. And she stayed because she had a strong fear of being alone, and Jack would keep her safe in a world that always had been cruel to her. "He was abusive, yet protective," she said.

As the months passed, Jack's brutality escalated. He slapped her, shoved her, and began to intimidate her with a knife which he would hurl in her general direction, close enough to frighten her without hitting her. He struck her on the buttocks with a flashlight, and kicked her. He slapped her and shoved her. And he humiliated her, calling her stupid and fat.

With his criminal record, Jack could not purchase a gun. Instead, he insisted that Betty buy one. She made the purchase, but he took control of the weapon. Often, he pointed it at her. Jack constantly complained about things, she said. He frequently harangued the landlord regarding matters that were not in the landlord's control. And he hated blacks. Sometimes he accused Betty of sleeping with them.

In time, Jack's drinking, abuse and intimidation had tightly melded with Betty's conflict about the upside of living with a protective monster. In early Fall 1994, around the time Betty's daughter married, Jack's violence worsened. On one occasion, Betty, clad only in her nightgown and robe, fled to a nearby Gino's restaurant where she called 911. As she pleaded with the operator for help, Jack arrived. He cut off her call and insisted she return home.

Following that incident, Betty continued to receive therapy, while Jack continued to drink. And Jack was becoming more dangerous, sometimes aiming his anger at individuals other than Betty. On September 29, 1994, William Claude Congleton filed a complaint against Jack for brandishing a weapon. But Jack's terror tactics were never reined in for long.

A week later, October 5, 1994, Betty left to do grocery shopping. She returned by cab around noon and, mistakenly thinking Jack was away, asked the cabbie to help her with the groceries. Jack met them on the porch. He was drunk, and the sight of the driver coming to the front door sparked his simmering jealously. The Yellow Cab driver, Jessie McComas Jr., later would say that he noticed nothing out of the ordinary about the couple that day. But when the cabbie drove off and Betty and Jack carried the last of the groceries toward the house, Jack began to slap Betty's face. They got the groceries into the house and soon Betty joined Jack in a drinking bout.

Betty had been seeing Huntington therapist Maria Stallo, who had a master's degree in psychology and also was a registered nurse. The therapist and patient developed a solid relationship and during one visit Betty disclosed to Stallo that Jack had threatened to tie her up and force her to leave Huntington with him, in the trunk of his car, if necessary. Despite the disturbing image, and although Maria Stallo urged Betty to make plans to leave the relationship, Betty remained with Jack.

Stallo suggested that having a pet might improve Betty's mood and sense of self-worth. Betty had always been a dog lover, and she responded positively to the suggestion. A pet enthusiast herself, Stallo drove Betty to the local animal shelter and paid for the puppy that Betty took home. However, the dog proved difficult to train, so the therapist and patient returned the pup to the shelter and, in exchange, Betty brought home a kitten. Stallo's suggestion worked out well. In the kitten Betty found a new sense of companionship. And responsibility for the kitten boosted her self-worth.

* * * * * * * * *

With the groceries put away and the drinking proceeding, Betty was hurting physically and emotionally. To find comfort, she laid down on the sofa and caressed her kitten. She was thinking, "The cat loves me..." Jack entered the room and saw her with the cat. Perhaps for no other reason than to taunt Betty, he pulled the kitten out of Betty's arms and threw the frightened animal across the room. He picked it up and tossed it again and again, with no evident purpose other than to bring Betty to a state of helpless outrage. She pleaded with him to stop, but the brutal activity continued. Betty recalled once, to get rid of a neighbor's cat, he had sprayed weed killer in its face.

When I examined Betty, she recalled that, despite her pleadings, Jack continued to hurl the terrified kitten about the room. Her memory of what occurred next remained clouded. But this much is certain. As she grappled with Jack to save her kitten, Betty's hand found the gun that he had insisted she purchase for him. Moments later, bullets stopped his mistreatment of her pet. Jack would never again harm the kitten, or Betty, or anyone else.

Police arrived at the home, located in the 900 block of Ninth Avenue, and arrested Betty. (Note: This is the same city block where the fatal confrontation between Timothy Scott Skeens and Walter Henry, described in chapter five, took place.) She told the officers, "I'm tired of him beating on me." She added, "I don't know how many shots I fired. I just wanted him to stop hitting me." She initially was charged with attempted murder. When Jack died from his wounds the charge was upgraded to first degree murder.

* * * * * * * * *

Betty was represented by the Cabell County Public Defender's staff attorney Charles Houdyschel, under the excellent leadership of Robert Wilkinson. Aware that Betty had an extensive psychiatric history, Houdyschel asked me to examine her to determine whether she was competent to stand trial and whether she may have been driven to a state of mental illness at the time she shot Jack Brown to death. One thing was certain, if attorney Houdyschel should decide to use an insanity defense, no one could accuse Betty Riley of creating a mental illness, on the spot, to exactly fit her actions during the homicide. Rather, Betty had a long history of mental illness, going back to her childhood. Betty was born in South Carolina and adopted as an infant. As a young girl, she kept away from her biological parents, who lived in the area, because she was afraid they would attempt to get her back. At the same time, she had ambivalent feelings toward her adoptive mother, who frequently beat her severely, sometimes drawing blood, from the time she was five or six until she was thirteen or fourteen. At times, her adoptive father stepped in and stopped the thrashings.

In 1955, at age sixteen, Betty married Thomas Cook and soon had a daughter, Donna. Her husband entered the military and deserted his young wife and daughter. Thus, at age nineteen or twenty, Betty filed for divorce. Aware she had filed the divorce papers, Thomas lured her away from her adoptive parents' home to a motel where he beat her, raped and sodomized her and even bit her severely. She told me she did not know how she was able to drive ten miles to her parents' home. The assault was not the last she would endure, but it was one of the worst.

In 1963, while still in South Carolina, Betty met a man named Linwood Sweat. He also frequently beat her. And he fathered her second child, which was placed up for adoption. Betty told me, with some regret, she never learned what happened to that child.

Soon Betty met and married Harold Riley, who adopted her daughter, Donna, and the trio relocated to Parkersburg, West Virginia. She and Harold were married for twenty-nine years. Harold was an alcoholic who abused prescription medications and who beat Betty throughout their marriage. At times, Harold would lock Betty and Donna out of the house then, once he had sobered up, beg them to return. Harold beat Betty viciously dozens of times and, when not physically abusing her, he abused her emotionally. After twenty-nine years of marriage, she divorced him in 1992, although she returned to him the following year. Ultimately, she could no longer endure his physical abuse, drinking and medication abuse, so she left him for good and began to live full-time with Jack Brown. Harold Riley was killed in an automobile accident in 1994.

* * * * * * * * *

I delved into Betty's psychiatric history, which was extensive. Although Betty was somewhat reticent regarding her mental health treatment history, she disclosed that she had been hospitalized several times and had undergone two series of electroconvulsive shock therapy (ECT) treatments, each series with about three applications. That told me that Betty's problems had been major, and probably had reached psychotic proportions. Typically, ECT is reserved for the most severe levels of depression, when all other treatment has failed. Occasionally, it is used for other severe disorders, as well. As a full-time practioner for more than ten years of my early career, I have seen psychotically depressed patients for whom ECT brought about improvement.

Most of the time the functioning of these patients had sunk to the point that they were not taking care of themselves – failing to get dressed, get out of bed or go to work, unable to take care of personal hygiene, even refusing to eat. Many times, ECT had brought about dramatic change. No one entirely understands the physiological or psychological mechanisms that effect improvement with ECT. Theories range from the physiological (that ECT rebalances the electrolytes or some similar phenomenon), to the classically psychoanalytic (the treatment fulfills a patient's need to be punished). Perhaps ECT's general shock to the individual's system simply jolts the patient to a new level of energy and activity, somewhat akin to heightened arousal and activity upon leaving the warm sun of one's cozy deck chair for a plunge into cold water. Although the mechanism of ECT's action remains unknown, its positive results have been demonstrated clearly.

ECT helps a percentage of patients who have become hopelessly depressed and who have stopped engaging in even the most routine activities of life. Many of us have seen the 1975 Oscar-winning film "One Flew Over the Cuckoo's Nest." I found its portrayal of patient life in a large, old state hospital to be realistic, as I had just moved on after working full-time for more than three years at Bateman Hospital, then called Huntington

State Hospital, in Huntington. The look of the film's hospital wards, the sterile hallways and the actors' realistic portrayals of chronically mentally ill patients were uncanny reminders of the atmosphere I had just left. However, ECT was misused in the film. Rather than as treatment for severe depression, the 'big nurse' used ECT as punishment for the lead character's refusal to bend to her overbearing, power-mad desire to maintain complete control over the patients. She exerted so much control, in fact, that she robbed her patients of any hope for improvement.

Although she was reluctant to discuss her treatment history, I learned a great deal by reviewing Betty's treatment records. In 1977, when Betty was thirty-eight, she was examined by psychologist Andrew P. Gershman, who suspected that her difficulties could be traced to her childhood. Perhaps she had experienced trauma "very early in life," he accurately suggested. Also, he found her IQ score to be 83, which placed her general intellectual functioning in the lowest part of the average range. Throughout 1977, Betty's functioning was so poor that she was admitted to St. Joseph's Hospital in Parkersburg on three occasions between March and December. On the first admission she told staff that she had "no choices." She elaborated, "Sometimes I feel like exploding and want to hurt him (her husband)." The examiner made a dead-on observation, "She is expressing much anger towards her husband and seems to have many unresolved problems."

The second admission of 1977 occurred on September 30. As with the first admission, her diagnosis was depressive neurosis, terminology that today does not exist in the diagnostic nomenclature, but may be interpreted to mean that Betty was very depressed, although not out of touch with reality. A report of an examination shortly after her admission quoted Betty saying, "I don't care what happens to him anymore (her husband). I've actually thought about killing him…either him or myself. He is just like a child…he can't do anything for himself." Her hospital stay did little to help Betty cope. She was soon discharged, then readmitted on December 15, with the same diagnosis.

By 1981, forty-two year old Betty again was brought to St. Joseph

Hospital. Her discharge summary, dated May 12, 1981, included a surprising statement: "Treatment with major tranquilizers in the past has induced a psychosis." Interestingly, we now know there is increasing evidence that certain psychotropic medicines, particularly the anti-psychotics that Betty took for years, may do just that – cause psychosis. During her stay, the night nurse, Eva Gillispie, noticed that Betty's problems with her second husband, Harold Riley, were anything but resolved. Gillespie's note of May 5, 1981 read in part, " Betty has been up and down all night. Very distraught about the way she says her husband treats her. Cannot get the anger out of her mind. Up, waited to call husband all night. Called him at 5:45 a.m. and expressed her anger loudly and appropriately to him…" Before long, Betty again was discharged, evidently with little change in either her functioning or her circumstances.

By the mid-1980s, Betty and Harold had moved to Huntington. Her coping problems remained unresolved and in 1987 she was admitted for inpatient treatment, this time to the psychiatric unit at St. Mary's Hospital with a diagnosis of major depressive disorder, a diagnosis that indicates she was seen as having become either psychotic, or very close it. She was admitted again in 1992 by psychiatrist Jack Dodd, who worked with therapist Maria Stallo. Betty told Dodd, "I meant my wedding vows and now I wish I could die." He added that she was disorganized, and somewhat disoriented, with "…strong suggestions of paranoid hallucinations and delusional thinking…" While in the hospital she also was seen by counselor Roger Swango. He concluded that she had been a victim of verbal and physical abuse by Harold throughout their marriage, although the two by then were divorced but still living together. Swango also discovered that Betty, at times, had thoughts of killing Harold. She was discharged on October 21, 1992, with a diagnosis of bipolar disorder, a clear indication that she had experienced episodes in which she was not bound to reality.

Betty followed up as an outpatient with Jack Dodd and his staff therapist, Maria Stallo. Her mental status waxed and waned. Dodd again admitted Betty to St. Mary's Hospital on

January 27, 1993, after she arrived for an outpatient visit in acute distress. She remained hospitalized for five weeks and continued to carry a diagnosis of bipolar disorder, terminology that meant she continued to experience difficulty staying in touch with reality. She was haunted by an abiding despair about her everyday life, Dodd noted. Following her discharge, Betty continued to see both Dodd and Stallo, as an outpatient. It was during that time that she and Jack Brown began to live together.

On September 1, 1993, Maria Stallo became concerned that Betty could turn violent. The therapist noted that Betty denied she would ever become violent and added she would never attempt to harm her "ex." At the next visit, a week later, Stallo commented on Betty's deteriorating relationship with Jack Brown: "She feels her relationship with Jack is a large mistake because he is drinking again. She wants out of the relationship, but is fearful of Jack's reaction. He wants to leave the area and force Betty to leave too regardless of her desires....(She is) fearful of living alone and walking out of the house alone. Some days she becomes confused and can't find her way back home, and gets frightful and unable to think, due to overwhelming anxiety."

Eleven days after that visit, on September 18, 1993, Stallo and Dodd concluded that Betty's condition had again declined to dangerous levels. Thus, they decided to re-admit Betty to the hospital, where she stayed until October 1. Jack Dodd noted the many sources of stress that impinged on Betty. She suffered from inadequate family support, financial stress, "frequent family conflicts with years' long history of illness dating to the 1970s."

Despite the efforts of Dodd, Stallo and the other mental health professionals who had worked with Betty Riley for several decades, Betty remained bound by the stressors that Dodd had described. Dodd again admitted her to St. Mary's hospital, on March 23, 1994, with diagnoses of bipolar disorder and alcohol abuse. In fact, drinking had become a daily coping strategy for Betty. She was drunk when admitted to the hospital. And she complained that her daughter, Donna, had been hounding her. She was discharged on April 8, then readmitted on June 1, where she remained for two weeks. She told psychology intern Karen R. Wickline that she had been living off and on with Jack Brown, but it might be best to end the relationship because there was too much arguing. Even so, she indicated to Wickline that Jack provided care and companionship. Unfortunately, Betty continued to feel tied to Jack, despite his substance abuse, alcohol abuse and his physical and emotional abuse. Betty admitted to the intern that she had been drinking up to twelve beers a day.

I concluded my review of Betty's psychiatric history. She had endured childhood abuse and was deserted by her first husband, who later raped her. She had given up a baby for adoption, had been systematically physically and emotionally abused for decades by her second husband and, later, by Jack Brown. She had been psychotic at times, suicidal at times and occasionally homicidal. She had undergone outpatient treatment and ten hospital admissions for treatment of her psychological problems. It added up to at least one conclusion: During the timeframe in which she killed Jack Brown, Betty was not pretending to suffer from a mental disorder.

* * * * * * * * *

As I examined Betty she underplayed her psychiatric history. When I asked her to tell me about her treatment history she said only that she had been hospitalized "several" times, adding that she had undergone ECT twice. She said nothing more — which was not typical of an individual who wished to fake a mental illness.

I learned that Betty was a high school dropout who occasionally had worked in low-skilled jobs. In the 1960s she had done factory work in South Carolina. While living in Parkersburg in the early 1970s, she worked as a clerk in various retail shops. She hadn't been employed since 1975.

I could see that Betty was both anxious and depressed. She seldom made eye contact. I judged her self-esteem to be awfully low. I found it somewhat surprising that she denied any history of hallucinations, although I knew from her records that she had experienced them. Again, such understatement was atypical for an individual who was feigning a mental illness.

As I got to know her better, I was forming a picture of Betty's mental functioning. Her insight into her problems was poor. She was chronically unsure of herself, easily intimidated and felt worthless and hopeless. Her attorney, Mr. Houdyschel, had asked whether she fit the pattern of "battered woman syndrome." Doubtless, she did, in my estimation.

At the time, the syndrome was acknowledged to exist by most professionals, although it was not recognized in the diagnostic nomenclature. Today, however, it is a syndrome that may be diagnosed, although not by the term battered woman syndrome. The Diagnostic and Statistical Manuel, 5th Edition (DSM-5), published in 2013 by the American Psychiatric Association, splits the diagnosis into physical and psychological components, under the general heading of "Other conditions that may be a focus of clinical attention."

"Spouse or partner violence, physical," is defined as occurring *...when nonaccidental acts of physical force that result, or have reasonable potential to result, in physical harm to an intimate partner or that evoke significant fear in the partner have occurred during the past year. Nonaccidental acts of physical force include shoving, slapping, hair pulling, pinching, restraining, shaking, throwing, biting, kicking, hitting with the fist or an object, burning, poisoning, applying force to the throat, cutting off the air supply, holding the head under water, and using a weapon.*

"Spouse or partner abuse, psychological," *encompasses nonaccidental verbal or symbolic acts by one partner that result, or have reasonable potential to result, in significant harm to the other partner. This category should be used when such psychological abuse has occurred during the past year. Acts of psychological abuse include berating or humiliating the victim; interrogating the victim; restricting the victim's ability to come and go freely; obstructing the victim's access to assistance (e.g., law enforcement; legal, protective, or medical resources); threatening the victim with physical harm or sexual assault; harming, or threatening to harm, people or things that the victim cares about; unwarranted restriction of the victim's access to or use of economic resources; isolating the victim from family, friends, or social support resources; stalking the victim; and trying to make the victim think that he or she is crazy.*

It is interesting that these diagnoses reveal nothing about the thoughts, feelings or overt behavior of the victim who receives the diagnosis. Rather, the cumbersome terminology describes the actions of the perpetrator. It is a clinical paradox that a patient may receive a mental health diagnosis based on the actions of someone else.

To add to the diagnostic picture, I administered the Minnesota Multiphasic Personality Inventory. This test provides a clinical practitioner with a description of the patient's functioning, based on the patient's self-report. Betty's results were consistent with the impressions I had formed during my lengthy interview and with my review of her voluminous treatment records. I concluded my examination of Betty on June 15, 1995. I found that, indeed, Betty was suffering from bipolar disorder, with associated psychotic features. As well, she fit the picture of the battered woman syndrome. The more difficult question was whether her mental disorder prevented her from acting within the constraints of the law when she pulled the trigger. In the end, I concluded that Betty Riley was briefly psychotic when she killed Jack Brown. Her emotionally impoverished existence was defined by a history of disorders of psychotic proportions, and it was reasonable to conclude that her history, combined with Jack's doorstep abuse of Betty followed by her kitten's torture, had vaulted her over the edge. The kitten was the only being in which she found comfort. The sight of Jack, as he repeatedly harmed the pet, had, I judged, sent Betty into temporary psychosis, and she pulled the trigger.

* * * * * * * *

While my testimony would be helpful to Betty's defense, it is standard practice for both the defense and prosecution to hire forensic experts to examine a defendant who makes a claim of insanity. On April 19, 1995, Betty was seen by psychologist Rosemary Smith and psychiatrist Ralph Smith. In contrast to my findings, the Smiths concluded that Betty did not fit the picture of battered woman syndrome. They concluded, in part,

"...at the time of the alleged crime Ms. Riley was criminally responsible...she had no mental disease or defect which would have prevented her from having the capacity to appreciate the wrongfulness of her conduct. She had long-standing depressive disorder, but there is no evidence that she was psychotic at the time of the alleged crime. A careful review of Ms. Riley's past reveals that she has had no criteria suggestive of manic episodes."

Rosemary Smith and Ralph Smith are responsible professionals whose work I respect. However, in Betty Riley's case, I disagreed with their conclusions, primarily for two reasons. First, Betty's depression frequently had been so severe as to require hospitalization, which suggested the likelihood that her disorder had escalated to psychotic levels. My thinking was reinforced by counselor Roger Swango's October 1992 finding that Betty had reported auditory hallucinations. Second, I knew and respected psychiatrist Jack Dodd, who had diagnosed bipolar disorder (manic-depressive disorder) repeatedly, each time based on Betty's functioning as she sat before him. Dodd would not have diagnosed bipolar disorder had Betty not experienced one or more episodes of mania, which is a form of psychosis. In my view, Dr. Dodd's repeated diagnosis was inconsistent with the Smiths' conclusion that there was nothing in Betty's past suggestive of manic episodes. And Dodd's findings were based on his repeated direct contact with Betty when she was at her worst over a period of years, rather than a one-time interview.

* * * * * * * *

The case went to trial and the prosecution worked hard to convince the jury that Betty Riley had suffered no mental illness at the time she killed Jack Brown. The state's case amounted to this: Betty got angry and shot Jack, minus any extenuating circumstances such as mental illness. I gave my testimony along the lines described above.

In my cross-examination, the prosecutor focused on a section of Betty's MMPI profile, her elevated score on the scale that attempts to determine whether an individual is faking a mental illness. It was absurd to think Betty was faking, given her history and the fact that she downplayed that history. On my direct questioning by Betty's attorney, I had discussed the two possible interpretations of an elevated "F" scale of the MMPI profile. Besides the possibility that the individual is malingering, it is quite common that an individual with an extensive, severe mental health history genuinely sees herself as functioning very poorly, which spuriously elevates the "F" scale. When Betty was honestly answering the questions in ways that indicated she functioned poorly, the false impression was given that she was faking a mental illness. Unfortunately, it can become easy to forget that, like all measurements, the MMPI and its malingering scale are imperfect.

The scale has twenty-four true/false questions. Betty answered ten of them in the same way as people who are known to be pretending to be mentally ill. Two examples from among the twenty-four items will illustrate the difficulty in interpretation that Betty Riley's prosecutor was willing to exploit: "Most people I meet like me," to which Betty answered 'false.' She also answered false to "Sometimes I have a great deal of energy." While malingerers tend to give the same answers, it should be no surprise that an individual with chronic depression, frequent hospitalizations, low self-esteem and a history of failure at relationships would respond honestly as Betty did. Despite the fact that I had explained these caveats during my direct examination, the prosecutor wanted the jury to prefer the least likely of the two interpretations of the F scale, as opposed to my overall interpretation of the ten clinical scales. As I explained to the jury, the group of clinical scales revealed that Betty suffered from severe depression, so severe that she likely became psychotic at times.

The prosecutor also focused on whether battered wife syndrome is recognized generally, as a disorder. I was asked whether it was listed in the DSM. It wasn't, at that time. I added that experts indeed recognized it as an actual disorder, and that battered wife syndrome surely would be included in the next edition of the DSM, which indeed it was, though by the names I have described earlier. I felt the prosecutor was squirming, doing anything possible to win the case, whether it served justice, or not. My cross-examination got worse. I was asked whether Betty should wear a warning label. It was a low blow. I replied, "Like a big red A? I don't think so." I felt that the prosecutor was implying to the jury that, if Betty ever re-entered the community she would be quite dangerous, perhaps roaming the streets with murder on her mind. It was absurd, but such images can influence jurors, everyday people who live in the same community as the defendant. Then, as I began to describe more of Betty's treatment records, particularly therapist Maria Stallo's documentation of Betty's report that Jack Brown had threatened to kidnap her, the prosecutor cut me off. Finally, and strangely to my thinking, I was asked why Betty would have described Jack's abuse to me, but never mentioned it to any of her neighbors. The answer was obvious. If Jack had heard word of such talk, Betty would have been in for another beating. I stepped out of the jury box and left the courthouse with the uneasy feeling that the prosecutor had wanted only to win, rather than doing a prosecutor's job — seeking justice.

And win he did. Betty was convicted of first degree murder.

However, Houdyschel and Cabell Public Defender Services Director Robert Wilkinson appealed her conviction to the West Virginia Supreme Court of Appeals. In his oral argument, Wilkinson stressed a number of factors. One of them was that my testimony had been unnecessarily limited. Specifically, trial judge John J. Cummings had ruled that I could testify as to the Betty's extensive history of abuse, but because it amounted to hearsay, the jury could consider it only as part of the basis for my opinion, rather than as direct evidence that the abuse actually had occurred. It may be a fine point of law, but it was vital to Betty Riley's case. The State Supreme Court's stilted legalese read, in part:

When Dr. Wyatt began to encompass particular instances of abuse, the prosecution raised the concern that such hearsay evidence should be admissible only for a limited purpose. The lower

court sustained the **530 *714 prosecution's objection, 5 and Dr.
Wyatt subsequently testified concerning the general nature of the
comments by the Appellant regarding her relationship with Mr.
Brown. Thus, the lower court did not preclude Dr. Wyatt from tes-
tifying regarding the factual underpinnings of his conclusions. The
court simply noted that any hearsay evidence which was encompassed
therein was being introduced only for the limited purpose of allow-
ing Dr. Wyatt to educate the jury regarding the foundations for his
medical conclusions. This same type of exchange transpired regarding
medical records, and the lower court noted that such hearsay evidence
could not be used as direct evidence of Mr. Brown's abusive behavior,
but could be used to build the foundation for Dr. Wyatt's conclusions.

Another of Robert Wilkinson's bases for the appeal was that
the prosecution had made improper statements regarding the
potential consequences of an insanity finding by the jury. At one
point in the trial, the prosecutor had remarked that "...forty days
is not a punishment," implying that a finding of not guilty by
reason of insanity might result in only forty days of incarceration.
In a similar vein, the prosecution had characterized such a finding
by the jury as a "license to kill." However, again, the court was
unmoved by the potentially prejudicial nature of such statements:

In addition to the comments which received no objection at trial,
the Appellant also alleges that she was prejudiced by the prosecu-
tor's remark that "forty days is not a punishment," referring to the
possible consequences of a not guilty by reason of insanity verdict...

The Appellant also alleges that she was prejudiced by prosecutorial
characterization of the insanity defense as potentially a "license to kill."
The prosecution argues that such comment was intended only to stress the
absence of any convincing evidence that the Appellant had lapsed into a
psychosis prior to shooting Mr. Brown. A similar comment, "if 40 million
people are depressed and we send out a message that this is a defense," is
also raised as prejudicial. Objections to these comments were overruled...

Upon our evaluation of the allegedly improper remarks by the pros-
ecution and the effect of those remarks upon the jury, we find that the
comments do not warrant reversal. We do not believe that the remarks

"clearly prejudice(d) the accused or result(ed) in manifest injustice."

In the end, the West Virginia Supreme Court of Appeals rejected each of Wilkinson's arguments, and Betty Riley's conviction stood, with no further hope for reversal.

*   *   *   *   *   *   *   *   *

In writing this book, I talked to Robert Wilkinson, particularly regarding the concept of battered woman syndrome which the courts had seemed reluctant to accept as compelling. Wilkinson recalled the case well, saying that, in its own way, the case had achieved a breakthrough relative to the syndrome. The legal atmosphere surrounding battered woman syndrome was evolving, and Betty Riley's case had been a milestone. Wilkinson added that a subsequent case, which he defended only a few years later, had succeeded in establishing the syndrome as a legitimate defense. Betty Riley, he said, ultimately served out her sentence and now is living with a family member.

*   *   *   *   *   *   *   *   *

Note: In my years of clinical practice and even more years training doctoral and master's students at Marshall University, I have frequently treated women who, like Betty, remained with their abusers, or left and returned to them, sometimes more than once. Often, such women have little understanding of why they stay. Some cite love, as the reason. "I guess I just love him," they have told me with uncertainty that belies the fact that such a rationale makes little sense, even to them. In contrast, there are some specific reasons that explain why women stay, and love is seldom one of them, in my opinion.

Here are a few of the more salient variables. For some women, he is the breadwinner. They are convinced that they, and their children, would starve unless they continue to endure his abuse. Fortunately, women have far more resources today, such as domestic violence centers, than in years gone by. Another rationale some women mention is outright physical fear. He has threatened to kill them, or their children, or her parents or other family members, if she should leave. It is understandable that a woman would be frozen by such a threat, although with care and planning, she still may break free. Another reason, tragically, is that a woman's own family members may keep her with an abusive man by telling her, "You made your bed, and you'll have to lie in it."

Some men employ guilt inducement to get a woman to remain. They may threaten to kill themselves, should she leave. "You will read in the newspaper that my body was found floating in the river, and it will be your fault," they tell her. Or they may convince her that their children would miss him, if he were out of the picture. That could be true, but it is not a healthy reason for either her or the children to remain. Other men may enlist religion as a means to control her. They may cite scripture, or invite the minister to "counsel" her about the sin of breaking up the marriage, notwithstanding the fact that there is little or nothing in any scripture with which I am familiar to suggest a woman must remain with a man who abuses her. Several women who were my therapy patients have said that they felt obligated to remain with their abuser because they were convinced that God was "testing" them, to see whether they deserve eternal life. A therapist is unwise to attempt to trump the Almighty. But more than once I have seen a woman find new life once I asked her whether God might intend that she pass his test by using the intelligence he gave her to get out of the abusive marriage.

There are other reasons that women remain with their abusers, but these are some of the most common. At times, I have found that simply articulating this list of causal factors brings a woman to a much better understanding of why she stays, than does her vague reference to "love" that, even to her, seems an unsatisfying rationale.

Seven

He Hammered His Stepfather to Death

IT WAS A WEEK BEFORE CHRISTMAS, December 18, 1990, when Logan County, West Virginia, resident Charles Walls was acting strangely, once again. The thirty-six-year-old complained that his head hurt and he was talking nonsense. Perhaps members of his family were not as alarmed as they should have been. After all, on three previous occasions the burly, hundred-and-eighty pound man had undergone inpatient treatment for mental problems. Charles' mother and stepfather, Charlotte and Ernest Adkins, hoped that a nerve medicine would calm him. Maybe, they thought, he would not have to be in the hospital during the holidays. They drove Charles to the Emergency Room at Man Appalachian Regional Hospital, where he was given a dose of anti-psychotic medication, and sent home.

Charles lived a half mile from Charlotte and Ernest Adkins in the tiny community of Crown, West Virginia, beside Buffalo Creek. It is the location of the 1972 Buffalo Creek flood, one of the worst industrial disasters in the state's history. That year, in the black of night and following days of rain, several miles above Crown an earthen dam had crumbled. Until that moment, the dam had held back millions of gallons of water and sludge, byproducts of cleaning coal before it is sent out by train. The deluge rushed fifteen miles down the tight valley, sweeping over Crown and several other communities. An hour later the flood had ended; a half dozen communities, including Crown, had vanished. Where towns had stood, now there were only mud flats, level and smooth, except for the occasional chimney, upturned auto or portion of a roof that eerily protruded from the muck as if to ask, "Where is everything?" One hundred and twenty-four people were dead. Those who lived had survived by fleeing to the hillsides, where they clung to trees and brush as they prayed that the deluge would not reach them. They had watched the torrent sweep away their loved ones, friends and homes. Virtually every sign of life they had known had ceased to exist. Then the decades began to roll by and a number of residents rebuilt. Some did so in Crown.

Although Charles Walls had received a heavy dose of anti-psychotic medication at the ER, by 3:15 the next afternoon his condition had worsened. His sister, Diana Lynn Vance of nearby Accoville, visited her mother and stepfather's home and noticed the deterioration in Charles' thinking. He was still complaining that his head hurt and he was uttering bizarre remarks, danger-ous things that made no sense. Diana's concerns escalated when Charles screamed at her, "You're taking my power!" In a while, her attempts to calm Charles met with some success, enough that a few minutes after 5:00 p.m., she asked Charles to drive her home. After dropping Diana at her home, Charles drove back to Charlotte and Ernest's house, where the three ate dinner. Also there was Charles' brother, David Walls, who lived elsewhere but, while visiting his mother and stepfather, had laid down to rest and fallen asleep. At her home, Diana Vance fretted about Charles and the safety of her mother and stepfather. As her worries grew, Diana put on her coat and began walking. A little before 6:00, Diana arrived back at the couple's home. She was relieved to see that Charlotte and Ernest were fine and her brother David, who had awakened, was still there.

Diana's reassurance was not to last. The remaining threads of Charles' tenuous grip on reality were unraveling. He stared at Diana and repeatedly screamed, "You're taking my power! You're taking my power!" Diana tried to calm him. "What are you talking about Bubby? I'm not doing anything to you," she said. Charles shouted back, "You're taking my power and I want it back, — NOW!"

Diana went to the living room and told her mother that Charles was "freaking." David Walls heard Diana tell her mother that she was leaving. Also overhearing her, Charles announced he again would take her home. Diana declined, insisting she would walk. But Charles insisted. Then, moments later, Diana relented, thinking it best to get Charles away from Charlotte and Ernest, even if only briefly. Although Charles had lapsed into psychosis, his sister once again permitted him to take her home.

Charles left with Diana. Charlotte, Ernest and David watched the clock. They knew the distance and time it would take for Charles to drive to his sister's home, and immediately return. When Charles pulled in, the three noticed the time. Evidently, Charles had dropped Diana and she was safe.

After greeting his mother and stepfather in the living room, Charles walked to the kitchen where, saying nothing, he sat down at the table with his brother David, who had begun to eat a hastily prepared dinner. David found his brother's silence unsettling and walked to the living room, carrying his plate of food with him. As David moved to the living room, his mother, Charlotte Adkins, walked past him, toward the kitchen and toward Charles. From where he sat in the living room, David overheard his mother say to Charles, "Honey, what are you going to do with that hammer?" Quickly, David returned to the kitchen. Charlotte was gently removing the hammer from Charles' grasp. She laid it out of sight, on top of a cabinet. Charlotte's calming words seemed to have quieted Charles. David wondered whether the calm would remain.

At 6:05 David and his stepfather Ernest Adkins stepped onto the front porch where they discussed what to do about Charles. Perhaps they could get Charles under control. Maybe he would be OK by tomorrow. Although David had to leave, he told his stepfather he would stick around a bit, just in case. The two men parted, Ernest returning inside the house while David made his way to the hillside, where he spent a few minutes burning trash. In ten minutes the initial flare of the trash fire had quieted. With the flames dying, David walked back toward the house. Through the window he could see Charles standing in the living room. His brother seemed calm enough. It was 6:15 and, without re-entering the house, David drove off.

Moments after David's departure, Charles, Charlotte and Ernest were seated in the living room, watching television. Suddenly, Charles shouted, "That mother fucker killed my son!" In an instant he tore the telephone from the wall and began using it to pummel his stepfather. When Charlotte attempted to intervene, Charles struck her with the phone, knocking her to the floor and cutting a large gash in his mother's head. He immediately returned to beating his stepfather. Charlotte ran to the kitchen and picked up the hammer. She rushed to the living room to assist her husband who by now was defenseless against the younger, stronger man. Ernest was on the floor, still being savagely beaten with the phone. Charlotte grabbed at Charles, attempting to save her husband. Charles turned on her and, twisting her arm, took the hammer. With Charles momentarily distracted, Ernest had gathered himself from the living room floor and retreated to the bedroom. Charles, hammer in hand, followed him. Falling backward onto the bed, Ernest made a final, futile effort to defend himself as Charles, in full psychotic fury, mercilessly hammered at his bleeding stepfather.

At 6:20, neighbor Perry Harvey heard a knock at his door. It was Charlotte Adkins, frantic and bleeding from her head and her arm. She shouted that Charles was killing Ernest. Harvey called both the State Police and an ambulance, then raced next door. He found Ernest sitting, slumped over, in a chair in the bedroom, blood streaming from multiple head wounds. The hammer lay on the bed. There was no sign of Charles Walls.

At her home, Diana Lynn Vance's heart sunk as she heard an emergency vehicle roar by. She rushed to her mother's home. Entering the bedroom she saw emergency workers James Kubow and Tom Takubo working to save her stepfather, who remained seated in the chair. Blood was everywhere. Ernest was partially conscious and was attempting to tell Kubow and Takubo what had happened. Diana ran next door to Perry Harvey's home, where her blood-drenched mother described what had happened. Diana called David.

At two minutes before 7:00 p.m., State Troopers W. E. Stroupe, W. R. Gibson and J.C. Chambers arrived. The EMS workers directed them next door to the Harvey residence, where they found Charlotte Adkins lying on the floor and conscious, her head still bleeding. Diana was with her. Charlotte told the troopers that it was Charles who had attacked her and Ernest. Diana added that she had not seen Charles, nor had she seen his white Nissan Sentra since she arrived.

The troopers conducted a preliminary search, secured the scene and left after talking to David Walls, who gave them Charles' address. Around 10:00 p.m., the troopers arrived at Charles' house on Crown Hill. They talked to several neighbors who said they had not seen Charles that day. While still interviewing Charles' neighbors, the troopers received a call. They learned that at 9:26 p.m., at Man Appalachian Regional Hospital, Dr. Maria Ibara had pronounced Ernest Adkins dead. The troopers also were told that in Ernest's wallet was $1,057. As Trooper Stroupe later would write in his extensive report, "...robbery was not a motive for these crimes."

Throughout the night, law enforcement officers searched the roads, especially Routes 10 and 80. But they found no trace of Charles Walls. David had suggested that Charles might travel to Greenbrier County, where his ex-wife lived. A check there revealed that Charles had not been seen. Then, at 6:45 in the morning, troopers received a report from the Virginia State Police. Forty-five minutes earlier, state trooper M. D. Spangler had attempted to pull Charles over for speeding on Interstate 81, near Abingdon, Virginia. The trooper had pursued Charles for twenty miles at speeds of 105 miles per hour until Charles had attempted to pass on the median and wrecked. Charles was in custody of the Virginia State Police.

Charlotte recovered from her wounds. Diana, David and their siblings dealt with the shock of what had happened. One ordeal had ended, and another had begun.

★ ★ ★ ★ ★ ★ ★ ★ ★

Charles Walls' psychiatric history could be summed up in a single word — extensive. Twice he had been admitted to Weston State Hospital, most recently in 1989 under a commitment order. While there he was diagnosed as suffering from paranoid schizophrenia. During that admission, Dr. S. B. Cruz noted that Charles had a long history of abusing alcohol, and also at times had used marijuana and cocaine. Also, Dr. Cruz took note of a fact that would play a crucial role in the outcome of Charles' trial in the homicide of his stepfather: When at home, Charles tended not to take his medicine.

The two stays at Weston State Hospital were not his first admissions for mental health problems. Earlier, he had been committed to Huntington State Hospital after becoming psychotic. At that time his symptoms were attributed to a blow to his head with a rock, during a bar fight. Charles had run from the hospital, leaving against medical advice prior to completion of his treatment. Interestingly, under the law, when an involuntary patient departs his treatment AMA, it is the responsibility of the hospital staff to notify the sheriff's department, which then bears the burden of locating the patient and returning him or her to treatment. However, often that is not what happens, for several reasons. If, in the opinion of the hospital's staff the involuntarily committed patient had been near the end of his treatment, a report to the sheriff's department may never be made. If a report is made, sheriff's deputies may have difficulty locating the patient. Moreover, apprehension of such patients generally is low on the priority list of law enforcement agencies. Thus, Charles never was returned to Huntington State Hospital.

On another occasion Charles was admitted to the psychiatric unit at St. Mary's Hospital in Huntington. He was examined by Dr. Jack Dodd, who prescribed Prozac and Lithium. Dodd's decision to prescribe Lithium indicates that the doctor saw Charles as psychotic. This time, Charles completed two weeks of treatment.

Records of his three earlier admissions showed he had experienced auditory hallucinations, paranoid delusions and at times was convinced that he could read people's minds. There were occasions when he believed others could insert their thoughts into his mind

Thus, there was no question that, prior to killing his stepfather, Ernest Adkins, Charles had become psychotic on a number of occasions, over a period of several years. That history, combined with the bizarre statements he had made minutes before killing his stepfather, provided powerful evidence that he had been insane at the time.

While in jail after killing his stepfather, Charles began to hallucinate. He told correctional personnel he was hearing voices of his family, "hollering for help," and voices of others whom he did not recognize and could not understand. Thus, Logan County Circuit Judge Eric H. O'Briant remanded Charles to Weston State Hospital for a full mental health examination.

On March 27, 1991, while at Weston, Charles was examined by psychologist Robert J. Rush, who described Charles's account of killing Ernest Adkins:

A delusional sounding version of the demise of his stepfather was presented. Professing his innocence, he asserted a 'vision' of the event. His ex-wife and his brother were reported to have been involved but he said he couldn't go into a courtroom and say (he'd) had a vision. According to the defendant, "It's a conspiracy...(the) reason I'm here is over my money...other people didn't want me spending." The subject asserted that brain and mind were separate and (he) had a previously prepared picture to illustrate this dichotomy. He continued that some people had special powers to control the minds of others. An illusion (sic) was made to "state police ninjas" with these special powers.

During the assessment, Dr. Rush administered the Wechsler Adult Intelligence Scale (Revised), which revealed Charles' full-scale IQ to be 80. Given the national mean score of 100, and the standard deviation of 15, Charles' score meant that his general intellectual functioning was well below average, "at the bottom of the low average range," Dr. Rush wrote. But given that such functioning is a bit above the level of mental retardation (which the DSM-5 now terms intellectual disability), the doctor added, "...thus, mental retardation will not be an issue in the matter before the court."

Charles also completed the Minnesota Multiphasic Personality

Inventory, twice. It is unusual that anyone fails to complete the test in a single administration. However, Charles had skipped many of the items on the first administration, which caused Dr. Rush to be concerned that Charles had difficulty reading the 566 true/false items. Thus, the doctor asked Charles to read aloud several simple sentences of instructions given to those who take the test, instructions that assume only a sixth-grade reading ability. Charles' reading difficulties were confirmed. As a result, a staff member read the items to Charles and he completed the MMPI. The test's scales indicated depression, paranoia and schizophrenia, with only slight elevation in the F scale, which is designed to catch those who may be faking mental illness. That modest elevation likely was explained by the fact that Charles admitted to so many bizarre thoughts, feelings and experiences that already had been documented in his other admissions.

Dr. Rush made a diagnosis of paranoid schizophrenia and concluded that Charles was not competent to stand trial, "due to his persecutory delusions." On the question of criminal responsibility, Dr. Rush demurred, "The question of criminal responsibility will therefore be deferred…(because), Many experts on psychiatry and the law argue that it is not appropriate to address criminal responsibility unless the subject is competent to stand trial."

Three days later, Charles was examined again, this time by psychiatrist B. M. Hirani, whose diagnosis differed only slightly from that of Dr. Rush. Charles suffered from schizoaffective disorder, the psychiatrist concluded. The odd-sounding term indicates that signs of both schizophrenia and a major depressive disorder were present. Charles again remarked to the doctor that the reason he was sent to Weston was because of money, and that his sister and the police were lying about the homicide. "In fact," the doctor wrote, "he also does not believe that his stepfather is indeed dead. When I read to him the police investigation report and the statement that was made by Mrs. Atkins (sic) he just yawned, seemed very unconcerned, and in a very nonchalant (way) stated that 'I didn't do it.'"

Like Dr. Rush, Dr. Hirani found that Charles was not competent to stand trial and, thus, the doctor offered no opinion regarding criminal responsibility. He prescribed both Lithium and Mellaril, commonly prescribed for psychosis, as well as Prozac for Charles' mood. The doctor also was in agreement with Dr. Rush in another way. Both recommended that Charles remain at Weston for six months for an extended evaluation.

As the months passed, Charles' mental status improved. He continued to take psychotropic medications, including Trilafon and Prozac. On November 15, 1991, he was examined by another Weston State Hospital psychiatrist, Patricia Williams. He exhibited insight into his psychotic episodes, telling Dr. Williams that in the past he had been paranoid after he was hit in the head with a rock, and that he had believed people could read his thoughts, and he had heard voices telling him he was going to die. Now, however, he said he had not heard voices for several months. He understood that, "it was all in my head." Regarding the question of criminal responsibility, Dr. Williams concluded, "During December of 1990, he was suffering from a psychotic illness which prevented him from conforming his behavior to the requirements of the law. He was not criminally responsible for his actions during December, 1990." His extended evaluation at Weston had come to an end and, in December, 1991, Charles was returned to the Logan County Jail.

* * * * * * * * *

Logan County prosecuting attorney Donald C. Wandling is an excellent lawyer who faced a dilemma in the case of Charles Walls. I have known Wandling and his wife Anne, who also is a lawyer, for many years and have consulted with them a number of times in their private practice. As a prosecutor, the issue he faced was whether to push ahead with the murder case in the face of Dr. Williams' finding that Charles was not criminally responsible. A prosecutor represents the state, the members of his community. Many Logan County residents had questions about Charles Walls. What might happen if Charles returned to the community at some point? What if he again stopped taking his medicine? Might he again become homicidal?

Wandling considered whether a second examiner would agree with Dr. Williams' finding that Charles was not criminally responsible. Thus, Wandling referred Charles to me for a forensic examination to determine whether Charles was competent to stand trial and, more importantly, whether at the time he hammered his stepfather to death, Charles was criminally responsible.

I reviewed reports of the previous examinations and agreed to conduct the examination. Charles was transported from the Logan County jail to my office at Marshall University on April 1, 1992. Like many individuals whom I have examined, he was clad in orange jail clothing. He remained handcuffed and the deputy stood watch outside the examination room's door. Charles said he had no memory of killing his stepfather, but had no doubt he had done it because his mother said so. She would not lie about it, he added. Charles insisted he had borne no ill-will toward his stepfather. In fact, by Charles' account, and based on reports from family members, the two men had a relatively good relationship. His biological father had not been very much involved with Charles. His mother married Ernest Adkins when Charles was about fourteen, and Charles could recall no animosity between them. As Charles talked about his family of four brothers and three sisters, he said all but one sister were supportive of him.

Charles told me more about his personal history. He was in special education classes, a "slow learner" he called himself, until he dropped out in the ninth grade. He had attended training in auto mechanics at the Job Corps, and later worked in construction. For a time he was a heavy equipment operator. He told me about his two marriages and his child from the first marriage and two adopted children from the second marriage, which also ended in divorce. He termed his first wife an alcoholic. He said he had custody of their child for about three years until she successfully petitioned for custody by convincing the judge that she was a changed woman, although in his opinion she was not. He admitted that he had a cocaine conviction in the late 1970s but it had been overturned, for reasons he did not understand. He also admitted to excessive drinking and abuse of pot.

We discussed his earlier inpatient stays, prior to his recent hospitalization at Weston. He seemed to consider excessive drinking to have been the primary reason for the prior admissions, but acknowledged that he also had been depressed. His other health problems were of interest too. He described the incident in which he had been hit in the head with a large rock during a bar fight, three or four years prior to killing his stepfather. I noticed he walked with a significant limp, which he said was the result of a motorcycle collision, and later a fall from a truck that caused him to be hospitalized, off and on, for a year and ended with placement of a rod in his back. As I sat with Charles, I wondered what, if any, brain damage he had suffered during his injuries. That question never has been satisfactorily answered.

During the examination, Charles did not seem depressed and wasn't overly anxious. He wasn't psychotic and did not describe any recent delusions. Nor was he actively hallucinating. He was calm and demonstrated acceptable insight into his legal situation. Although he did not volunteer information about any unusual thoughts and feelings in recent years, when I brought it up Charles admitted that he had seen visions of his wife, his brother and others, when they were not present. On one occasion he had become so upset about his hallucinations that he had run to his brother's house in tears. The more we talked, the more relaxed and open he became. He described the period of time in which he was convinced that his mind was in touch with the minds of others. He seemed obsessed with the fact that, back then, he had become convinced it had happened. Now he was at a loss to explain it. Although he was uncertain as to the timeframe, my impression was that some of these episodes had occurred not long before the killing, and some of them had happened during his hospitalization at Weston.

By the end of our interview, I had come to know Charles well. He understood the charges against him and how serious they were. He understood the roles of a judge, jury, prosecutor and defense lawyer. He knew the results if he were to be found guilty and if found not guilty. In short, he was competent to stand trial. He could assist his attorney in his own defense, a requirement before anyone may be brought to trial on any charge. Then came the question of criminal responsibility. As is usually the case, the evidence cut both ways. He had fled the crime scene, which tended to indicate he knew he had done something wrong. And he had tried to avoid arrest while running from the law in Virginia.

But the heaviest weight of factors went to the alternative conclusion. Specifically, due to mental illness, Charles was not responsible for his actions at the time he killed his stepfather. In my report, I wrote:

This evidence includes the fact that he had not been in a heated argument with his father just prior to the crime, and I could find no evidence that there had even been a mild disagreement at the time. Additionally, I could find no evidence of a longstanding feud between them. This is based on his statements as well as those of witnesses given to state troopers investigating the crime. Second, he has a history of mental disorders that pre-dates the crime. It is not as if he concocted a story about mental disorders after the fact of the crime. Third, the statements of others to the police indicate that he was engaging in unusual talk, indicating that someone had taken his "power" just prior to the crime. This is consistent with his reports of a history of paranoid ideas in which he felt individuals could communicate with him via mind power. Considering all these, pro and con…the killing of his stepfather was the product of a mental illness.

I made a diagnosis of chronic paranoid schizophrenia with acute exacerbation. I added that I felt his schizophrenia would re-emerge from time to time over the next few years and, while dangerousness is not predictable with complete accuracy, should he stop taking his medicine, he could again become dangerous. I recommended long-term inpatient treatment because of that concern, but added my opinion that, after years of treatment, he might again be able to live in the community. I submitted my report and wondered what would become of Charles Walls.

Earl McCoy is led into court in Hamlin, West Virginia, to
stand trial for the killing of Emmett Brooks.
Photo Credit: Lee Arnold, *Lincoln Journal.*

Emmet Brooks died here,
shot by Earl McCoy, near
Kiahsville in Lincoln County.

Emmet Brooks
pulled off the road
at this intersection
to threaten Earl
McCoy. Later that
day, McCoy killed
Brooks.

IN THE SUPREME COURT OF APPEALS OF WEST VIRGINIA

January 2006 Term

No. 32860

STATE OF WEST VIRGINIA,
Plaintiff Below, Appellee,

V.

EARL RAY McCOY, JR.,
Defendant Below, Appellant.

James Spurlock,
Attorney for
Earl McCoy

Appeal from the Circuit Court of Lincoln County
Honorable Jay M. Hoke, Judge
Criminal Action No. 03-F-02
REVERSED AND REMANDED

Submitted: April 11, 2006
Filed: May 24, 2006

-
-
-

.....This error was particularly egregious and reversible because "[t]he prosecutor exploited that lack of corroborating testimony in his closing argument to the jury when he repeatedly portrayed [Mr. McCoy] as a 'liar'[.]" *State v. Turner*, 771 A.2d 206, 215 (Conn. App. Ct. 2001). (See footnote 16)

IV.

CONCLUSION

The circuit court's conviction and sentencing order of May 19, 2004, is reversed. This case is remanded for a new trial consistent with this opinion.

Reversed and Remanded.

Earl McCoy's attorney James Spurlock successfully appealed his conviction to the West Virginia Supreme court of Appeals, arguing the case on April 11, 2006.

Nick Mauro with attorneys Patrick Wilson and James Shields, and an investigator;
James Mauro family; Fairmont, WV, murder scene.
Photo courtesy of *Fairmont Times West Virginian*.

Nick Mauro, on trial for
quadruple murder.

Nick Mauro attempted to escape during
his trial, by leaping from the second
story window of the courthouse.

Rustic Motel where Bobby Lowe lived with Misty Cabral.

Room 127 Rustic Motel, where Bobby Lowe lived with Misty Cabral.

JB's Gentlemen's Club, Jefferson, WV, where Misty Cabral worked as a stripper.

Timothy Scott Skeens lived in the building on the right. His confrontation with Walter Henry occurred in front of the Speedway on the left.

Walter Henry lived here, a block from Scott Skeens' apartment.

he Herald-Dispatch

st Virginia   www.herald-dispatch.com   2-3-07   Home Edition 50¢

Teen gets 25 years

Skeens sentenced for his role in the fatal stabbing of Walter Lee Henry in 2005

By CURTIS JOHNSON
The Herald-Dispatch
cujohnson@herald-dispatch.com

HUNTINGTON — Timothy Scott Skeens' youth, intelligence, aggressive nature and hope for rehabilitation were all put on the stand Friday morning, moments before Cabell Circuit Judge Dan O'Hanlon sentenced the 18-year-old murderer to 25 years in prison.

Skeens of Point Pleasant, W.Va., apologized for using a 17-inch sword to fatally stab Walter Lee

WEB EXTRA

Share your thoughts about crime in the Tri-State at our crime and safety forum at www.herald-dispatch.com.

Henry on Oct. 13, 2005, but in the same breath admitted "anything I say will never bring back the life that I took."

"I think about it every day," he said. "My nightmare is seeing him every day and then

having to live with what happened. I never saw myself ever being up here, standing up here for a murder charge."

Skeens also asked the court for a second chance, but the victim's sister Minnie Martin testified that she is hurt, devastated

and torn. She told the court it's unfortunate that such a young man would kill her brother, but in the end she pleaded for O'Hanlon to punish Skeens to the fullest extent of the law.

Please see SENTENCE/2A

Timothy Scott Skeens, 18, of Point Pleasant, W.Va., sits at his sentencing hearing Friday morning. The convicted murderer was sentenced to 25 years in prison for using a sword to kill Walter Lee Henry in October 2005.

Curtis Johnson/The Herald-Dispatch

Timothy Scott Skeens pled, and received a length sentence.

Murder suspect to be tried as adult

Curtis Johnson/The Herald-Dispatch

~mothy Scott Skeens, 17, of Point Pleasant, W.Va., exits a Cabell County courtroom after hearing he will be ~ed as an adult if a grand jury indicts him in connection with the October stabbing death of 45-year-old Walter ~e Henry.

~efense attorney claims self ~efense in sword-stabbing case

y CURTIS JOHNSON
~e Herald-Dispatch
johnson@herald-dispatch.com

HUNTINGTON — A ~tal sword-stabbing case ~volving a 17-year-old boy ~s been transferred to ~ult court. Circuit Judge ~lfred Ferguson made the ~ecision during a closed-~oor juvenile transfer ~earing Monday morning, ~ccording to attorneys ~rguing both sides of the ~se.

Ferguson's ruling allows ~urt officials and police to ~eat Timothy Scott Skee-~s, 17, of Point Pleasant as ~ adult defendant, mean-~g the teen's identity and ~any court filings can be ~eleased to public.

Police arrested Skeens two days after they say Walter Lee Henry, 45, of Huntington walked into a convenience
store/ser-
vice sta-
tion along
8th Street
with a
sword
wound to
his chest.
They esti-
mated the sword to be 18 inches long.

Cabell County Prosecutor Chris Chiles and defense attorney John Laishley said they anticipate the case being presented to the Janu-ary grand jury.

Henry

"This child is detained right now, and in order to get the case moving along and resolve it for him, we have to get this procedur-al bump out of the way," Laishley said of Monday's hearing.

A list of possible wit-nesses includes Joe Wyatt, a Marshall Uni-versity psychology pro-fessor, but Laishley said that an insanity defense is not part of his client's strategy.

Instead, Laishley said he will argue the fatal stab-bing was the result of self defense, but he declined comment when asked if Skeens participated in the incident.

"It looks like a classic self defense case," he said.

Chiles said he is aware of the self defense strat-

egy, and he responded by saying he believes Fergu-son found probable cause Monday that a crime was committed.

Laishley's resume includes his defense of teenage convicted mur-derers DeAaron Fields and Michael Day.

"The biggest problem is communication with children that do not have the worldly experience necessary to make good decisions," he said of his experience. "We think, with the help of the judge and the court, we've put together a team and (Skeens) has been com-municating with us, and we've been communicat-ing with him and that's what is important."

Please see SUSPECT/2A

Timothy Scott Skeens appears in court, charged with the murder of Walter Henry.
Photo Credit: Curtis Johnson, *Huntington Herald Dispatch*.

Timothy Scott Skeen was tried as an adult, although he was seventeen at the time he killed Walter Henry.

Jim Richardson at the scene of Kelli Gilfilin's murder. Photo credit, Lawrence Pierce. Reprinted by permission of *The Charleston Gazette*.

John Noble, left, and Cpl. David Tackett, right, escort Betty Riley to a police car at 943 Ninth Ave., Huntington, where she shot boyfriend Jack Brown. Photo credit: Frank Altizer, *The Herald-Dispatch*.

Robert Wilkinson appealed Betty Riley's case to the WV Supreme Court.

* * * * * * * * *

No doubt the case was deeply troubling for everyone involved. A man was dead. The individual who killed him, by all accounts and based on examinations by several professionals, had been insane at the time. Community members were concerned that Charles should not be walking freely among them. In the end, Prosecutor Donald Wandling decided to try the case and, thus, allow community members themselves to hear the evidence and reach a decision on what would become of Charles Walls.

Several additional variables played roles in the case. Defense attorney Mark Hobbs was relatively young and probably had never tried such a case before. As well, Judge Eric O'Briant was fairly new to the bench. The trial played out in the Logan County courthouse on Stratton Street, with each side doing its best to succeed. Attorney Hobbs had the experts uniformly on his side, and we gave our testimony, in line with our examinations of Charles. On direct examination by Hobbs, I described my credentials, methods and conclusions. On cross-examination, Mr. Wandling asked me only a few questions, but one of them turned the case around. The prosecutor asked me about the statement in my report concerning my fear that Charles could become dangerous again, if he returned to the community and stopped taking his medicine. The jury heard my acknowledgement. It was a realistic concern.

Jurors are required to consider the evidence and decide accordingly. Most jurors do not know what is done with a prisoner who is found to have been insane at the time of a horrible crime such as the one committed by Charles Walls. Many jurors believe that such a person is immediately released, free to roam the community minutes after their verdict, although nothing could be further from the truth. Typically, individuals found not guilty by reason of insanity spend as much time incarcerated in a mental hospital as if they had been convicted of their crime and sentenced to prison. In fact, some defendants have ended up spending more time committed to a mental hospital than if they simply had pled guilty. Most potential jurors are unaware of those facts, and it is forbidden that they consider possible sentences, as they deliberate. Rather, following the jury's verdict, the disposition of the prisoner's fate lies in the bailiwick of the judge. However, jurors are human beings, complete with their fears and misperceptions and it is difficult to blame them for feeling fearful about the fictional possibility that they could find 'not guilty by reason of insanity' one day, and meet the defendant walking down the street the next day. It doesn't happen.

The jury concluded its deliberations and announced it had found Charles Walls guilty of first degree murder. Judge O'Briant sentenced him to life in prison, without mercy.

* * * * * * * * *

Over the next sixteen years, Charles went through an unsuccessful appeal plus two unsuccessful *habeus corpus* appeals. By then in his fifties, it appeared that Charles Walls would spend the rest of his life in prison. But in 2008, Pineville, West Virginia, lawyer Tim Lupardus was assigned to the case. For three years, Lupardis delved into every detail of the case – Charles' psychiatric history, the opinions of experts, and the events of the homicide itself. On March 9, 2011, Mr. Lupardus contacted me with some startling news. He had uncovered sufficient errors in the case that Charles' conviction had been reversed by the West Virginia Supreme Court.

The state's high court had found an improper instruction by the judge. Specifically, Judge O'Briant had instructed the jurors that they could presume malice and intent, which are necessary for a verdict of first degree murder, from the fact that Charles had used a weapon, the hammer, to kill Ernest Adkins. Although O'Briant's jury instruction was consistent with the law, conceptually that law always had seemed to make little sense. If a person is not responsible due to mental illness, why would it matter that he used a weapon? A mental illness defense should not rest on whether an individual was able to lay his hands on a weapon. As Lupardus explained, Judge O'Briant's instruction had been permitted in 1992 but, years later, the West Virginia State Supreme Court had ruled such an instruction to be improper, and the justices had made their ruling retroactive. Thus, Charles was entitled to a new trial, after nineteen years of incarceration. In anticipation of a second trial, attorney Lupadus contacted me to discuss Charles' case.

Interestingly, Charles had continued to receive medication during his nearly two decades in the state's maximum security prison, Lupardus said. He added that when the jail staff were late with his doses, Charles again tended toward psychosis, sometimes becoming almost incoherent. Also, Lupardus told me that Charles' general health had declined and he was now mostly confined to a wheelchair because of his longstanding back problems.

Over the years, I had not forgotten Charles Walls. I agreed to meet with Mr. Lupardus and, if necessary, to again provide my opinions to a new jury. Two months later, On May 10, 2011, I received the following startling e-mail from Tim Lupardus:

Dr. Wyatt,
Please accept my apologies for not corresponding sooner. I want to let you know that Mr. Walls' long ordeal is over. He has been released into the care of his brother, and long-time supporter, Ballard.
Sincerely,
Timothy P. Lupardus

* * * * * * * * *

Note: There never was another trial. I contacted Mr. Lupardus when writing this book. He told me that Charles' declining physical condition — he could stand for brief periods but essentially was confined to a wheelchair — had played a role in the decision to release him to his brother, rather than to re-try him.

Eight

Counterfeit Kingpin, Or King of Pranks?

WHEN FIFTEEN-YEAR-OLD ALIJAH COOK was caught in an episode of petty misbehavior at his middle school in Charleston, West Virginia, on March 23, 1999. Authorities found $180 in counterfeit twenty dollar bills in his pocket. The U.S. Secret Service was notified, and Alijah wasted no time in telling the officers how the money was produced and that his half-brother, twenty-six-year-old Steven Arlo Cook, had made it. The agents interviewed Arlo, who immediately admitted he made the counterfeit twenties. But Arlo claimed he had no intention to use the bills as real cash, and he hadn't been aware that his little brother had tried to spend any of them. He told the agents that he thought it was within the law to print bogus money, provided he had no intention to use it as currency. Arlo was mistaken.

He told the agents that Alijah, who was aware the bills were counterfeit, evidently had been unable to resist temptation, after Arlo made the bills on his computer. Two days before the Secret Service showed up at his house, he made the phony cash after hearing Alijah say that some girls were coming over. Arlo thought that flashing a roll of bills would impress them. It appeared that the agents accepted Arlo's version of events because there was no evidence Arlo had tried to spend any of the bills. Moreover, after talking to Arlo, they may have con-

cluded that he suffered from mental problems. If that was their conclusion, they were correct as Arlo had a lengthy history of baffling
mental problems. Whatever their thinking, they did not arrest Arlo
and it seemed that a stern warning would take care of the problem.
The next day Arlo brought the remaining bills to the agents,
including some that never had been cut from their sheets.

A few days later, one of the counterfeit bills was discovered
to have been used to make a purchase. Probably, Alijah had spent
it before he was caught. The fifteen-year-old told his mother that
he may have spent one. Upon learning of the bogus twenty that
was in circulation, agents took Arlo to the U.S. Secret Service
office in Charleston on the evening of March 29, 1999. His mother,
Dreama Cook, went with Arlo. She told an agent that Arlo had
serious mental problems, that he was learning disabled, and she
asked to sit in while Arlo was questioned. The agents refused,
although Dreama sat just outside the door to the interrogation
room and listened for more than four hours as the diminutive
Arlo, who stood five feet, four inches tall and weighed one
hundred and thirty pounds, underwent a bruising interrogation.

Dreama listened as the agents escalated the intensity and
volume of their questions and accusations. Occasionally, she was
able to hear part of what was happening. They hammered away
at Arlo, shouting things like, "Smiling means you're guilty!!" and,
"Rubbing your nose means you're guilty!!" They accused Arlo of
using his juvenile brother to pass the bills so that Arlo would not go
to jail. They repeatedly called him a liar. They were attempting to
break him down, Dreama concluded. Ultimately, they succeeded.

For most of the intense four hours, Arlo had denied that
he intended to pass any of the bills. Finally, however, as the
night grew late and Arlo's physical and mental energy were
tapped out, he caved to the demands of the Secret Service agents
and told them to believe whatever they wanted. By the time
Arlo broke he was consumed with a single desire – to end the
abusive questioning so that he could go home. An agent placed
a written confession in front of him and Arlo signed it. The statement concluded, "It was my intention to purchase better quality

computer equipment to make better quality counterfeit so I could get away with passing it. Because of my current financial status, it was my intention to print counterfeit money to purchase items that I could not afford with my present income." He had given them what they wanted, and they let him go home.

* * * * * * * * *

Soon, however, Arlo Cook was indicted on federal counterfeiting charges. His attorney , Assistant Federal Public Defender Brian J. Kornbrath, met with Arlo and his mother and quickly understood that Arlo's mental status was anything but typical for a twenty-six-year-old man. Thus, Mr. Kornbrath wrote to me on November 18, 1999, with a request that I conduct a forensic examination of Arlo, who by then had recanted his confession. Lawyer Kornbrath asked me to address three questions in my examination of Arlo. Were Arlo's disabilities, as Dreama described them, still present? If so, would they have affected the voluntariness of the confession he had signed? If the confession were admitted at trial, should a jury be skeptical of it, given his disabilities?

Six days later, on November 24, 1999, Dreama Cook brought Arlo to the examination in my office at Marshall University in Huntington. I spent considerable time with the two of them together, and with each alone. Additionally, I administered several psychological tests to Arlo.

Arlo freely admitted that he had printed the bogus money, but he insisted that, at the time, he felt there was nothing wrong with doing so because he had no intention to spend it. He realized he was in trouble when the federal agents showed up at his home. He described how Alijah had been caught with some of the bills and he said it had come as a surprise to learn that Alijah had attempted to spend them.

As my clinical interview continued, it became clear that something essential was missing from Arlo's psychological makeup. Initially, I noticed he lacked sufficient understanding of the seriousness of the trouble he was in. He said he was not worried about the charges or a trial, because he continued to believe that printing the money wasn't wrong, assuming he had no intention to spend it. The charges against him should have awakened him to the realization that his opinion was at odds with the law. I asked myself why that awakening had not happened. As we talked more, I began to see that Arlo's naïve perspective on his legal problems was characteristic of his approach to almost everything. Evidently, he was without the typical level of social and situational perceptiveness that most adults possess. Something was seriously wrong with him but, for the moment, the precise nature of his mental problems remained out of my reach.

When I interviewed Dreama Cook alone, she expanded on several of the things she had only hinted at while the three of us were together. She said that Arlo always had been different, a loner, with a strange sense of humor and insufficient perception of how his actions would be interpreted by others. She said, "Arlo doesn't know where to draw the line." Once, Arlo had taken a pair of handcuffs to school and, while the principal was distracted, Arlo had put them on the man. It had taken two hours to get the handcuffs off. Arlo saw the episode as a funny, harmless prank, one that should have been appreciated for its humor, his mother said.

Arlo once hacked into the Capitol High School computer system and put out a message that students would be dismissed from school at noon and they all should stop by the cafeteria to pick up free pizza on their way out. Dreama said that Arlo was astonished to learn that the school's administrators were outraged over this highly disruptive prank. One day he lifted a teacher's car keys and, as a joke, moved the teacher's car to another side of the school's parking lot. He considered the teacher's frantic search for the "stolen" car to have been hilarious. The flustered faculty member strongly disagreed.

Arlo had held a number of jobs, most of them only briefly. One was at McDonald's, Dreama said. Arlo was working in the back of the restaurant when the line of customers backed up. The manager told Arlo, "Get up on the counter," and Arlo jumped up on the counter with both feet. He was the only one who thought it was funny, she said. He had done things like that all his life, a discouraged Dreama Cook told me.

She said Arlo had wrecked, or blown the engines out of, six cars in about two years. Once a friend of Arlo's called her to say he had been frightened when Arlo took the car to 120 miles an hour on the interstate. When she talked to Arlo about it, he seemed unconcerned that driving at that speed could be dangerous. She added that Arlo had received many vehicular-related tickets, and blithely had thrown them away. When he received a letter saying his license would be revoked if he failed to pay off the tickets, he threw that away as well. In time, she ceased all efforts to rescue Arlo from his traffic-related jams. He could get along without a car and without a driver's license from now on, she said. I suspected that, aside from the tough love message she was sending, she may have decided that both Arlo and the driving public would be healthier if he never drove at all.

Arlo's mother described a recent tactical mistake she had made. In hopes of getting her son into a hobby or activity, she had suggested that he learn scuba diving. Arlo passed the written test and did well enough on some of the in-water tests. However, his insufficient appreciation for danger had raised its head yet again when, on a recent trip to Florida, Arlo swam beyond the limits of depth and danger set by the instructor. He even had attempted to pick up an eel. I formed an impression of Dreama Cook: She had tried her best to be a thoughtful, conscientious mother to Arlo, despite her numerous disappointments.

Records supplied to me by Brian Kornbrath revealed that, starting at age four Arlo began to have grand mal seizures. The seizures continued until he was eleven, although Dreama felt that her son had continued to experience petit mal seizures throughout high school, and occasionally had them at present. She described a recent episode that happened while he was working as a deejay, a hobby he engaged in about twice a year, for twenty dollars each time. A person at the party called her to say that Arlo had become non-responsive and was semi-conscious. Perhaps the party's strobe light had triggered the episode, Dreama said. Fortunately, he came around later, at home. Dreama also described a dangerous incident in which Arlo had neglected to take his anti-seizure medication, the highly toxic drug Tegretol, for at least three days. Arlo attempted to catch up by taking several days' doses at once. Such an overdose of Tegretol can be fatal. Luckily, Arlo, after a brief stay in the hospital, survived.

Both Arlo and his mother said that his school performance had been poor. In elementary school he received mostly grades of C, or lower. In the third grade he was diagnosed as learning disabled. In middle school he was placed in special education classes where he earned what Dreama termed "modified" grades of B and C. After high school, he attended Carver Vocational School and received a certificate in electronics. Then he began a checkered series of jobs at four or five electronics businesses, as well as jobs at restaurants such as Shoney's, Red Lobster, a pizza shop and the McDonald's job. Arlo admitted he lost most of those jobs because of his inability to conduct himself in "socially appropriate ways." Aside from the McDonald's episode, he once was dismissed after breathlessly rushing into his workplace and telling the manager that the man's car had been smashed in the parking lot. When the manager discovered there had been no accident, Arlo was fired.

Arlo first was referred for a psychological evaluation by psychologist Ronald Pearse when Arlo was ten, in 1983. He was examined again at age eleven, by school psychologist Kathleen Klaus Strosser, and underwent three examinations at age twelve, by psychologist Joseph Shaver, child psychiatrist John Kelly and by psychologist Eugene Quarrick, who was one of my supervisors when I was an intern at the West Virginia University School of Medicine's Department of Behavioral Medicine and Psychiatry. As I read the conclusions of one report after another, it occurred to me that those professionals had been stumped. Each, in turn, had accomplished a thorough examination. Yet, there was no consensus among them regarding either a proper diagnosis or even how best to describe Steven

Arlo Cook.

The numerous childhood evaluations were filled with findings such as "absence of social and emtional reciprocity and empathy, and inability to read social cues...he was very friendly and outgoing...auditory discrimination difficulties...learning disability...a history of seizures...problems stemming from the parents' separation and divorce...verbal sequencing deficits...arrested development...likely attention deficit disorder...daydreaming and withdrawn behavior..." The evaluations from Arlo's years in elementary school pointed in several directions. They could be summarized to say that every examiner knew something was wrong with Arlo, but not precisely what.

As Arlo got older and went to high school, the evaluations continued. Kanawha County school psychologist Harold McMillan evaluated Arlo when he was seventeen, after Arlo's over-the-top pranks had caught everyone's attention. Psychologist Stephen O'Keefe examined a nineteen-year-old Arlo at the request of the Social Security Determination Section. In his extensive report, O'Keefe noted that Arlo was capable of doing most daily functions. But O'Keefe also found that Arlo "...sometimes engages in dangerous activities, but does not intend to hurt himself. He had several incidents of magical thinking. He believes he has precognition and telekinesis." Dr. O'Keefe, who later became my colleague at Marshall University, concluded that Arlo could be successfully rehabilitated, although he would need supportive employment.

At age twenty, Arlo saw psychologist William Phelps, whom I have known for forty years. Phelps administered the Luria Nebraska neuropsychological test battery. Arlo scored in the brain dysfunction range on two of the test battery's five general indicators. "This profile indicates a chance of brain dysfunction..." Phelps wrote in his report.

It was around that time that Arlo shot himself in the chest with a pellet gun or a .22 caliber hand gun. It remains unclear whether this was a suicide attempt, a suicidal gesture or a fluke accident. Dreama insisted that he should go to the hospital, although Arlo was reluctant to be hospitalized. He told hospital staff that his mother was overly concerned, that she "just lost it." A staff member wrote that Arlo believed his "protector ghost, called the shadow, cocked the bullet," and kept him from coming to any harm. Dreama told hospital staff about her son's unusual behaviors, including his squandering of money on odd purchases, such as a very expensive sword, when he didn't have enough cash to buy necessities. As well, evidently unaware of how his words would come across, Arlo also told staff members that he had plenty of friends, including several who were children in grade school. He was diagnosed as suffering from "brief reactive psychosis" and soon was discharged.

It was around this time that U.S. Administrative law Judge Harry C. Taylor II found Arlo to be disabled due to "organic and personality disorders..." Judge Taylor strongly recommended that a payee be appointed for Arlo, and perhaps the payee should be a mental health center, to help Arlo manage his benefits. Ultimately, his mother was made payee.

Arlo's file was one of the more extensive I have ever reviewed. And his mental health history was unique in another way: Despite all the evaluations, there was a noticeable absence of consistency in the opinions of those who had examined him.

* * * * * * * * *

It is routine that I administer one or more psychological tests, and Arlo's case was no exception, although his results were exceptional. I gave him the most widely used test of intellectual functioning, the Wechsler Adult Intelligence Scale (3rd edition). The test involves assessment of about a dozen different tasks, from vocabulary and general reasoning ("How are an apple and a banana alike?") to more performance-related activities such as putting together puzzle pieces to make an object and using colored blocks to match a design shown by the examiner. The subtests result in three IQ scores, full scale, verbal and performance. (Since then, the verbal and performance scores have been broken down further, to yield four separate scores.) For each of the three scores, the population's mean is one hundred, and the standard deviation is fifteen. This means that two-thirds of the population score between eighty-five and one hundred fifteen. Extending outward, to two standard deviations on either side of the mean, about ninety-five percent of the population obtain IQ scores between seventy and one hundred thirty. Scores below seventy are within the intellectual disability range (then called the mental retardation range). Conversely, scores above one hundred thirty place the individual in the brightest two or three percent of the population.

It is statistically unusual that an individual's verbal and performance IQ scores differ by more than fifteen points. Arlo's differed by forty-four. His verbal score was seventy-five, while his performance score was one hundred nineteen. In my report, I wrote, "The verbal score puts him in the lowest five percent of the general population. This accounts, in part, for his problems perceiving dangerousness, threat, social appropriateness, and the like." I added that, conversely, his performance IQ score, "...is in the high average range, in the highest ten percent of the population....In my memory, I can recall only, perhaps, one or two other cases in which a discrepancy was that great." But it was nothing new for Arlo. A review of his records showed that when Arlo was initially tested at age ten, the verbal performance IQ discrepancy was twenty points. At age twelve it was thirty-three points. And now it had widened to forty-four.

I continued my report: "The practical significance of such a discrepancy is unclear. However, one interpretation does present itself: That Arlo's verbal learning and functioning, although adequate perhaps in some respects, place him at a substantial disadvantage when dealing with people verbally. This would also include the nonverbal cues which, as substitutes for words, are indications of people's feelings and thoughts."

Besides the Wechsler test, I gave Arlo the Rey's Sixteen Items Test, to assess whether he was malingering. He scored a perfect sixteen. He was not faking a disorder. Last, I wondered about Arlo's reading ability. With a history that included diagnoses of learning disability and placement in special education classes, I wondered whether he could have read and understood the confession he had signed. Thus, I administered the passage comprehension section of the Woodcock-Johnson Achievement Test (second edition). Arlo was reading and understanding at a twelfth grade level, which was but one more curiosity given that his verbal IQ score was far below average. But perhaps that finding should not have surprised me, since nothing about Arlo could be easily predicted. As with so many things about him, the swirl of characteristics presented an enigma. I was beginning to feel a bit of Dreama Cook's pain. Surely, she brought Arlo into the world assuming he would be a typically developing child who would become a typically developed adult. The outcome was wildly outside her expectations.

* * * * * * * * *

I diagnosed Asperger's disorder, a condition that then was not well known to professionals, much less to the public: At the time I made the diagnosis, the disorder was listed in the Diagnostic and Statistical Manual (4th edition), along with specific behaviors that would establish the presence of the disorder. Even so, there was debate among professionals as to what, exactly, this disorder was. It was generally seen as a specific disorder, somewhat akin to autism, but on a plane of its own, unique and different from autism. Today, the debate about the nature of Asperger's disorder continues among the professionals. However, the most recent edition of the diagnostic nomenclature, the DSM-5, published by the American Psychiatric Association, has dismissed the notion that Asperger's is an entity separate from autism. Instead, the DSM-5 describes a broad category called "autism spectrum disorder." Individuals such as Arlo, who in 1999 were diagnosed with Asperger's disorder, now are said to be "on the (autism) spectrum." Thus, the clusters of behaviors that historically gave rise to diagnoses of either Asperger's or autism, now are seen as fitting within one large family of behaviors, a spectrum of problems in functioning that differ mainly in degree, rather than in their essential natures.

Beyond my diagnosis of Asperger's disorder, I summarized the basis for my conclusions, employing the jargon and terminology of the DSM-IV:

The diagnosis of Asperger's Disorder is based on the qualitative impairment suffered by Arlo with regard to social interaction and as manifested by his failure to develop typical peer relationships, his lack of interest in others, his absence of social and emotional reciprocity and empathy, and his inability to read the social cues contained in various situations and the nonverbal actions of individuals. It is also based on his stereotyped and narrow patterns and interests (action shows on TV and computer activities). Finally, it is based on the fact that this disturbance in functioning causes enormous problems for him in social, occupational, and legal areas of life's functioning. As is typical with Asperger's, there is no noticeable significant delay in some kinds of cognitive development or age-appropriate self-help skills or adaptive behavior. And, also as is typical with Asperger's Disorder, there is no known clinically significant general delay in the development of language.

I contacted Arlo's attorney and told him I had the answers to the questions he had posed. Indeed, Arlo suffered now from the same disabilities as previously were diagnosed, and they would have affected the voluntariness of the confession he made. I concluded my written report to Mr. Kornbrath this way, "Asperger's disorder renders Arlo much more susceptible than a typical person to coercion, suggestion and intimidation and, thus, certainly affected the voluntariness of his March 29, 1999, statement to authorities." Aside from that written conclusion, personally I told Brian Kornbrath that I suspected the federal investigators easily had perceived Arlo as psychologically weak and they may have concluded that, given time, they could browbeat and intimidate him into saying what they wanted to hear, if only so that the yelling would stop and he could go home. Mr. Kornbrath did not disagree.

On February 18, 2000, a suppression hearing was held before Federal District Judge John T. Copenhaver, in Charleston. Brian Kornbrath hoped the judge would bar Arlo's confession from being used as evidence against him. I provided extensive testimony under direct examination by Mr. Kornbrath and cross-examination by Assistant U.S. Attorney Karen L. Bleattler. Although the judge was not a mental health professional and had never examined Arlo, he ruled that Arlo did not suffer from Asperger's Disorder and that his confession was, "...knowing, intelligent and voluntary." Judge Copenhaver's decision was preposterous.

The Judge's decision to allow Arlo's confession into evidence at his trial was based, in large part, on a report co-authored by psychologist Rosemary Smith and her brother, psychiatrist Ralph Smith, who practice in Charleston. They had examined Arlo on January 10, 2000, at the request of the federal prosecutor. I respect their work, although prior to my testimony at the suppression hearing, I had read the Smiths' report and found myself in disagreement. Drs. Smith and Smith were aware of my diagnosis of Asperger's disorder. And, given that I had quoted directly from the DSM-IV to show how Arlo fit the diagnostic criteria for that disorder, they referenced the same criteria but concluded just the opposite, that Arlo "does not have Asperger's disorder." Although they had read the same documentation of Arlo's history of examinations as I had read, and though they devoted five pages of their report to an extensive review of that mental health history, they concluded, in part, "As for the criminal responsibility issue, I (sic) found no evidence of a severe mental disease or defect." In my view, they were wrong on both counts. Even so, I didn't begrudge them for disagreeing with my opinion. Arlo's case provides evidence enough that opinions may well differ, even when professionals have done their best to diagnosis a disorder. If it was easy, those of us in the field of mental health never would disagree. The Smiths had their opinion and I had mine. At Arlo's trial the jury would have the last say.

Although the judge had decided that Arlo's coerced admission of guilt could be admitted as evidence at his trial, Brian Kornbrath was not barred from re-litigating the voluntariness of Arlo's confession in front of the jury. The trial began on February 22, 2000, in the Federal Courthouse in Charleston. The government put on its case on the first day. On day two, Brian Kornbrath called his witnesses. I was his last. My testimony to the jury paralleled my testimony at the suppression hearing. I reviewed Arlo's extensive history, my methods, and conclusions. I described in detail how Arlo fit the picture of Asperger's disorder. I told the jury that such a person would easily be intimidated into falsely confessing, if only to put an end to the misery of an interrogation that was characterized by a bombardment of intensely shouted, accusatory statements and questions. I added something else. Given Arlo's verbal IQ score of seventy-five, he functioned intellectually at roughly the level of a twelve-year-old. I wanted to add that this would be true of his functioning in most matters, including during a hostile interrogation. However, the judge sustained the prosecution's objection to my saying that.

As I was being cross-examined, I watched Arlo as he sat at the defense table with Brian Kornbrath on his left and the lawyer's investigator on his right. In his characteristic fashion, Arlo appeared unconcerned about the proceedings. He seemed possessed of the same inability to read people and situations that had haunted him all his life. I noticed his mother. Dreama Cook's face reflected the gravity of her son's circumstances. As usual, she was doing the worrying for both of them.

The prosecutor concluded my cross-examination. After a few more questions on re-direct and re-cross, I left the courtroom. Each side then presented its closing arguments and the jury deliberated, but only briefly. Despite the efforts of both the Secret Service investigators and the federal prosecutor to portray him as the kingpin of a counterfeiting ring, the jury found Steven Arlo Cook not guilty, and he went home.

* * * * * * * * *

Note: Given Arlo's difficulty in reading situations and nonverbal communication, it was ironic that a non-verbal matter may have had an unexpected impact on the jury, although I never will know that for certain. The possible factor was this: At the height of six feet, four inches each, both Brian Kornbrath and his investigator towered over the five-foot, four-inch Arlo. Every time the three stood up to acknowledge the entrance or exit of the jurors, Arlo looked like a sixth grader, compared to the two very tall men. And though he was twenty-six, Arlo had a youthful face. Were jurors influenced, even if only subconsciously, by the size discrepancy? It was something I considered, particularly in light of my analysis for the jurors that Arlo's verbal intellectual functioning was akin to that of a twelve-year-old. Like so much about Arlo himself, that is a question that will never be answered.

As I wrote this chapter, one additional thought occurred to me. For those who wish to better understand Asperger's syndrome (or, to use contemporary terminology, the Asperger's place on the "autism spectrum" continuum) consider the popular sitcom, Big Bang Theory. *The role of Sheldon Cooper, expertly played by actor Jim Parsons, presents a compelling version of the disorder, even if somewhat overblown.*

Nine

Wrongly Convicted

JIM RICHARDSON STOOD in the yard outside his home in the Charleston suburb of Cross Lanes, West Virginia. Calm turned to panic when he noticed smoke coming from the home of neighbor Kelli Gilfilin. Aware that Gilfilin was the single mother of a three-year-old little girl, Richardson, thirty-two, rushed into the flaming house. Scarcely able to breathe amid the thick, dark smoke, Richardson searched for any sign of either Gilfilin or her daughter. Gasping for air, he located the little girl and brought her to safety. By then, the house was fully ablaze. The roils of smoke meant that re-entry in search of the child's mother was no longer possible.

Media reports of the May 18, 1989, tragedy quickly hailed Jim Richardson as a hero. However, within days the case took a surprising turn. It was discovered that neither Jim Richardson nor anyone else could have rescued Kelli Gilfilin. An autopsy revealed that she had been raped and beaten to death, before the fire was set. Another twist in the story soon took place. When police looked into Richardson's background they discovered he had engaged in some petty crime, years before. As a result, Richardson quickly became the police's prime suspect in the case of murder and arson.

As Richardson later would tell me, when he was twenty-two he and a buddy made a stupid mistake after drinking too much. They foolishly convinced themselves that an elderly neighbor had hoarded huge wealth in her modest home. They broke into the home and stole several guns and jewelry, but the house contained none of the riches they had drunkenly imagined. Fortunately, no one was injured. The two were caught and found themselves on the receiving end of well-deserved, though brief, sentences. Jim had put the incident behind him and had endured only one other scrape with the law, which occurred several years later. Police showed up at his door to accuse him of injuring a child whose mother he had dated. Jim adamantly denied harming the child. He insisted he wasn't present when the child was injured and had no idea how it happened. He offered to take a lie detector test to prove his innocence. Charges against him were dropped. Later the mother evidently was found to have been neglecting the child and lost custody to the child's grandmother. Otherwise, Jim Richardson's life had been unremarkable. He was a high school dropout who had done various types of construction work. He married in 1979, had a son in 1981, and was divorced in 1987.

With no other major suspects in Kelli Gilfilin's death, prosecutors pressed the case against Jim Richardson. He went to trial two months later and on July 27, 1989, was convicted of murder. There had been no eyewitnesses, no fingerprints, nor any other evidence of the terrible crime, except for a single stunning finding. State Police serologist Fred Zain testified that semen taken from the dead woman could be found in only one percent of the population and Jim Richardson was in that one percent. It was all the jury needed to hear. Jim Richardson, still proclaiming his innocence, was sent to prison for the rest of his life, with no chance of parole.

There was, however, a glaring problem with Fred Zain's testimony — it was false. As re-analysis of the serology samples later revealed, Zain should have testified that no one, much less ninety-nine percent of all men, was eliminated by his serology testing. In other words, Zain's laboratory findings were useless as evidence, whether as evidence against Jim Richardson, or any other potential suspect.

* * * * * * * *

Fred Zain had become a West Virginia State Police chemist

in 1977, when he was twenty-six. But he got the job, in part, by falsifying his credentials. He had graduated from West Virginia State College (now University) with a major in biology, and he claimed to have minored in chemistry, although he had not. He had taken several chemistry courses, but not enough to have minored. Additionally, he had either failed, or barely passed, the chemistry courses in which he had enrolled.

That Zain embellished his academic credentials may have gone unnoticed as a relatively insignificant line on an insignificant resume of a police laboratory worker who otherwise did his job well enough. But enhancement of his college record turned out to be the tip of the falsification iceberg. A dark web of lies was about to be revealed.

In 1985, four years prior to Kelli Gilfilin's murder, two of Zain's lab staff members had become concerned about irregularities in his work. Lynn Inman Moreland and Sabrina Gayle Midkiff wrote to Larry L. Herold, Director of the State Police Criminal Identification Bureau and to Kenneth W. Blake, who replaced Herold that year. They wrote that they had seen Zain record results from enzyme test plates that, to them, appeared to be blank. If Moreland and Midkiff were correct, Zain had been going to court and describing "results" of tests that he had not performed. Worse, it was likely that Zain's testimony had sent innocent individuals to prison. Midkiff said later that she had seen Zain do this at least a hundred times and that Zain's reports almost always pointed the finger of guilt at the accused individual. Astonishingly, the lab workers' warnings went unheeded. Later, Herold and Blake said they had no copy of such a letter and that they recalled only that Zain and his staff tended to bicker about various matters within the lab.

There was another reason that Zain's findings should have come under scrutiny by his superiors. Earlier in 1985, prior to Moreland's and Midkiff's warning letter, FBI lab director James Greer informed the West Virginia State Police that Zain had failed its basic courses in serology and testing of bloodstains. There is little evidence that any corrective action was taken.

If warnings from Zain's laboratory staff and the FBI official had failed to bring sufficient scrutiny of Fred Zain, another factor should have set off alarms that something was badly amiss. In the the late 1980s, Zain moved to San Antonio, Texas, where he was hired as chief of physical evidence at the Bexar County medical examiner's office. But because Zain's testimony was central to ongoing cases back in West Virginia, it was not a surprise that he often returned to testify. But alarms should have sounded when prosecutors began sending samples from new cases to Zain, even though the samples already had been tested in West Virginia's police lab and found to be inconclusive. Zain would re-test the West Virginia samples in Texas. Many times, Zain's results came back as positive. He then would be brought back to his home state, and paid five hundred dollars each time where his testimony aided prosecutors' efforts to gain convictions.

Although authorities had ignored, or covered up, the internal suspicions about Fred Zain, his house of cards began to crumble publicly in the mid-1980s when a Huntington, West Virginia, man named Glen Dale Woodall was accused of several crimes. Among Woodall's alleged crimes were two rapes that began with abductions at the Huntington Mall. Although Woodall maintained that he was innocent, Zain's 1987 trial testimony was central to the conviction. Woodall was sentenced to more than three hundred years in prison.

This was the dawn of the DNA era. Although Woodall's attorneys' request for DNA testing had been denied prior to his trial, a year later Cabell County Circuit Judge Dan O'Hanlon made history by becoming the first judge to allow DNA test results as evidence in a state case. Woodall's initial DNA results, which were conducted by an independent laboratory, proved inconclusive. But as the science advanced and more refined DNA test methods became available, samples from Woodall's case were retested. Finally, in 1992, the newer tests proved that Glen Dale Woodall was not the Huntington Mall rapist. He was released that year, after five years in prison. Eventually, another man was found to have committed the crimes.

Because Woodall could not have committed the rapes, his lawyers were suspicious of Zain's serology testing that had been crucial in sending their client to prison. Also, Zain had testified that a hair found at one of the crime scenes had come from Woodall's beard. Now it was clear Zain's testimony about the hair could not have been accurate, because Woodall had not been at the crime scene. Thus, Woodall's attorneys had the serology and hair samples retested by outside laboratories. The new results showed that Zain had used improper blood-typing procedures. Woodall's attorneys uncovered another surprising fact. A close reading of the records showed that Fred Zain initially had concluded that the hair could not be identified, but then testified it was from Woodall's beard.

The Woodall case set off alarms that could not be ignored. As Jim Richardson followed events from his prison cell at the state's maximum security lock-up in Moundsville, back in Charleston Kanawha County prosecuting attorney Bill Forbes, who had relied on Zain's testimony numerous times, decided it was necessary to begin an investigation of his frequent expert witness. Forbes asked the West Virginia Supreme Court of Appeals to intervene. The state's high court formed a blue ribbon commission of lawyers and scientists whom the court charged with the investigation of Zain and the activities of the West Virginia State Police serology lab. Retired Putnam County Circuit Judge James O. Holliday was appointed to oversee the commission's investigation. In November 1993, the special panel concluded its work and forwarded its findings to Holliday, who rendered a final report to the state's Supreme Court.

The report was a bombshell. The investigators had uncovered an astonishing level of misconduct and fraud, and much of it could be traced to Fred Zain. The report detailed how Zain repeatedly had falsified test results and given false testimony about the serology lab's findings. He had written reports on untested materials as if the testing had been done, as Moreland and Midkiff had alleged eight years earlier. He had reported negative results as if they were positive. He had testified that inconclusive results were conclusive. In the summary of investigators' findings, Holliday wrote that Zain had reported results that were not scientifically possible. As many as one hundred and thirty-four individuals may have been wrongly convicted, the report said. Holliday concluded, in part, "…any testimony or documentary evidence offered by Zain at any time should be deemed invalid, unreliable and inadmissible." On November 12, 1993, the West Virginia Supreme Court accepted the Holliday commission's findings. The high court deemed Zain's actions "egregious violations of the right of a defendant to a fair trial." What Zain had done amounted to nothing other than a "corruption of our legal system," the justices wrote.

* * * * * * * * *

Meanwhile, in Texas the few remaining strands of Fred Zain's credibility rapidly unraveled. An investigation there found that he had engaged in improper conduct in nearly two hundred Texas cases. With his sixteen-year career in police work over, the disgraced serologist left Texas and began working in Florida for that state's Department of Health. Texas authorities attempted to convict Zain on perjury charges, but the statute of limitations had expired and the charges against him were dropped.

Back in West Virginia, Zain was charged with perjury in 1995. He went to trial claiming that he was a victim of politics, and was acquitted. However, West Virginia officials then charged Zain with four counts of obtaining money under false pretenses because of the payments he had taken for his return trips in which he provided false testimony. Because there had been extensive pre-trial publicity in Charleston, Zain's second trial was moved to Beckley, West Virginia, where it began on September 4, 2001. By then, dozens of cases on which Zain had testified had been re-opened. Other inmates, such as Charleston rape suspect William O'Dell Harris, and St. Albans rape and kidnapping suspect Gerald Wayne Davis had been exonerated by DNA evidence. Highly regarded, longtime chief Kanawha County public defender George Castelle, in an interview with *The New York Times*, termed Zain's actions "a blueprint on how to convict an innocent person." Despite the efforts of special prosecutor Jim Lees, the second jury was deadlocked and a mistrial was declared. A re-trial was set for July, 2003, but it never took place. Zain, who already was gravely ill with liver cancer, passed away in December 2002. He was fifty-one.

* * * * * * * * *

By the time that Glen Dale Woodall was released from prison in 1993, Jim Richardson had served four years for the rape and murder of Kelli Gilfilin in Cross Lanes. But with the floodgates of wrongful convictions burst open, Jim Richardson's conviction was overturned. Zain's testimony that the serology sample could have originated only within one percent of the male population (and that Jim Richardson was in that one percent) had imploded. Equally unfortunate, it was discovered that police had not turned over a blood-covered flashlight found at the scene of Gilfilin's death. DNA testing showed the blood had not come from either Kelli Gilfilin or Jim Richardson. There was only one possible conclusion — another person had been there and had committed the awful crime. With overwhelming evidence that Jim Richardson was not guilty, he was released on home confinement in 1996. In July 1999, all charges against him were dropped. After seven and a half years of incarceration, plus an additional three years in which the cloud of suspicion hung over his head, Jim Richardson, forty, was a free man.

* * * * * * * * *

Jim Richardson, Glen Dale Woodall, William O'Dell Harris, Gerald Wayne Davis and several other wrongly convicted individuals, decided to sue the state of West Virginia because of the years of imprisonment they had endured wrongly. The men correctly claimed that, if authorities had paid heed to the warning signs about Fred Zain, they never would have been convicted. Charleston attorney Arden J. Curry, II contacted me in late December, 2000, with a request that I examine Jim Richardson. Richardson was suing the state of West Virginia, Kanawha County, the law firm of Steptoe and Johnson which represented the State Police, along with the firm's individual partners and one of its attorney s, Steve McGowan, because the prestigious law firm had represented the state police. Curry had learned that McGowan evidently was aware of Zain's possible wrongdoing early on, because McGowan had been alerted to the complaints raised by lab workers Moreland and Midkiff in 1985, and no evident corrective action had been taken, as innocent individuals languished in prison.

Arden Curry asked that I examine Jim Richardson to determine the extent of the stress he had undergone relative to his wrongful conviction. It doesn't take a forensic psychologist to understand that a wrongful conviction and prison life are stressful. But Curry needed an expert witness to examine his client and confirm the extent of it.

I examined Richardson in my office at Marshall University on February 1, 2001. He was thoughtful and forthcoming during the examination. Surprisingly, he wasn't depressed, nor was he overly anxious. In fact, his mental status was quite good, given everything he had endured. He described himself as "happier than ever," as he talked about his relationship with his wife and children. The couple met shortly after he was released to home confinement and now had a thirty-month-old toddler. His wife had a son, age thirteen, by a previous marriage. They, and Richardson, were getting along well, he said, with one exception. He continued to be plagued with dreams about prison life.

I learned he had earned his G. E. D. in prison and since his release he had worked installing and servicing communications equipment. Unfortunately, it had been nearly impossible to maintain steady work because of the time involved to pursue the litigation. His lawsuit involved numerous visits with doctors, meetings with attorneys and depositions. He had decided that, until conclusion of lawsuit, he could not continue working. Thus, he had spent the past seven months fixing up a home that he and his wife had purchased.

Richardson described a single positive outcome of his prison experience: It provided time to think about his life, his mistakes, the things he valued and how to live his life. He had clarified his goals, which involved meeting a good woman, having a family and getting on with life, which he was doing. He was surprisingly lacking in bitterness. My testing confirmed the impressions I had formed during the interview. His Beck Depression and Anxiety Inventories revealed little of either of the two common difficulties.

Interestingly, Richardson felt that conditions were better

during his six years at the state's old northern panhandle prison at Moundsville than at the new facility in Mt. Olive, near Montgomery, West Virginia, where he spent the final eighteen months of incarceration. At Moundsville there were shop activities, jobs and crafts, all of which kept the inmates busy and, thus, more at ease. When inmates were doing something useful, everyone was more relaxed, he said. Moreover, he felt Mt. Olive was "harder time" because the staff was less predictable and more "hard core" in their approach to the inmates. Jim was convinced the differences were due to an administration at Mt. Olive that kept life in constant flux, so that inmates often did not know what to expect.

For example, at Mt. Olive the inmates initially were not allowed to have new computers, then they were permitted to have them, he said. Later, only those inmates who initially had computers were allowed to keep them, while other inmates had to relinquish their computers. Other policy changes suggested that the administration at Mt. Olive was unsure of itself, he added. For example, at first, inmates could wear jeans, then they could not. And regulations regarding various creature comforts were constantly changing at Mt. Olive. For example, battery-powered television remotes were not allowed, then there was an about face and the "clickers" were permitted. The net effect of such changes was to keep inmates unsettled, which added to fear of assaults and the like, Richardson said. But, to be clear, neither place was good. He summarized his prison experiences at Moundsville and Mt. Olive saying, "Take the worst thing that has ever happened and make it last eight years." He added that, for him, it was made worse because he was innocent. I didn't doubt it.

In both prisons, there existed a constant low-grade fear for one's physical safety, he told me. Though many inmates were reasonable, some were "nuts," and the latter group included many who were quite unpredictable. Some prisoners could be friendly one minute, then try to kill you the next, Jim said. As a safety precaution, he developed the habit of sitting or standing with his back to a wall, as did many inmates. Perhaps ironically, the most relaxed time was being locked in his cell, he said. There were constant fights and the way to survive was to keep one's mouth shut, to always be vigilant and to know whom to associate with, and whom to avoid, even though those variables were not always under his control. He was aware of one murder while he was at Moundsville, and others throughout the prison system, he said.

Fear for one's life was not the only source of stress. He described the absence of privacy, and the absence of dignity that went with it. Guards and inmates were always looking into the open front of his cell. The constant noise interfered with sleep. There was never a quiet time because people always were laughing, shouting and screaming. Televisions and stereos blared, doors were slammed. Interestingly, researchers have discovered that extreme sleep deprivation can lead to psychosis. Fortunately, I uncovered nothing to suggest that Jim Richardson was, or had been, psychotic.

He described his feeling of low-grade "paranoia" due to the unpredictability of the other inmates. He constantly scanned the prison environment and the people and things in it. It was important to always take stock of who was where, and what was happening. His "radar" for potentially dangerous situations never was turned off, with the exception of when he was locked in his cell.

There was another, perhaps more difficult, source of nagging distress – the realization that, in his home community, he was seen as a murderer. Although his immediate family and a few close friends always remained supportive, he was burdened with the knowledge that he was stamped a criminal. And he was away from everyone whom he cared about. He told me that doing time in prison would have been easier if he had had no family, even though he loved them deeply. He explained that he appreciated his family's support, but he wished he hadn't missed them so much or worried about them. And he had plenty of time to think about what might have been. His son, by now nineteen, was seven years old when Richardson entered prison. Father and son had missed out on a lot.

I asked him how he had coped with the knowledge that he was an innocent man. He described the frustration, the helpless feelings and the confusion as extremely stressful, but added, "I had a goal — to get out. That kept me from going wacko." I concluded my interview with Jim Richardson feeling that now he was getting along pretty well, considering what he had been through.

* * * * * * * * *

Inhumane conditions at the Moundsville prison went back decades. In the 1970s, more than thirty inmates had petitioned for writs of *habeas corpus* on the basis that conditions at the prison violated the Eighth Amendment's ban on cruel and unusual punishment. In 1982, a legislative committee concluded that the prison suffered from lack of upkeep and neglect, and was difficult to operate and keep secure. Moreover, it was an impossible environment in which to even attempt the rehabilitation of an inmate, legislators concluded. As a result, in 1984 the state's Supreme Court appointed Donald Poffenberger to be Special Master/Monitor of the prison. Thus, Poffenberger became the eyes and ears of the court, as the prison undertook improvements that the court had ordered.

To provide attorney Arden Curry with a more complete report of the prison experience at Moundsville, I turned to a 1996 report by Mr. Poffenberger. He began his review saying, "In fulfilling the role of Special Master/Monitor, I have spent thousands of hours of on-site observation, reviewed and analyzed countless written documents and records and conducted hundreds of interviews with prisoners, prison personnel and central office administrators, including individuals holding the office of Commissioner of Corrections."

Most people understand that prison conditions often are anything but optimal. While prison is not supposed to be luxurious, the state is supposed to provide an environment that is safe and clean. Poffenberger's report was scathing. He found the physical plant at Moundsville to be "antiquated, dilapidated, dirty, unsanitary, malodorous and dangerous." He wrote that "the conditions of confinement, when considered in their totality, were indeed cruel and unusual." He criticized the space. A one-man cell was seven feet by five feet. One large area housed three hundred nineteen inmates. A court already had found that the space situation violated the Eighth Amendment.

Sanitation was awful, Poffenberger wrote. Plumbing was defective. Once, an inmate had found maggots in his food. An inspection located a dead rodent in the crawl space above the prisoner's dining table. Part of the infested carcass had dropped onto the prisoner's tray. When toilets were flushed, toilet water came up in an inmate's sink. A five-gallon pool of sludge composed of sewage and rotting food had accumulated in a break area. Poffenberger himself observed numerous rodents, some of which he described as evidently unafraid of people. There was inadequate ventilation and the odor of sewer gas reeked through many areas.

On some of the coldest days of winter, ice formed in the toilets in the lowest tier of cells, the tier on which showers were located. The cold caused inmates to be reluctant to take showers, which added to the unsanitary atmosphere. In summer, the heat could be unbearable. Standards called for temperatures between sixty-six and eighty degrees in summer, but on two occasions the heat registered thirty-two degrees above the outside temperature. Poffenberger found fungus in the showers, deficient electrical wiring and fire hazards. In fact, Poffenberger noted, a court earlier had found "the entire institution (was) ...a fire hazard and in total non-compliance with the existing state fire code." Food was poorly prepared and the "generally unsanitary conditions of the kitchen precluded me from ever eating a meal at the institution," the Special Master concluded.

Poffenberger also expressed concerns about inmates' physical safety. He described an incident the year prior to Richardson's incarceration when three prisoners were shot during an attempted takeover of the prison. During the 1988 melee, there were numerous stabbings, severe beatings and several prisoners were set on fire by other inmates, while locked in their cells. Two years prior to that, a prisoner revolt occurred in which seventeen correctional officers were held hostage for three days. That year alone, six prisoners were murdered. These incidents, and others, including a recent decade during which eleven prisoners were murdered, contributed to "a tangible fear" that sometimes permeated the entire prison, as well as to a decision that the prison had to be closed and replaced,

Poffenberger said. He concluded his exhaustive report saying, "During my tenure as Special Master/Monitor I observed first-hand the results of years of inadequate funding, mismanagement and apathy. Imprisonment in this facility meant daily exposure to health hazards and real concern for one's physical safety."

Somehow, Jim Richardson, Glen Dale Woodall, William O'Dell Harris, Gerald Wayne Davis and several others who had been wrongly convicted had managed to survive the inhuman conditions, even though they never should have found themselves in the prison at all. One more thing was clear. In contrast to the courtroom statements of Fred Zain, when Jim Richardson described the stress of living in prison, he wasn't making it up.

* * * * * * * * *

I concluded my examination of Jim Richardson and wrote my report to Mr. Curry. The following was among my conclusions:

James Richardson suffered extreme stress throughout his prison experience. This stress increased somewhat during the time he was at Mount Olive due to the unpredictable nature of his incarceration there. The stress was due to the factors described above including the feeling of helplessness, knowing that he had been wrongfully convicted, the constant noise, loss of dignity, awareness of his lowered reputation in the community, knowledge that he was missing his son's development along with other good things in life, the substandard living conditions described by Mr. Poffenberger, and the constant frustration and confusion that accompanied general life in prison.... It is my opinion, to a reasonable degree of psychological certainty, that Mr. Richardson has suffered severe emotional distress during his prison stay and that this distress was, at a minimum, as bad as, or slightly worse than) at Mt. Olive, as compared to Moundsville.

As I wrote this book, those words from my report to attorney Arden Curry seemed hollow, bones without flesh that were unable to convey what Jim Richardson had experienced in prison. Maybe no words ever could do that.

Arden Curry took Jim Richardson's lawsuits against the state and against Kanawha County to their conclusions. As I had suspected would happen, there was no trial against either entity. Fred Zain's actions had been so egregious that there was little point in the state or county wasting the taxpayers' money on trials, only to hear juries award the maximum that could be paid by the state's Board of Risk and Insurance Management. Thus, Jim Richardson's cases were settled out of court. He was awarded one million dollars from the state of West Virginia, because it was responsible for activities at the serology lab, and another million dollars by Kanawha County, where Kelli Gilfilin had been murdered and Jim Richardson had been prosecuted and convicted.

At age forty, Jim was still a relatively young man. But I wondered whether the constant stress of prison had taken an immeasurable toll on his mental and physical integrity, a toll that would shorten the life he now termed "contented." Although I would never know the answer to that question for a certainty, Jim Richardson died of a heart attack on January 8, 2011. He was fifty-four years old.

* * * * * * * * *

Note: There was a time, many years ago, when I believed in capital punishment. But as I got older, I better understood the human capacity for error, not to mention outright malfeasance. James Richardson likely would have been sentenced to death if West Virginia had been a capital punishment state. I am thankful it isn't. A life sentence leaves hope that an individual such as Richardson can be exonerated, an option not available to the dead. For the more mercenary minded, a life sentence is six times less expensive to the state than are the numerous rounds of appeals that tend to accompany a death sentence. Moreover, researchers have established that the death penalty is not a deterrent to crime. I doubt that anyone who was about to commit a horrible crime ever said to himself, "Maybe I'd better not do it, because if I should be caught and convicted, I might be executed."

Moreover, we know from the research on eyewitness testimony that memory of events is fluid rather than static and, as fallible humans, we may recall events, people and circumstances that never happened. It oc-

curred in the case of William O'Dell Harris, whom I have mentioned above, and who was another victim of Fred Zain's false testimony. At Harris' trial, the victim identified him as her attacker (and Zain testified that the recovered semen samples tied Harris to the rape). Later DNA tests proved that Harris was not the perpetrator.

There are individuals who support the death penalty, saying that it should be used only in cases where the evidence is certain. But the evidence is always certain — until it isn't. In my thinking, the only way to protect the innocent is to rid ourselves of the death penalty completely. A life sentence protects society as well as a death sentence. In 1824, the British scholar Thomas Starkie expanded on an earlier statement by William Blackstone saying, "It is better that ninety-nine offenders shall escape than that one innocent man be condemned." And where a life sentence replaces the death penalty, the perpetrator has not avoided severe punishment.

Note: Reading Special Master/Monitor Donald Poffengerger's report reminded me of a well-known experiment in psychology, Philip Zimbardo's 1971 prison simulation at Stanford University. In the study, Zimbardo received permission to remodel the Psychology Department's basement as a prison. He selected twenty-four volunteers, all university students, tested them to make sure they were mentally healthy, then split them randomly into two groups, guards and prisoners. The "prisoners" were arrested, fingerprinted, assigned to cells and told they would be paid fifteen dollars per day for the duration of the two-week study. The "guards" received the same pay and were instructed to keep the prisoners in line. Initially, the prisoners remained united against the guards. But after two days, several individuals on both sides began to exhibit signs of stress. The prisoners began to fight among themselves, and the guards helped them do so. The conditions rapidly deteriorated to the point of brutality. To prevent further harm, the experiment was halted after only six days. Zimbardo's experiment revealed something about prison stress, even though this was not an actual prison, and the students were able to drop out of the study at any time. Zimbardo's work revealed even more about the human capacity for inhuman behavior. Perhaps that brings us back to Fred Zain. Why had Fred done it? For a few hundred dollars? For prestige? Or was he telling himself that lying didn't matter, because if the accused hadn't done the crime, he probably was guilty of some-

hing else? Did he do it thinking that his role amounted to little more than helping prosecutors do the right thing? Although the questions are intriguing, the answers remain known only to God.

Ten

A Case of Child Sexual Abuse?

Note: The names of many individuals in this case were changed because the case involved children. The exceptions are the names of defense attorneys Jack Laishley and Neil Bouchillon, private investigator Greg Cook, Public Defender Services Director Robert Wilkinson, Judge Alfred Ferguson, Judge Paul Farrell and Victor Veith.

I BELIEVE THAT THE MAJORITY OF ALLEGATIONS of child sexual abuse are true. Unfortunately, some are false. Determining the difference can be as difficult as untying the Gordian knot. Researchers have discovered the disturbing fact that false allegations are surprisingly common, occurring in between five percent and thirty-five percent of all cases. For example, a Denver study found that twenty-four percent of cases were unfounded. In Michigan, researchers looked at the subset of cases that also involved divorce. They found thirty-three percent were unlikely to be true, based on Child Protective Services and court-appointed examiners' findings.

The most difficult cases involve children aged six and under. Young children are generally less credible than are adults because they are more easily led than adults, are more likely to confuse fantasy with reality (which is developmentally normal), and more likely to tell a biased grownup what they think the grownup wants to hear. Years ago, there was a mistaken belief among professionals that children, in their innocence, could not be wrong about a matter as serious as sexual abuse.

But the days of believing "If it's out of the mouths of babes, it must be true," are over. A tangle of issues come into play when an adult becomes suspicious that sexual abuse may have happened or when a child makes an outright allegation of sexual abuse: It is vital both that the child be protected, and that the accused not be wrongly deprived of his liberty based on an erroneous allegation. I have examined many children who may have been sexually abused, and consulted with attorneys on many other such cases where my role came down to reviewing the examinations of children by other professionals. Anyone who is convinced that the job of child sexual abuse assessment typically is straightforward should know this — the case that follows is not unusual.

* * * * * * * * *

On May 8, 2011, four-and-a-half-year-old Annie Sims was taken to the emergency room at St. Mary's Hospital in Huntington, West Virginia, by her great aunt, Rhonda Felix. Felix reported that, hours before, Annie had disclosed sexual abuse at the hands of thirty-year-old Johnny Nathan, who was the boyfriend of Annie's mother, Jen Banks. ER nurse Frances James talked to Annie. The preschooler told the nurse that Johnny had taken her and a playmate, Betty Frame, age seven, to the basement. Johnny had kissed her "ladybug," Annie Sims told Nurse James. Annie also told the nurse, "Him put his finger up in my butt crack and it hurt real bad." She added that Johnny Nathan had showed her his "wiener" and had asked her to touch it, "but I wouldn't." Nurse James wrote that Annie was "…pleasant, laughing, (and) appears close to (her) 'great aunt', who is holding (the) victim. Mother is present at times. She is teary (and) states child has never told her anything." The nurse had done her job, which was to screen for possible abuse and report any findings to the authorities.

The preschooler's disclosure seemed clear enough. However, a troubling fact had not been disclosed during the ER examination of Annie Sims. Well prior to the emergence of the sexual abuse concerns, Rhonda Felix, to whom Annie's initial disclosure had been made, had not disguised her intense dislike for both her niece Jen Banks, who was white, and Johnny Nathan, who was black.

Following the ER visit, Huntington Police Detective Frank Boyd investigated the complaints against Nathan. One of Boyd's first responsibilities was to conduct an interview with Annie. Boyd had been trained in an interviewing method called Finding Words. The method, which is fairly widely used with children who may have been sexually abused, was developed by three prosecutors and a social worker. To become a certified Finding Words forensic examiner of children requires one week of training.

Detective Boyd employed the Finding Words technique on each of the two occasions that he interviewed Annie. Additionally, the detective spoke to numerous other individuals as he followed a meandering trail of evidence. The others he talked to included Rhonda Felix; Annie's mother, Jen Banks; two of Annie's frequent playmates, Betty and Cynthia Frame, ages seven and twelve, respectively, and their mother, Lila Nathan, who had been married to John Nathan; a Mr. and Mrs. Diaz, parents of a young boy who was Annie's cousin; and the accused, Johnny Nathan.

On September 28, 2011, Detective Boyd presented the findings of his investigation to a grand jury in Huntington, West Virginia, with the result that John Nathan was indicted on charges that he had performed oral sex on Annie, and had digitally penetrated both her vagina and her anus. Nathan, who vehemently denied the charges, now faced the strong possibility that he would spend much of his life behind bars.

* * * * * * * *

I received a call from private investigator Greg Cook, who asked me to consult on the case. Cook was working with Nathan's attorney, Jack Laishley, and the two men had serious misgivings about the validity of Annie Sims' accusations. Later, attorney Neil Bouchillon joined with Laishley in defending Nathan. I had worked with Laishley before, on the case of seventeen-year-old Timothy Scott Skeens, who had fatally stabbed a Huntington man. That case is described in chapter five. I also had consulted with Bouchillon on an earlier case, when he had been with the Cabell-Wayne Public Defenders Service under the leadership of Robert Wilkinson.

Jack Laishley had obtained a voluminous file of documents as well as videos of Detective Boyd's interviews. First, I watched Boyd's interview with Annie. It had taken place the day following her ER visit. After chatting about innocuous matters in order to establish rapport with Annie, Boyd showed her a pair of anatomically detailed pictures, a boy and a girl, and began talking to her about "touches." She repeated her story of the previous day — Johnny had kissed her "ladybug." However, I found it curious that, by the end of the discussion with the detective, Annie's story diverged in three important ways from her report of the previous day. First, Annie pointed to the "wiener" on the boy's picture and indicated that Johnny Nathan's wiener had touched her "ladybug," an allegation she had not reported to the ER nurse. Next, she said that Nathan had touched her "boobies," which was a second disclosure that had not been reported just a day earlier. Third, Annie denied that Nathan had touched her anywhere else, making no mention of any anal digital penetration. I asked myself why Annie was adding new allegations and subtracting another.

Evidently, I was not the only one who noticed that Annie's report to the detective differed significantly from her account to the ER nurse. Discrepancies in her story must have been clear to Detective Boyd, because next he showed Annie a pair of anatomically detailed dolls and asked her to show him what had happened. Annie placed the girl doll's face on the crotch of the boy doll, a display that presented a fourth departure from her report to the ER nurse. At that point, and for reasons unknown, Detective Boyd prompted Annie to reverse the doll's positions. He went further, asking a leading question, "His wiener never touched your ladybug, did it?" She nodded, indicating "yes," and placed the male doll's penis in the vaginal area of the girl doll. This was a fifth way that her report to the detective differed from her report to Nurse James. I wondered why Detective Boyd was conducting the interview with prompts and leading questions, unless he was making an effort to rehabilitate her wandering descriptions of what had happened. The detective may have sensed that Annie's credibility was quickly falling apart. She had yet to tell the detective anything about digital penetration, as she had described to the nurse. Again leading the child, the detective asked, "Did he put his finger in you?" Annie responded that he had.

When the fifteen-minute video ended, I processed what I had just seen. It appeared the detective had attempted, and failed, to massage Annie's divergent reports into a consistent whole. While her report that Johnny had kissed her vagina was consistent across the two interviews, now she added that his penis had touched her vagina, and that he had touched her breasts. Moreover, Annie had failed to mention digital penetration, until the detective asked whether Nathan had "put his finger in you?" I found it surprising that she had described penetration to the ER nurse and characterized it as quite painful, but a day later made no mention of it to the detective, until he brought it up. Also, the detective's re-positioning of the dolls seemed more an effort to help Annie get her story straight than to find out what actually had occurred. The detective's actions did not fit with acceptable forensic interviewing techniques.

There was more. Detective Boyd had failed to directly test Annie's ability to separate fantasy from reality, which is important in dealing with young children. And, although he had asked whether she understood what "the truth is," he evidently had accepted her affirmative response at face value, rather than to ask that she explain the concepts or give some examples of each. Moreover, he had not directly evaluated the ease with which she could be led to report something that was untrue. I was left to ponder why the detective had not simply reported the fact that Annie could not keep her story straight from one day to the next and, barring more convincing evidence, conclude there was little reason to proceed with a case against Johnny Nathan. Had the detective possessed a mindset of, "Where there is smoke, there is fire"?

Two days later, Boyd interviewed Johnny Nathan, who had waived his rights and agreed to the meeting. Boyd described the little girl's accusations to Nathan and added that Annie "even used anatomically correct dolls." But the detective did not tell Nathan that Annie's story differed from one day to the next. Rather, Detective Boyd told Nathan that he had conducted close to a hundred such interviews and in this case, "The problem...is how graphic it was." Nathan was taken aback by the allegations. He told Boyd he had assumed they were meeting because someone in the family had reported him to Child Protective Services because he had whipped Annie. Earlier, someone in the family had threatened to report him for that. Throughout his meeting with the detective, Nathan insisted there had been no inappropriate touching.

* * * * * * * * *

Eight days later, on May 19, 2011, Detective Boyd interviewed Annie again. In the initial interview, Annie had claimed the abuse occurred in the basement. During the second interview, the detective again asked where it happened, leading Annie with a remark about the basement. Annie now answered that she didn't remember where it took place. When he asked, "Who did that?" she gave no answer. Leading her, he rephrased his question, "When your ladybug got touched, who did that?" She answered that no one did it. Annie claimed she didn't even remember telling him about it ten days earlier. In the style of, "Do you still beat your wife?" the detective asked, "Does he do it anymore?" She answered that he did not. Annie's aunt, Rhonda Felix, initially had said that she suspected a different perpetrator. But after watching both of the detective's interviews with Annie, I was surprised he hadn't asked questions about the possibility of a different perpetrator. Rather, Boyd appeared to be looking at the case with tunnel vision – something happened, and Johnny Nathan did it. The second interview concluded with Annie denying the allegations altogether, although she added something else to put yet another twist on the case. She said that her mother had told her she would get in trouble if she did not recant. It was no secret that Annie's mother, Jen Banks, was in disbelief about whether Johnny had molested Annie.

Had Johnny Nathan sexually abused Annie Sims? Perhaps he had, I thought. But could Annie be believed? I found it troubling that, from her interview with the ER nurse to the following day's talk with the detective, she had changed her description of the alleged abuse in ways that were not mere peripheral details, but were central to the allegations. And if her mother had indeed easily coerced her to deny the abuse, could someone else just as easily have prompted her to make an allegation in the first place? The likelihood of getting clear answers to those questions was slipping away.

* * * * * * * *

Between the dates of his interviews with Annie, Detective Boyd met with Betty and Cynthia Frame, ages seven and twelve respectively, who were playmates of Annie's. They were the daughters of Johnny Nathan's former wife, Lila Nathan, by her earlier marriage to another man. Although they were not biologically related to Annie, she thought of them as her sisters.

As I watched the detective's interview with Betty Frame, it was clear that, at age seven, Betty was more mature and cooperative than Annie, who was but four and one half. When the detective brought out pictures of the boy and girl and began to talk about "touches," Betty cut him off. "He's not touched me anywhere like (indicating her pelvic area), anywhere like down in there and he's not beated (sic) me." Betty described having heard about the allegations but said they weren't true. She denied that anyone had told her what to say.

Cynthia Frame was next. She, too, denied any inappropriate touches by Johnny Nathan. She doubted that Nathan had sexually touched Annie. When Nathan and Annie were in the basement, "We're always there," the twelve-year-old added. Boyd asked why Annie would say she had been touched. The twelve-year-old girl told the detective, in essence, that bad blood within the families probably had given rise to Annie's accusations. Cynthia Frame added that Annie would repeat anything that somebody told her to say.

Next, Detective Boyd talked to Lila Nathan, Betty and Cynthia Frames' mother and the former wife of Johnny Nathan. The interview was unremarkable, with a single, jaw-dropping exception. The topic of true and false allegations of child sexual abuse came up. The detective said, "Seventy percent of them (allegations)…are not legitimate." As his next several remarks made clear, the detective's remark was not a slip of the tongue. I could scarcely believe what I had heard. A detective, supposedly well-trained in forensic examination of children, had just told Lila Nathan that the vast majority of allegations of child sexual abuse were false. As a long-time professional in the field, I was bewildered. There is no research evidence to support such an outlandish claim by the detective. Had Detective Boyd gotten that from his week of training in the Finding Words method? From another source? Or was he purposely misleading Lila Nathan for some unstated reason? One thing was clear, if the detective genuinely believed what he had said, his training regarding matters of child sexual abuse had been woefully inadequate.

On the same day of his second interview with Annie, Detective Boyd interviewed her mother, Jen Banks. He peppered the interview with falsehoods. He told Banks that Annie, in her second interview, was "still telling the same story," when, in fact, Annie had recanted. He added that Annie's story could not have been rehearsed. That may have been his opinion, but which version of her story was he referring to? And they discussed whether Johnny Nathan might have taken and failed a polygraph test. The test is "one hundred percent accurate, unless you are insane," the detective said, which also is false. Moments later, the voice of an unknown female added a chilling perspective. From out of camera range a woman could be heard telling Jen Banks, "We're the ones that determine visitation…" Those words may have shaken Banks, but she remained calm and the interview soon was over.

I suspected the voice came from a member of the prosecution team. The person who said those words was delivering a not-so-veiled threat to Jen Banks: Implicate Johnny Nathan, or risk losing custody of Annie. The reader may draw his or her own conclusions regarding what the formless voice had implied, but one thing is undeniable: the speaker had put herself in a position in which I, or anyone else viewing the recordings, could interpret her words as such a threat.

Soon, both Annie and her sister were removed from Jen Banks custody. Moreover, the one-two punch of the detective and unknown woman, along with the detective's other interviews, led me to another conclusion. Perhaps the detective had lapsed out of the role of the unbiased forensic examiner and into the role of a member of the prosecution team. If so, had his training in the Finding Words method taught him that such a switch was acceptable?

* * * * * * * * *

I watched three additional videos as the detective interviewed additional witnesses. The first was with Mr. and Mrs. Robert Diaz, relatives whom Annie sometimes visited. They once had caught Annie and their same-aged son touching each other's genitals, while the children played in the bathtub. They talked to the children about the incident and nothing more had come of it, they said. However, the benign interview was interesting in another way. Of Annie's allegations, he told the couple, "At that age, they really don't lie. They may have little deviations." But discrepancies in Annie's accounts had not been "little deviations." They were major additions and subtractions.

We know that young children may come to believe they have been sexually abused, even though they have not, as I will discuss in the next chapter. As I have testified to many juries, this phenomenon is akin to a child's rush up the stairs from the cellar, in tears, convinced he has seen a monster. The child isn't lying, in the usual sense of the word. Rather, he or she is in the grip of an emotionally charged fantasy. This is a nuanced matter that is not given the attention it deserves by anyone who reduces the issue to simplistic terms, such as that the child either is lying, or telling the truth. Thus, it is possible both that Annie's allegations were wrong, and that she did not intend to lie.

Curiously, Boyd also told Mr. and Mrs. Diaz that Annie's mother, Jen Banks "blew up in here." Although I am not aware of any off-camera reactions by Banks, during her recorded interview she had been composed. I doubt that anyone seeing her interview would describe her actions as a blow up. The detective also told Mr. and Mrs. Diaz that he had the feeling that Betty and Cynthia Frame had been "coached." That may have been his feeling but there was nothing in the interview to support such a statement. And the detective told the couple that Annie "froze" during her second interview. But his term implied that Annie had refused to talk, when the truth was that she had recanted. I shut off the video player and asked myself a question. What had the detective hoped to accomplish with his misrepresentations to Mr. and Mrs. Diaz?

* * * * * * * * *

Twice, the detective interviewed Annie's great aunt, Rhonda Felix, to whom Annie had made the initial disclosure of abuse. In the interviews, Mrs. Felix made no attempt to hide her intense dislike of both Johnny Nathan and Jen Banks or the fact that her dislike was present well before Annie's allegations. She said that Jen mainly screamed at Annie and said of Johnny Nathan, "I know he drinks a lot. He drinks every day." She continued, "I don't like him. I've never liked him. I just didn't like his attitude…" And she added something else. Annie had told Felix that playmate Betty Frame also was in the basement when the abuse happened, and Nathan sexually abused Betty too.

As he had said to Mr. and Mrs. Diaz, now Detective Boyd told Rhonda Felix that Annie "froze up" in the second interview. Rhonda Felix told the detective she had heard that Nathan had passed a polygraph test, which the detective quickly disputed. I was struck by the detective's eagerness to correct that particular misunderstanding, as it stood in contrast to his numerous misrepresentations to various witnesses.

Then I watched the final interview. It was Johnny Nathan's. Nathan denied everything. In discussing the allegations against the man who sat before him, Detective Boyd said, "The problem...is how graphic it was." He could have added "and how inconsistent it was," but he didn't.

* * * * * * * * *

On September 28, 2011, Detective Boyd gave his testimony to the grand jury. He made no mention of Annie's recantation. Rather, he repeated the erroneous statement that she "froze." He made no mention of the inconsistencies in her reports. He failed to describe how the older girls, Betty and Cynthia Frame, doubted the abuse claim. Nor did he tell the grand jurors that Annie claimed to have seen Betty abused in the basement, which Betty then denied. Perhaps most surprising of all, the Detective testified that he could not recall whether he had used the anatomically detailed dolls with Annie, even though he had "corrected" her placement of them to fit with her testimony to the ER nurse.

The grand jury indicted Johnny on six counts related to child sexual abuse of Annie Sims.

* * * * * * * * *

Having reviewed the recorded interviews and read the documents supplied to me by attorney Jack Laishley, I expressed my deep concerns about the detective's investigation. The lawyer said he intended to mount a vigorous defense.

As Jack Laishley and I discussed the case, I expressed another concern about Detective Boyd. Specifically, it appeared the detective had found himself in conflicting roles. He was acting as both a forensic examiner of Annie Sims and as the person who then conducted the ongoing investigation of her case. It was a burden that Boyd should not have attempted. Rather, the detective would have maintained more credibility if he had acted as either a forensic examiner or an ongoing investigator, not both.

As I explained to Laishley, there was a parallel to the American Psychological Association's position that a forensic examiner should not also be an ongoing therapist for the same child, because the roles differ and may conflict. That is, an ongoing therapist often cannot help becoming an advocate for the child, while the forensic examiner simply must assess whether the abuse happened or did not happen. The APA's position is that once a forensic examination establishes the fact of abuse and determines that therapy would benefit the child, a referral is made to another professional, who then undertakes therapeutic treatment.

Although it is not an exact parallel to Detective Boyd's situation, he had conducted a forensic examination, then gave the appearance that he had become an advocate for the child as he conducted his investigation. Perhaps the detective's dual roles explained why he told Annie's mother that Annie was still "telling the same story," even though the child had recanted. Perhaps his conflicting roles explained his feeling that Annie's playmates had been coached and his statement that Annie had "frozen" (rather than that she had recanted). And perhaps the detective's role conflict explained why he did not reveal to potential witnesses that Annie's disclosures contained important inconsistencies, or that the older girls' statements were consistent with Nathan's claim that he was innocent, or that great aunt Rhonda Felix had possessed an intense dislike for Annie's mother and Johnny Nathan, well before Annie's disclosure. Perhaps the detective had indeed become an advocate, rather than a dispassionate forensic investigator. If so, it would have been an entirely human response to his work within the case. And it would have shown why good practice requires that the role of forensic examiner of a child stop when the interview ends and the recording has concluded.

I told Jack Laishley about my concerns regarding the inadequacies of the Finding Words training itself. Bluntly, I told Laishley that Finding Words seemed to be deeply flawed. I was well aware of the inadequacies in the Finding Words method, even before I began my consultation with Laishley.

Several times, I had reviewed forensic interviews in other cases in which a law enforcement officer or social worker had been trained in Finding Words. Thus, I was not entirely surprised at some of the inadequacies in the detective's interview methods.

First, Finding Words is prosecution driven. It was developed by three prosecutors and a social worker. Its lead author, Victor Veith, claims that the success of Finding Words is evidenced by increases in conviction rates, once the method comes into use in a given state court district. In my view, that is not an acceptable criterion by which to judge the usefulness of the method. Instead, as with any assessment technique, the success of Finding Words ought to be judged by whether the results are valid and reliable, rather than by whether the method helps one side against the other. What matters is learning what happened to the child, rather than whether prosecutors gain more convictions.

In his writings, Victor Veith has openly expressed his disdain for accused individuals who do nothing more than exercise their right to a defense. As well, Veith is openly hostile toward professionals who have devoted substantial portions of their careers to study of the best ways of interviewing children. In an article, Veith wrote that "…these experts often have a Ph.D… (but) they frequently do not understand even the most fundamental principles of forensic interviewing." Mr. Veith has offered no research support for such a rash, counter-intuitive statement. Nor has he attempted to reconcile the conflict inherent in his disgust for extensively trained professionals, with his belief that his method can train virtually anyone to be a forensic examiner in one short week.

Working on other cases, I had been surprised at another bit of Finding Words' publicity. Its website emphasizes that the method is "…taught in a course that includes intense hands-on training." However, in contrast to that claim, the training involves only two mock interviews, totaling less than an hour. At the end of the week's training, each attendee first interviews a child about non-abuse matters, then interviews an adult who role-plays an abused child. I know of no professional who would consider that to be "intense hands-on training" as the website says is provided to attendees. Rather, most professionals would term two such practice interviews as nothing more than a good beginning in learning how to talk to young children who may have been sexually abused.

I described my concerns about Detective Boyd's training in the Finding Words method to Jack Laishley. Mainly, I told the lawyer, without a broader, deeper base of knowledge of child development, learning processes, interview techniques, and the essentials of assessment including an understanding of how reliability and validity of the process may best be achieved, Finding Words was insufficient to bring an individual to an acceptable level of competence as a forensic examiner. I added that the method may be helpful for an individual who already has a background in those areas, but for one who has little or no such other training, Finding Words could backfire. Poorly done interviews, such as Detective Boyd's with Annie Sims, risked further clouding an already uncertain complaint about abuse.

In summarizing my findings, I said I harbored concerns that Laishley was dealing with a perfect storm of conditions that may well have fomented false allegations against his client, Johnny Nathan. That is, there was an initial disclosure to an individual who already possessed an intense dislike for the accused. The accuser was a very young child who might easily have been coached. And there were seriously flawed forensic examinations by a Detective who found himself in conflicting roles and whose grand jury testimony reflected that conflict. Jack Laishley got the message.

* * * * * * * * *

On June 6, 2011, roughly a month after her initial allegation, Annie Sims entered therapy with local therapist Lisa Bonner, whom I knew slightly from the several years that I had consulted with Family Services of the Kanawha Valley, where Bonner used to work full-time. Over the next three years, Annie underwent nearly four dozen therapy sessions with Bonner. Reading Bonner's treatment notes of those sessions, Annie Sims' progress might best be described as a roller coaster ride of disclosures, recantations, changing stories, unfounded accusations of drug use by a member of her extended family, new allegations against Johnny Nathan, changing feelings about whether she wished to testify or even remembered what Johnny had done as well as general misbehavior that concerned Bonner, Annie's foster parents and others. Representative excerpts of Lisa Bonner's therapy notes are revealing:

On June 29, 2011, Annie initially told Bonner that her dad touched her ladybug when he was wiping her bottom. Minutes later, Annie said that was a lie. Before the session ended, she told Bonner, "I keep forgetting." Later, during a November session, she told Bonner that her mother was in the basement with them when Nathan touched her, which was a major detail that Annie had never voiced up to that time.

Over the months that followed, Bonner led Annie through educational books about sexual abuse and engaged Annie in frequent therapeutic conversations about Johnny Nathan's alleged abuse. By the fifteenth session, on May 1, 2012, Annie's frequent misbehavior at her foster home had become a focus of treatment. During that session, Annie stripped the clothing off the child dolls and placed one on top of the other, as if kissing. "I told her it wasn't nice and to stop," Bonner wrote. As I read Bonner's notes, I was beginning to wonder whether the alleged sexual abuse, or frequent discussion of sexual matters, or both, were causing Annie to develop a hypersexualized slant on the world.

At the following session, Annie told Bonner that Nathan had done the touching five times, which was at odds with her initial account to Detective Boyd. Months later, following a treatment session on February 27, 2013, Bonner contacted Child Protective Services because, she wrote, "I believe that her (Annie's) little sister, Judith, is being sexually abused when she goes to see Johnny." If Bonner had a reason to suspect, it wasn't reflected in her notes.

Over the next months, Annie sometimes told Bonner she would like to go to court and testify against Nathan, and at other times she demurred. During her twenty-sixth session, on July 9, 2013, more than two years after the initial allegation, Annie dropped another bombshell. She told Bonner that her mother had forced her to touch Johnny's wiener and that her mom whipped her when she refused. "She whipped me for not touching him! My butt was so red!" Reading that treatment note, I asked myself why this new disclosure had come out now, so long after the initial allegation. Was it because she now was comfortable enough and felt safe enough to implicate her mother? Possibly, but that seemed unlikely, given that her initial disclosure about Johnny had been just as serious. The largely-discounted psychodynamic theory was that a child might recover traumatic memories that had been repressed to the unconscious part of her mind. However, research on the recovered memory phenomenon essentially had disproven this. Instead of grasping at preposterous theories to "explain" why a little girl couldn't keep her story straight, I concluded that, in the style of the Arabian Nights, Annie was making it up. And why would Annie do that? Because, in her thinking, such tales were what Bonner wanted to hear, as had great aunt Rhonda Felix and Detective Boyd. I reached another conclusion, as well. Therapy was not making Annie better.

On September 26, 2013, social therapist Bonner met with Jen Banks. Bonner expressed no doubts that the allegations against Johnny Nathan were true. The therapist, sounding more like a prosecutor conducting a cross-examination, repeatedly asked Jen why she had not protected Annie. Banks replied, "She didn't tell me or I would have done something." Banks pleaded with Bonner that, following Annie's disclosure, "I kept asking her and she kept telling me 'no.' Since she told me no, I believed he didn't do anything." Annie had told her that great aunt Rhonda Felix had told her what to say, Banks added. Bonner asked, "Do you believe Annie when she reports that Johnny sexually abused her?" Jen Banks answered that she did. Bonner asked what had convinced Banks of that. Watching the forensic interview recording was what she found compelling, Banks said.

Upon reading that, I thought back to the same recordings

and how they had revealed Annie's inconsistencies, the officer's leading questions, and other reasons to doubt the accuracy of Annie's disclosures. But given that Jen Banks wasn't a trained professional in the field, the child's mother would not have watched the interviews from a dispassionate, critical perspective, as I had. And she would not have known that the detective who conducted Annie's interviews was capable of saying that seventy percent of child sexual abuse reports are false.

Over the months that followed, a major outcome of Bonner's therapy appeared to involve an escalation of Annie's animosity toward her mother. In a session on October 3, 2013, Lisa Bonner asked Annie what she would like for Bonner, as a therapist, to say to her mother. Annie replied that the therapist should tell her mother, "You know what you did! You are a liar!..I hate you! I want to beat you up!" Annie added, "I don't care if she cries!" As I read Bonner's notes, I took pains to remind myself that therapeutic techniques, and treatment goals, may well differ from one therapist to another. Still, I wondered whether this therapy was helping Annie Sims, or was toxic.

* * * * * * * * *

Jen Bank's initial skepticism about Annie's disclosure had caused Banks to lose custody of both her daughters. For more than two years, Annie and a sister had lived in a foster home and had seen their mother only during supervised visits. Annie now was claiming (to her foster mother) that Jen had threatened Annie during one of the visits, while out of the hearing of the visitation supervisor. The foster mother had told Bonner of Annie's report. Bonner's January 9, 2014, notes reflected her discussion with Banks of Annie's latest allegation. Annie, Banks and Bonner were in the therapy room:

I told Jen that I understood that she had also said the same things at her last two visitations. Jen got really upset and asked me what I was talking about. I explained what (the foster mother) had told me about Annie's (and her sister's) statements. She said to Annie, 'Annie, this is not the time to be lying!' Annie told her, 'It's the truth!' Jen said, '(the visitation supervisor) did not leave me alone with my kids! I want you to call her now. Here's her number!' Jen insisted that I call (the visitation supervisor) and when I told her I was not going to, she told me she wanted me to call (the supervisor) after the session...

Reading Bonner's note, I was troubled that the therapist, with an opportunity to clarify whether Jen Banks was being honest, had taken a pass. The session deteriorated from there and, in the end, Bonner wrote, in part, "It is not in the best interest of these children to return to their mother's home." It was becoming clear that Jen Banks probably would lose custody of her daughters forever.

I reviewed Bonner's notes of six additional sessions, the last occurring on July 30, 2014. Bonner wrote that Annie's "future mother" had caught Annie telling lies about drug use by the grownups while Annie had visited an aunt (not Rhonda Felix). Bonner wrote that the future mother called the aunt, who said that, every bit of Annie's tale was a lie. "(When) confronted with this, she (Annie) hung her head, but then acted like a smart aleck and like she was justified about telling lies," Bonner wrote. By the next session, Bonner's treatment note indicated that she "attempted to process the lies she (Annie) was telling...and she had an 'I don't care' attitude...I tried to get her to understand that she should not treat people this way, but it left no impression, other than she can do what she wants."

There had been more than three years of therapy that involved forty-six sessions. The issue of Annie's court testimony had arisen several times. By the session of July 30, 2014, Annie was refusing to testify. Bonner wrote, "She told me, 'I'm done with it!... I've already moved on...I'm being adopted...I'm not sure if I remember...' Annie does not want to testify." My review of therapist Lisa Bonner's treatment notes had come to an end.

* * * * * * * * *

Jack Laishley already had attempted a number of maneuvers in defense of his client. Then, based on my review of Detective Boyd's forensic interviews, on September 14, 2012, he moved to exclude the recordings as evidence. His "motion to exclude" cited the unresolved inconsistencies in Annie's reports, as well as Boyd's excessive use of leading questions and other concerns I had outlined. Additionally, Laishley's motion listed inadequacies in the Finding Words method, citing its development by individuals "who were openly biased and hostile to defendants," as well as the training course's lack of depth and other concerns. Annie Sims' credibility had fallen apart. Not only had her initial reports been inconsistent regarding central elements of her allegations, now she was refusing to testify, telling Lisa Bonner she couldn't remember what had happened. Moreover, Annie was increasingly seen as a child who would carelessly fabricate a tale of illegal drug use by an extended family member.

During the course of Johnny Nathan's case, Jack Laishley had decided to retire and was gradually closing down his practice, with the exception of Johnny's case and a few others. Thus, Laishley contacted attorney Neil Bouchillon, who agreed to work with Laishley as the case proceeded through the summer and fall of 2014. At one point, the prosecutor offered a plea deal. Johnny Nathan rejected the offer because it would have required that he register as a sex offender for the rest of his life. Several trial dates were set, each followed by a continuance. As Bouchillon and Laishley continued negotiations with the Cabell County prosecuting attorney's office, it was clear that the case against Nathan had degenerated into a crumbling house of cards. The foster parents, who by now had adopted Annie, told prosecutors that Annie would not testify. Without a credible complaining witness (Annie), the prosecutor was left with little beyond some poorly executed forensic interviews and several witnesses such as ER nurse James, great aunt Rhonda Felix and therapist Bonner who would be able to report, in essence, only the conflicting accounts that Annie had given them.

A trial was set for March, 10, 2015. It never took place. Without a credible case, Judge Paul Farrell dismissed the charges against Johnny Nathan and, for the first time in in more than three years, Johnny Nathan was free to get on with his life.

* * * * * * * * *

In the end, I believed that justice was done, at least from the perspective that Johnny Nathan was neither convicted nor even put on trial. But there were many ways in which, in my opinion, justice was not done. During Detective Boyd's interview with Johnny Nathan, Boyd mentioned that he had conducted "pretty close to a hundred" forensic examinations of children. I wondered whether he had routinely tweaked children's reports or had misrepresented witnesses' statements as he talked with other witnesses. How many children had been removed from their homes as a result of his examinations? How many alleged perpetrators had been found guilty, even though they were not? If the case of Johnny Nathan was any indication, I could not confidently assume that justice had been done in those nearly one hundred other cases.

I wondered what would become of Annie Sims. It is highly probable she will grow up and live to the end of her days believing that she was sexually molested by Johnny Nathan, and that her mother had rejected her by siding with Nathan. Probably she will always believe that the legal system let her down. True or not, she had repeated her story so many times that, most likely, she had come to believe it was true. In the future, would Annie experience life's common rough spots, routine hurdles like a breakup or a bout of anxiety or depression, and assume they were caused by sexual abuse? What if Annie's initial allegation was the product of an overzealous great aunt Rhonda Felix who was possessed of such an intense dislike of Johnny Nathan that she felt justified in probing for anything negative about him? And what if Rhonda Felix, even with good intentions, had inadvertently asked sufficiently suggestive questions that Annie told Mrs. Felix what the little girl thought her great aunt wished to hear? Could such a discussion have been the initial nudge at a string of dominoes, a sequence that wasn't over until the final domino fell, three years later?

And what of Annie's mother, Jen Banks, who, because she believed a man who ultimately was found guilty of nothing, lost her child? Authorities initially placed Annie Sims with foster parents, who later adopted her, thus severing all of Banks' parental rights. Banks will go on with life aware she has little or no hope of reunification with Annie, at least not during Annie's childhood. As Neil Bouchillon and I discussed the case during my writing of this book, he and I agreed that this was the lowest point in a case with plenty of low points.

I asked myself whether the detective would come to appreciate the ease with which a child can be led to make a false allegation, and whether he would refine his interview techniques so that he would simply allow an alleged victim to tell what, if anything, had occurred. And I wondered whether a faceless person on the sidelines of an interview video would give thought to the enormous power she wielded when she implied that a relatively helpless Jen Banks could lose her child, if she did not implicate Johnny Nathan.

Surely a system capable of putting families through such misery is in need of reform. It can begin with scrapping the belief that virtually anyone may become a qualified forensic examiner in a week and without supervised practice in real cases. We live in an age that has brought us instant video coverage of questionable actions by the police and prosecutors in places like Ferguson, Missouri; Staten Island, New York, and North Charleston, South Carolina. In contrast, the case of Johnny Nathan offers no evidence of brutal beatings. His case suggests a different unfortunate phenomenon – the destructive power of unbridled confidence in the rightness of one's position.

Eleven

What Must We Do When a Child Alleges Sexual Abuse?

MY CRITIQUE OF DETECTIVE BOYD must not be taken as an indication of my feelings about law enforcement officers generally. On the contrary, I have enormous respect for law enforcement officers. Their work is difficult and dangerous, and the pay is meager. Most of them conscientiously do their jobs, and often with little thanks. I offer my gratitude to law enforcement officers everywhere. Several times, I have ridden with one of them and watched and learned as he went about his work. The officer is a sergeant on a police force in another West Virginia city, and he is my son.

* * * * * * * *

I have examined many young children where sexual abuse was alleged and I have testified in many such cases. As it became evident to me that many professionals were making a mess of their forensic examinations, I developed a training workshop that I have presented to professionals of every stripe, including law enforcement officers, attorneys and those in almost every helping profession who may find themselves in the role of forensic examiner. My first goal is to teach attendees that the mix of variables is complex and that it is easy to go wrong. Second, I hope to impress on attendees that, while the broad body of research remains a work in progress, behavioral science beats non-science, every time. Also, I have authored articles in academic journals to illustrate some of the difficulties inherent in assessment of child sexual abuse assessment, and to suggest research-based best practices. A representative article may be downloaded at no cost at http://www.baojournal.com/BAT%20Journal/VOL-8/BAT%208-2.pdf. Below are several high points of that article, starting with brief descriptions of three cases that drew nationwide attention.

* * * * * * * * *

Kelly Michales was a staff member at the Wee Care Nursery School in Maplewood, New Jersey, where she was accused of sexually abusing numerous children. The accusations began when a four-year-old was having his temperature taken rectally by his doctor and said, "Her takes my temperature." The child's mother contacted Child Protective Services and the boy was interviewed by an examiner who used anatomically detailed dolls. The child disclosed that Michales had also molested two other boys, although they denied it when they were interviewed. At that point the school's staff sent letters to all parents advising them of the disclosures. The parents attended a social worker's presentation on the topic. Many parents, convinced that the allegations were true, placed their children in therapy. Following many interviews by therapists, prosecutors and mental health professionals who were hired by the prosecution, twenty children accused Michales of molestation.

Many of the accusations seemed incredible, such as that Michales had penetrated children with a sword, smeared peanut butter all over their bodies and licked it off, and had done all of these things in the school's classrooms while the room was open and accessible by parents and staff at all times. No adult had ever seen anything suspicious. In August 1988, Kelly Michales was convicted of one hundred and nineteen counts of abuse and sentenced to forty-seven years in prison. However, after serving five years, Michales was ordered released on bail. New Jersey's Supreme

Court found the children's testimony had been tainted by the questionable, suggestive inteview tecniques used by the proffessionals.

The court also placed a burden on the prosecution. Before Michales could be re-tried, the prosecution would have to appear at a pre-trial "taint hearing" and show that the children's testimony should still be considered reliable. Faced with such a burden, the prosecution dropped all charges against Michales and she was again a free woman, although her life had been forever changed, as had the lives of the children.

A similar case occurred in 1989 in the coastal community of Edenton, North Carolina, at the Little Rascals Day Care Center. Complaints cropped up when a parent claimed that the owner's husband, Bob Kelly, had molested her son. Within a month three other children had made similar claims. Eventually ninety children accused Kelly and other staff members of similar acts. The children's incredible claims included that they had been abused in numerous locations: at the school, in outer space, on supervised boat outings, and that babies had been murdered (none were missing) during rituals of abuse.

The children also said that the molestation had been photographed (no photos ever surfaced). As in the New Jersey case, the nursery school was open and parents were free to drop in at any time. None had ever witnessed any suspicious activity. In April 1992, Bob Kelly was convicted of ninety-nine counts of sexual abuse and sentenced to life in prison. A staff member, Dawn Wilson, also was convicted. Two other staff members, fearing they would spend their lives in prison, pled guilty to lesser charges and received much lighter sentences.

In May 1995, the convictions of Kelly and Wilson were overturned by the North Carolina Supreme Court, for reasons similar to those cited by the New Jersey Supreme Court in the Michales case. The professionals had used far too many suggestive, leading interview techniques. In May 1997, all charges against Kelly and Wilson were dropped, and the two were released, although those who had pled guilty continued to serve out their sentences.

Astonishingly, once the charges against Kelly had been dropped, the prosecution announced that it would pursue a new charge against him, claiming he had molested another child in 1987, ten years earlier. Sadly, prosecutors appeared to have little appreciation for the likelihood that they were pursuing innocent people.

The McMartin Preschool case occurred in Manhattan Beach, California. It began when a parent, who was known to have previously made false allegations of sexual abuse against her ex-husband, went to police, claiming that her two-year-old had been sexually molested by Ray Buckey who worked at the preschool, which was owned by Buckey's grandmother. Following forensic interviews with numerous children, Buckey, his grandmother, his mother and five other staff members were accused of three hundred and twenty-one counts of child sexual abuse, some of which the children said occurred in tunnels beneath the preschool. By 1986, all charges, except several against Buckey and his mother, had been dropped for lack of evidence. In January 1990, following what was, up to then, the most expensive trial in California history, the jury returned not guilty verdicts on fifty-two counts, but remained deadlocked on twelve others against Buckey and one against his mother. The judge dismissed the single count against Buckey's mother but Ray Buckey went to a second trial, which also ended in a mistrial. At that point the prosecution decided not to re-try Buckey and the case ended, after seven years and at a cost to the public of $16 million. Throughout both trials, defense lawyers had emphasized to jurors the suggestive, sometimes to the point of coercive, questioning of children by the professionals who had conducted the forensic examinations.

A number of lessons were learned from these and similar cases. In both human and financial terms, the costs were enormous. Also, many children grew up convinced that they had been molested when indeed they had not. The children believed that the legal system had let them down. Defendants, who by all accounts were not guilty, spent years in prison, their lives forever changed. Professionals and professions suffered lost esteem. And financial costs to the defendants were enormous. It is possible that the cases' adverse publicity influenced juries in subsequent cases, who may have assumed that allegations in most child sexual abuse cases are overblown. Despite the hostility demonstrated toward defendants by individuals such as Finding Words developer Victor Veith, (see previous chapter), the tainted interviews in these cases make clear the value of both the research and extensive clinical training required when assessment of child sexual abuse is undertaken.

One may ask, specifically, what went wrong in these cases? Generally speaking, it was the absence of a science-based approach. Much of what happened may be reduced to the forensic examiners' evident failure to appreciate what is termed the situational control of behavior. Those who conducted the examinations frequently failed to appreciate their own influence over the children's reports. A common difficulty was thinking "Where there is smoke, there is fire," as may well have occurred in the case of Annie Sims. Too little attention was given to the possibility that the child's great aunt, Rhonda Felix, may have (even with good intentions) inadvertently coached Annie to make her complaints against Johnny Nathan.

A second frequent error was that examiners in these high-profile cases were guilty of looking at the children with tunnel vision. Examiners pursued a single hypothesis — that any child adjustment problems must have been due to sexual abuse. If a child demonstrated regressed toileting, excessive nightmares, fingernail biting or other anxious behaviors, it was thought by examiners that sexual abuse was the culprit. Little thought was given to whether there may have been alternative causes of the child's distress. No one asked whether the children's difficulties in adjustment could have been due to worrisome events, such as a move away from familiar friends and surroundings to a new neighborhood, or the death of a grandparent to whom the child was close, or marital strife between the parents, or any of dozens of similar events that, for a young child, may create distress. Interestingly, one-third of children who are known victims of sexual abuse exhibit no measurable problems in their overt behavior, thoughts or feelings, as Karen Saywitz and her colleagues at UCLA discovered in a 2000 study. Further, those who do exhibit problem behaviors do not do so in predictable ways.

Third, it was common for children to be interviewed numerous times, including by examiners who proceeded as if the abuse had occurred, regardless of whether a disclosure had been made. It was not uncommon for the examiners to engage in several other unfortunate tactics, each of which was evident in the case of Annie Sims: They often used anatomically detailed dolls, devices that are plagued by concerns about their suggestiveness. They asked many leading questions. At times, they did not accept children's exculpatory statements. And they erroneously assumed that graphic details indicated a valid report of abuse.

Also similar to Annie Sims' case, interviewers frequently failed to directly assess the child's tendency to be easily led. Some believed that, although a child might fabricate enjoyable events, that same child could not fabricate unpleasant or frightening events, a theory that researchers have disproven. Typically, they failed to directly assess the child's understanding of the concepts of either fantasy and reality, or truth and non-truth. Finally, once an allegation was made, parents and professionals often became so emotionally involved that all semblance of objectivity was lost.

While it is not the purpose of this chapter to fully review the research on assessment of child sexual abuse, brief descriptions of several relevant studies will shed light on matters that seemed to have been lost in the three cases above and in Annie Sims' case.

Some individuals believe that the accuracy of a child's report depends on whether pleasant or unpleasant events are being reported. Could a child possibly be wrong or fabricate events as troubling as sexual abuse? If so, does that relate to whether interviews are suggestive or repeated? These questions were examined in a 1997 study in which preschoolers were interviewed regarding four kinds of events. Two of the events had actually occurred within sight of the children, and two events were fictitious, although it was suggested to the children they had occurred. Furthermore, one of the actual events was positive (helping a school visitor who had tripped, an event staged for the children), while the other actual event was negative (a recent punishment by a parent or teacher). Of the fictitious events that were suggested by the interviewers, one was positive ("Remember when we helped that lady look for her lost monkey in the park?") and one negative ("Remember when we caught that man stealing food from the school's kitchen?"). The children were interviewed on five occasions. At the first interview they were asked whether these events had happened and for any details. The second, third and fourth interviews were suggestive and included peer references ("Suzie said you saw it. Did you?") Visualization also was employed ("Try to think what might have happened."). Questions were frequently repeated and children were praised for assenting to the suggestions. Then, a fifth interview was conducted by a new interviewer, who used non-suggestive questions. By the third interview more than fifty percent of the children assented to all of the events, whether the events were positive or negative, and whether the events had actually occurred or were fictitious.

The children's tendency to assent held through the fifth interview as well. Thus the crucial variable for most of the children was not the events, but the interview techniques. Clearly, the assumptions that children cannot be wrong, or may not be easily led to report negative events, are erroneous. The implications for interviewing a child such as Annie Sims seem clear: Avoid both repeated interviews and suggestive questions.

Some professionals have assessed children for sexual abuse based upon the assumption that children, in their innocence, could not be wrong about allegations of sexual abuse. It is unfortunate and unnecessary that jurors sometimes feel they must choose between only two options, either the alleged perpetrator is guilty, or the child is lying. Such a mindset is unnecessarily restrictive, especially when the child seems earnestly to describe sexual abuse, but all other evidence is equivocal or suggests the accused is innocent.

When jurors find themselves in that quandary, there is a third, more realistic, option: The non-abused child has erroneously come to believe he or she was abused. Such a child is not lying, in the usual sense of the term. This may explain why children in the above cases gave testimony in earnest, with no signs of lying such as shifty eyes or the like. In those cases the children had been interviewed repeatedly, typically with suggestive questions that were coupled with praise of their accusatory statements, and sometimes with continued urgings to "really try to remember" when they made exculpatory statements. As a result of such interview processes, the children came to believe they had been abused, although they had not.

When a family member, or an interviewer, describes the accused in negative terms, as may have occurred in the Annie Sims case, that likelihood increases chances that the child will say that sexual abuse occurred. Quite obviously, it would be ethically reprehensible to intentionally abuse children in order to study their reactions. However, there are studies that shed at least some light on what may happen when young children listen as grownups talk negatively about an individual. In one study, children aged three to six were told that they would be visited in their classroom by a man who was very clumsy. He visited the children and talked with them, but did nothing clumsy. Over the next ten weeks the children were interviewed about his visit on four occasions. Interviewers, frequently using leading questions, asked them whether their visitor had ripped things or had carelessly tossed things into the air, or done other clumsy things. Among three-year-olds, seventy-two percent said he had engaged in one or more clumsy behaviors, and forty-four percent said they had seen him do so, even though no such behavior had occurred. Among six-year-olds, eleven percent said they had seen the man do something clumsy. The children quite sincerely described seeing the fictitious clumsy events right before their eyes.

In a follow-up, over one thousand researchers and professionals in the area of child testimony were shown videos of the children's interviews. When asked to make a determination about which of the children's statements accurately described what had happened, the experts were wrong somewhat more than fifty percent of the time.

Sexual behavior in young children is statistically normal, a fact that is at odds with opinions sometimes offered on the witness stand. This was a factor for Annie, as her foster mother described how she had begun to engage in sexualized behaviors. In a study of more than 1,000 children who had not been molested, it was found that sexual behaviors, including sexual self-stimulation, exhibitionism, sexually rubbing up against someone and the like, were reported by their mothers as fairly common—too common to be employed as markers of sexual abuse. In Annie's case, the behaviors likely were taken as evidence of sexual abuse, although her behaviors could as easily have been taken either as the result of dozens of interviews and therapy sessions in which sexual touching was the topic, or even as developmentally normal behaviors. Interestingly, I once listened to a West Virginia circuit judge claim that young children could not possibly engage in sexual play unless they had been molested. The judge would have benefitted from a basic course on child development, if his own childhood had provided him with no clues as to the absurdity of his understanding.

Similarly, a child's sexual knowledge "beyond her years" must not be taken as evidence of sexual abuse. We are awash in a culture with sexual images in magazines, on television, in videogames, and in other media. Moreover, in many instances, sexually suggestive television programming is not confined to hours that children ordinarily would not be watching. Thus, what has historically been thought to be a marker for sexual abuse must be discarded.

In each of the three cases described above, only a few professionals examined dozens of children. That was problematic because when a professional concludes that a child has been sexually abused, a second opinion also has been formed – that the accused is a pedophile. If the professional then should examine additional children relative to the same alleged perpetrator, the probability of positive findings for the additional children increases. Thus, it is preferable that, in any case in which several children may have been abused, a given professional should examine only one child. Other professionals will be needed to examine additional children.

The professional's job would be much easier if abused children disclosed in similar ways. Unfortunately, such a pattern does not exist. An early effort to define such a pattern was known as the Child Sexual Abuse Accommodation Syndrome (CSAAS). The theoretical model held that the child would go through stages of secrecy, helplessness, entrapment and accommodation, disclosure, and recantation. Many professionals came to accept the CSAAS and rely upon it in examining children, although it was never validated for diagnostic use.

Similarly, there is no consistent pattern of diagnostic signs among children who are known to have been sexually abused. About one-third of them exhibit rather serious problems in adjustment, while another one-third show only minor, subclinical, problems. The last third exhibit no measurable problems at all. Thus, the twin notions that there is a pattern to how children disclose and that there are behaviors that are diagnostic of sexual abuse must be abandoned.

Looking at the body of research as a whole, below I have outlined some of the major parameters that follow from the findings of individuals nationwide who have studied how best to assess child sexual abuse:

• It is important to avoid the assumption of a predictable pattern of disclosure. Research suggests that the only exception is that many, though not all, sexually abused children exhibit a tendency to delay their disclosures. There is no tendency to recant. Thus, a recantation must not be taken as evidence that the abuse occurred.
• Similarly, there are no standard diagnostic "signs" of sexual abuse. Although anxious behaviors are the most common, they are observed only in a small minority of children. One-third of sexually abused children exhibit no problem behaviors at all, and another one-third exhibit only minor, subclinical, problems in adjustment.
• There are no consistent linguistic markers within children's descriptions of sexual abuse. Interestingly, researchers have discovered that a great many details may signal a false report. Upon reflection, that makes sense. The child who was abused tells what happened and stops. The child who is confabulating may see no reason to stop talking as he or she adds allegations and details.
• A single well-done interview is preferable to multiple interviews.

•Because anatomically detailed dolls may suggest that the examiner wishes to focus on matters of sexuality, the dolls should not be used during the assessment process. However, once the fact of sexual abuse has been established, the dolls may prove helpful with children who need treatment.

• The examiner must consider and explore alternative hypotheses that might account for a child's disclosures or her problem behaviors. Anxiety signs such as fingernail biting, regressive toileting and the like may be triggered by any number of events. It is important that the examiner search out all potential causes of a child's adjustment difficulties, rather than automatically assume sexual abuse has occurred.

• Leading questions are to be avoided. Typically these are questions that can be answered either yes or no. It should be noted, however, that at some point an examiner must gently explore whether the child has experienced sexual touches. If the child responds affirmatively regarding touches, the examiner should ask the child to tell what happened, rather than leading the child through a series of questions that may be answered yes or no.

• In general, repetition of questions and interviews leads one away from a valid description of events. Repetition implies that the preferred answer has not yet been heard. At the same time, an examiner is probably wise to assess the consistency of the child's report. This may be assessed on a one-time basis by feigning forgetfulness and asking the child to describe the events again.

• The examiner must avoid negatively stereotyping anyone whom the child has accused, or may accuse, and should assess whether anyone else, such as a family member, has described the alleged perpetrator in highly negative terms, within the child's hearing. If that has not happened, a case is strengthened. If it has occurred, further inquiry may prove useful.

• It is vital that a forensic examiner possess adequate knowledge of child development and of what are, and are not, statistically normal sexual activities of children.

• If multiple children are thought to have been abused, a

given examiner should assess only one of them. Other children should be referred to other examiners, if at all possible.

• The examiner should actively assess the child's understanding of the difference between truth and non-truth. This may be done by asking the child to describe or define these concepts, then quizzing the child with a few simple questions. ("If I said your name is Jill, is that the truth or a lie?") It also is wise to ask the child to tell the examiner something that is true and something that is a lie. ("Tell me the truth about the weather outside,"… "Now tell me a lie about it.") This approach will assess the child's understanding more completely. In the case of Annie Sims, the detective merely asked whether she knew what the term "truth" meant, then accepted her affirmative response at face value.

• Similarly, the examiner should actively assess the child's understanding of the difference between reality and fantasy. The examiner may ask whether certain television characters are real (humans) or not real (cartoons). However, one must be alert to the fact that the perceptive child may conclude that neither is real because even the humans in situation comedies and dramatic programs are playing roles. Careful inquiry may sort out any misunderstandings.

• It is developmentally normal for a young child to be easily led. Thus, following a disclosure the examiner should actively assess the extent to which a child will assent to suggestion. This may be done by asking the child whether a specific event (one the child never has reported) actually happened. For example, assume the child has never alleged that she was forced to touch the accused's penis. The examiner (feigning poor memory) may ask, "I don't remember whether you said this, but did you say he made you touch his penis with your hand? Did that happen?" It must be remembered that suggestibility is not diagnostic of sexual abuse, because both easily suggestible and non-suggestible children may be abused. Rather, whether a child is easily suggestible may be useful information which the jury may consider as it deliberates.

• The examiner should ask the child whether anyone has promised or suggested that her disclosure, or denial, will result in some sort of reward, such as money to be won in a lawsuit, or special rewards or attention, or is a way to get an alleged perpetrator in (or out of) jail, or the like.

• The examiner should assess, and use, the child's terms for its body parts.

• Once a child has made a disclosure, the examiner should inquire as to the number of people the child has told, as well as the number of interviews, formal and informal, the child has undergone, and under what circumstance the child has disclosed. This is important, given what is known about the problems of interview repetition. Annie Sims' initial interview was with her great aunt, Rhonda Felix. Within two days, she had been interviewed by the ER nurse and by the detective, who conducted Annie's fourth interview ten days later. She then underwent at least forty-six therapy sessions, with sexual matters about Johnny Nathan and her mother, Jen Banks, the topic of many of them. Most likely, the myriads of discussions took Annie further from the truth, rather than closer to the truth of whether any abuse occurred at all.

• Finally, for a given child, an individual professional must undertake either a forensic examination or therapy, not both. The roles of forensic evaluator and ongoing therapist are different. The forensic evaluator must not become an advocate, a roll that often is difficult to avoid when one is an ongoing therapist. For this reason the American Psychological Association's Guidelines for Psychological Evaluations in Child Protection Matters holds, "Psychologists generally do not conduct psychological evaluations in child protection matters in which they serve in a therapeutic role for the child or the immediate family or have had other involvement that may compromise their objectivity." In a similar vein, I recommend that a police officer who conducts a forensic examination should not also continue in the case as a criminal investigator.

Twelve

A Flash of Cash

AT AROUND 9:30 on the evening of February 20, 2009, a masked figure slipped through an unlocked bedroom window and into the Lincoln County, West Virginia, home of eighty-four-year-old James Topping. As the beefy, white-gloved intruder moved about the house, he abruptly found himself face-to-face with Topping. The intruder quickly overpowered the elderly man, pulled the wallet from Topping's pocket and pushed Topping to the floor where his head struck the hardwood and began to bleed. Standing over his cowering victim, the thief removed eleven hundred dollars from the billfold, then tossed it back to Topping. As quickly as he had entered, the intruder was gone, exiting through the same window that had been his point of entry. Along with the cash, the thief took sixty-five Lortab pills. The speed of the attack and the efficiency with which it had been carried out suggested the thief had known what he was looking for and exactly where he would find it.

Moments later, James Topping phoned his neighbor, Gary Price, saying he had been robbed. Price, whose trailer he rented from Topping, rushed across the yard, found Topping and called 911. Momentarily leaving Topping's side, Price ran to the downstairs apartment that Topping rented to David "Scott" Lambert and his live-in girlfriend, Stephanie Michelle "Shelly"

Plumley, telling the couple what had just happened upstairs. Lambert, who had come home from work minutes earlier and was just getting into the shower, pulled on his underwear, took a spotlight and shined it around the area, but saw no one. As Lambert would tell the police investigators the next day, upon entering his apartment from work, he found it odd that his girlfriend's sister-in-law, Tiffany Plumley, had rushed past him without saying hello and gotten into a truck where an unidentified person sat, with the engine already running.

* * * * * * * * *

State Trooper N. W. Samples arrived at the scene and talked to James Topping, who was being treated by paramedics for a contusion on the left side of his head as well as for minor injuries to his cheek and knee. Topping was able to describe only a little about the lightning fast attack. A second trooper, G. H. Ellis, arrived and spoke with Lambert. At about midnight, a canine handler, Trooper M. L. Vance, arrived and began a search. The dog picked up a scent at the bedroom window where the thief had entered. The dog followed the trail down a set of steps, around the house and to the door of the downstairs apartment, and from there to a phone junction box on the side of the house. Twice, Trooper Vance took the dog back to the bedroom window. Each time the canine followed the identical path. The troopers talked to Scott Lambert and ran a background check on him. It came back clean. In contrast, a background check on Lambert's girlfriend, Shelly Plumley, revealed outstanding warrants. At 1:30 in the morning, the officers arrested Shelly Plumley and departed, taking Shelly Plumley with them. Upstairs, a shaken James Topping went to bed and tried to relax.

At the state police detachment in Hamlin, West Virginia, troopers talked to Shelly Plumley. She told officers she might have heard a thump upstairs, but wasn't sure anything was wrong until Gary Price had come to her door saying that Topping, whose wife was out of town, had been attacked and robbed. She added that her sister-in-law, Tiffany Plumley, had been with her in the apartment from "about 6:30 until 8:00." She added something else that caught the troopers' interest: The day before the attack, James Topping had told her and her boyfriend Scott Lambert that they were being evicted because Topping believed that Shelly had stolen a gun and a check from him. At 4:30 a. m., the troopers concluded their conversation with Shelly Plumley and drove her to the Western Regional Jail in Barboursville, West Virginia.

As dawn broke on February 21, Shelly Plumley was settling into her cell. Back on Harts Creek, James Topping was feeling worse. Around 8:30, Lincoln County 911 informed troopers that Topping had slipped into unconsciousness and was being transported by ambulance to Logan General Hospital. While in route, Topping's condition quickly deteriorated. The ambulance crew was forced to abort the transport and call Health Net, which located the ambulance and flew Topping to Cabell Huntington Hospital in Huntington, West Virginia.

* * * * * * * * *

A little after 4:00 that afternoon, Troopers N.W. Samples and G. H. Ellis talked more extensively to Topping's neighbor, Gary Price. Price described how, the previous day, he had driven James Topping to the home of Topping's daughter in Danville, and from there to the courthouse where Topping paid some taxes. After a second stop at the daughter's house, the two men returned home. Gary Price added, "He always carries a lot of money."

Price recalled taking dinner to Topping around seven or eight o'clock, then having no more contact with the elderly man until picking up the phone and hearing Topping say, "I've been robbed!" Perhaps aware that he was a suspect, Price spontaneously told the troopers, "Ershel was with me!" He was referring to a friend with whom he had been playing cards in his trailer at the time of the robbery. Price added that he had seen a white male standing at the corner of Topping's home, near the phone junction box, just prior to the attack. He said that he called 911 as soon as he got in the door of Topping's home, and that Topping told him that both money and pills had been taken. Hearing that, one of the troopers replied, "When we arrived on scene…he (Topping) had no idea any medication was stolen." In contrast to what the trooper was telling Price, the officer's written report noted that Topping had said both money and pills were taken. If the trooper was testing the neighbor, evaluating Price's possible involvement in the crime, that portion of Price's account did not budge as he maintained that Topping had told him at once that both money and pills were missing.

However, as the troopers and Price continued talking, Price became confused about the timeframe, saying he had seen Scott Lambert doing something at the telephone junction box when he was carrying dinner to Topping around 7:00 or 8:00 p.m. But Lambert had not come home from work until shortly after nine o'clock. Questioned about the timeframe discrepancy, Price adjusted his report, saying it may have been as late as 9:00, or even shortly after, that he had taken dinner to Topping. And a nervous Gary Price again reminded the troopers that he and Ershel were playing cards when the robbery occurred. Price added that the downstairs renter, Shelly Plumley, had stolen a gun from Topping and pawned it. Price had seen the pawn ticket with Shelly's name on it, he said. And Price added another detail. He was aware that James Topping was on "twenty-seven different medications, including Lortab and Xanax," which Topping kept in a "little brown chest" in his kitchen.

As their discussion drew to a close, the troopers asked Gary Price if they could search his trailer. Price agreed. In the trailer, officers found some white latex gloves, several empty pill bottles, and something else: On Price's kitchen table was a prescription bottle "containing twelve white oval pills, with James Topping's name on it."

* * * * * * * * *

That afternoon, Troopers Samples and C.E. Stump interviewed Scott Lambert at the Hamlin detachment. With his girlfriend Shelly in jail, Lambert exhibited no hesitancy in telling the officers that she had a drug problem. She was using Lortabs, he said, and more than once he had overheard her talking about the pills on the phone. The couple had a son together, but Lambert was becoming increasingly disgusted with her, he told the troopers. Recently her doctor had cut off her prescriptions, and she was running around with bad people, he said. Their fighting had escalated in the past few weeks, as his suspicions about her drug use had mounted. She had told him a lot of lies lately, Lambert said, and he knew that she had stolen a check from James Topping some time ago, which had caused Topping to fire her as his housekeeper. Lambert said, "There's a lot of stuff about her I don't know and I'm finding out." Although she already had called him from the jail, he had talked to her for only a couple of minutes, telling her he wanted no more to do with her, Lambert added. He told troopers that Gary Price had spoken to him saying, "They're trying to blame us." Did Price have problems with money or drugs, the Troopers asked? Lambert knew of no such difficulties but added that once Price had borrowed a car from him and failed to return it, telling Lambert he had parked it at the home of a previous landlord to whom he owed money.

Troopers asked Lambert whether they could search the apartment. Lambert agreed, but, scarcely containing his disgust with Shelly, added that he didn't want to be there when they did so. Instead, he would ask his mother to unlock the apartment door and remain there while troopers searched. At the interview's conclusion a trooper said to Lambert, "We feel like you're telling us the truth."

Samples and Ellis also interviewed "Ershel," who confirmed that he and Gary Price indeed were playing cards when Topping called to say he had been robbed. On hearing of the robbery, he left Price's trailer and went to his nearby home to determine whether it had been robbed. When had Gary Price taken dinner to James Topping? After a lengthy pause, Ershel said it was around nine o'clock, or perhaps five minutes after.

A little after seven o'clock that evening, troopers arrived at the Salt Rock home of Tiffany and Corbet "Shawn" Plumley. Shawn's sister, Shelly, was there, having bonded out of jail. The officers talked with Shelly first. She told them that she had been in her apartment playing video games with her sister-in-law Tiffany until

Scott Lambert came home from work, at which time Tiffany had gone home to Salt Rock. Minutes later, Gary Price had informed them of the assault and robbery upstairs. Shelly told the officers that, while in jail earlier that day, she had talked to Tiffany three times, "Just talking…asking her to come and get me…" She added a comment that, doubtless, aroused the troopers' suspicions: During those three phone conversations, Shelly said, the sisters-in-law had not spoken about the assault and robbery of James Topping that had occurred less than twenty-four hours earlier while the two women played video games in the apartment below.

Next, the troopers interviewed Shelly's brother, Shawn Plumley. He told the officers that on the previous evening he and Tiffany had been arguing and, around six or seven o'clock, Tiffany had gone to her sister-in-law's apartment beneath James Topping's home to calm down. When Tiffany returned home at around nine-thirty or ten o'clock, Plumley said that she told him that "something was going on at Jim's (Topping's)." Shawn said he knew James Topping, and always had got along well with the elderly man. Of Scott Lambert, Shawn Plumley said, "Scotty is a good guy…he's always been nice to me." He didn't know James Topping's other renter, Gary Price. He added that, if his wife or his sister Shelly or David Lambert had drug problems, he wasn't aware of it. Officers asked Shawn about a pair of white gloves they had noticed lying on a table, as the men talked. His father had given the gloves to him when they were moving furniture at his father's home in St. Albans, Plumley explained. Plumley's father later confirmed his son's story. Plumley admitted to the officers that he took Lortab and Valium for back pain that originated with an injury in 2000. Asked about his employment, he said, "I don't miss work," except to take his wife to the doctor, he added.

* * * * * * * * *

Two days elapsed with no major developments in the case. Early on the morning of Wednesday, February 25, 2009, a member of James Topping's family called the Hamlin detachment of the West Virginia State Police. Troopers were told that, shortly after midnight, James Topping had passed away due to his head injury. This now was a case of felony murder, and the person or persons who had done the crime faced life in prison.

By eleven o'clock that morning, officers were at the Western Regional Jail getting copies of phone conversations between Shelly Plumley and her brother Shawn. Troopers listened as the siblings discussed the robbery and the amount of money that had been taken. At three o'clock that afternoon, Troopers Samples and Ellis again interviewed Shelly Plumley, this time at the Hamlin detachment. Asked to tell what happened, the emotional woman took a lengthy pause, then told the troopers that, while she and her sister-in-law were playing video games in the apartment, Shawn came in and told them he had just robbed James Topping. He described how he had shoved James Topping down, taken the money from his wallet and departed.

Shelly told troopers that Shawn had been carrying a mask that appeared to be a pair of baby pants with eye holes cut out, and that he had a pair of white gloves. She said that she watched him place the gloves in a trash can at his residence. It was her understanding he had thrown the mask over a hill as he drove away. Then she added that, although Shawn had just told the women of his robbery, Shelly had insisted that Shawn go to the phone box outside and fix whatever was wrong with her land line phone. Although Shawn had replied, "I need to get the hell out of here!" Shelly insisted that he see to the phone box, prior to leaving.

Finally, Shelly Plumley gave the troopers information that would become the lynchpin of their case. Her sister-in-law, Shawn's wife, Tiffany Plumley, was pregnant and, Shelly explained, if the troopers pushed their case against Tiffany, Shawn would admit to the crime and take all the blame, so that Tiffany could avoid jail and the baby would not be taken and placed in foster care. Thus alerted to leverage that would help them solve the case, the troopers began tracking down Shawn and Tiffany Plumley. Shelly tipped officers to the fact that the couple probably could be found that evening at the office of Dr. Anita Dawson in Milton, West Virginia, where Shelly had an appointment.

Officers caught up with the couple at the doctor's office. One officer went to the rear of the building while the other entered the waiting room and asked whether Shawn Plumley was there. Shawn identified himself and was arrested. Tiffany was in an examination room.

* * * * * * * * *

Sixty-eight minutes later, troopers had transported Shawn Plumley (Tiffany followed in her vehicle) to the detachment and were recording Shawn Plumley's statement. Prior to giving his statement, troopers told Shawn Plumley that James Topping had passed away in the wee hours that morning. Quickly, he took sole responsibility for the crime. Later, he would claim that, during the sixty-eight minute interval between the time of his arrest and his statement, one of the troopers had used the baby's fate as leverage to obtain his confession. If true, a crucial point of law could come into play: Is such a tactic justifiable, or would it be reasonable to conclude that his confession was coerced? Also, if a trooper had suggested that failure to confess could jeopardize the baby's fate, would the resulting focus on Shawn Plumley alone permit any of several possible co-conspirators to wriggle off the hook?

* * * * * * * * *

Plumley told troopers that he had needed money because he was a month behind on his rent and because the baby was coming. He had given thought to asking his sister for a loan but reconsidered because she seldom had money. He knew that Topping carried large amounts of cash because once he had observed the elderly man's cash-stuffed wallet as Topping was loaning money to a neighbor. On the night of the robbery he had driven to a wide spot near the house, parked and walked from there. He entered the house through the bedroom window, accosted Topping, took the money, tossed the wallet back to the man who remained sprawled on the floor, and left through the same window. He told troopers that he had not cut the house's phone line and, in contrast to his sister's statements, claimed he had not gone to the apartment downstairs following the robbery. He insisted he hadn't known his wife was at the apartment and added that he had talked to no one about fixing the phone box. Instead, he claimed, he had retreated to his truck, tossing the mask out the window somewhere along the way. He couldn't recall what he had done with the gloves. He strongly denied beating Topping, but admitted he had, more or less, grabbed the man and laid him on the floor. Throughout his statement, Shawn Plumley repeated that his wife was not involved in any way.

Tiffany talked to the police next. In contrast to her husband's statement, she told them that she and Shawn had ridden together to his sister's apartment. Beyond that, she knew little about the crime, but implied that Shawn had done it. She denied seeing a mask, but added that there had been several pairs of gloves atop her refrigerator, although the gloves had vanished in the past day or two. She told officers they could search her home for the gloves and anything else that could help them. They did so, but found nothing related to the crime.

That evening, a few minutes before midnight and less than twenty-four hours after James Topping had been pronounced dead, Trooper Samples prepared warrants for murder, robbery and nighttime burglary against Shawn Plumley. Samples took him to Cabell County magistrate court for arraignment where Plumley's bond was set at $200,000 and after which he was transported to jail. Tiffany Plumley went home, evidently having avoided implication in the crime.

* * * * * * * * *

In January, 2010, while Shawn Plumley was still held in the Western Regional Jail, a Lincoln County grand jury indicted him on charges of first degree murder and robbery. His defense attorneys, Robbie Long and Vic Navy, contacted me two months later, asking that I consult with them. Specifically, Long told me, the attorneys were nagged by the thought that Troopers may have coerced a confession from Plumley by making explicit or implicit threats that, without his confession, they would bring charges against Tiffany and, with the pair in prison, his baby would be taken by the state and placed in a foster home. Long added that perhaps other family members were involved in the crime, but the central question was whether Shawn Plumley's confession was given knowingly, intelligently and voluntarily, as the law requires. If not, it would not be admissible at trial. In a follow-up letter authored by co-counsel Vic Navy (with whom I had consulted in the Earl McCoy case that is described in chapter one), I was asked to review all the written and recorded materials in the case. Navy included the police reports and other relevant documents, as well as recordings of Troopers' interviews with the various suspects and witnesses.

I concluded my review on April 5, 2010, and met with Robby Long and Vic Navy eight days later. I shared my feeling that the case, with its numerous players and its convoluted familial constellation, resembled a Russian novel. I shared a number of other impressions and questions that had arisen in my thinking. Chief among them was my concern about what had been said to Shawn Plumley during the sixty-eight minutes between the time he was found in Dr. Dawson's waiting room and the onset of his recorded confession at the police detachment in Huntington. Conversations, if any, in the parking lot or on the ride to the detachment were not recorded. I told the attorneys that, in my opinion, if a trooper had given Plumley to believe that the baby would be placed in foster care if he didn't confess, then a reasonable person well might conclude his confession had been coerced.

There was much more that concerned me, I told Long and Navy. Based on police written reports, evidently Shelly had lied to police in her first interview, which was not recorded. I questioned whether Gary Price and his card-playing friend Ershel were involved. They had, essentially, alibied for each other. How had James Toppings' medication found its way into Price's trailer? It was somewhat suspicious that Price volunteered that he knew Topping was taking numerous medications and knew that the elderly man typically carried large amounts of cash. Why had Price been confused about the timeframe of his delivery of dinner to Topping, first saying it had been between seven and eight o'clock, later saying it was nine o'clock, or after?

And what of Shelly Plumley? Her boyfriend, Scott Lambert, said she had a drug problem, and her doctor had cut off her prescriptions. Lambert added that she ran with a bad crowd. Was she involved? Shelly had given two different stories to the troopers. And she had given troopers leverage which could accomplish dual ends: Her brother would confess, and she, Shelly, would be in the clear. Was she merely attempting to save herself by giving up her brother? Also, to what extent, if any, was Tiffany Plumley involved in a plan to rob the elderly Mr. Topping? She had given more than one account of the events. Scott Lambert appeared to be the most credible of the group, and he told troopers that Tiffany had exited the apartment and ridden away in a truck driven by someone he couldn't see, just moments prior to the arrival of Gary Price at their door. Finally, could someone else, perhaps one or more of the "bad people" whom, according to Scott Lambert, Shelly was running with, have been in on the incident?

The lawyers agreed that the case contained many unanswered questions. I suggested to Long and Navy that an examination of Shawn Plumley might shed light on the numerous gray areas. They arranged for the examination, which I conducted at the jail on June 29, 2010. I asked consulting psychologist Sandra Kiser-Griffith, who had been my student and who ran a successful local practice, to participate in the examination. I knew Dr. Kiser-Griffith to be an excellent psychologist with an analytical way of teasing out the intricacies of human functioning. I asked her to begin the examination with an administration of the Wechsler Adult Intelligence Scale (fourth edition) to Plumley. This was important because low functioning individuals are more susceptible to coercion, suggestion and promises than are individuals who function within the average range of intelligence. The test's results could not reveal whether Plumley had been coerced, but would indicate whether he suffered a heightened vulnerability to coercion. Results showed Shawn Plumley's general intellectual functioning to be far below average. His Full Scale IQ score was seventy-two, which is within the lowest three percent of the population, just three points above the level that would bring about a diagnosis of mild mental retardation. Thus, we had confirmed that, indeed, Plumley was more susceptible to coercion, threats, and the like. However, I wondered whether he might be malingering, attempting to fake low functioning. Thus, I administered two tests that are designed to catch those who are faking. Although the results of the two tests were mixed, I concluded that his history of school failure (he had dropped out of the eighth grade at age sixteen), combined with his history of working only at menial, unskilled jobs, indicated that any effort to distort his score would have made little or no difference.

Then I extensively interviewed Plumley. In order to conduct any clinical interview, it is necessary to get a complete history from the individual, which I did. Shawn Plumley described a dysfunctional childhood. His father was an alcoholic who abused his mother, although his father eventually got sober and Shawn now had a somewhat shaky relationship with both parents. He told me about his work history, a succession of unskilled jobs. After dropping out of school at sixteen, he had worked in a saw mill, as a timber cutter, and in a junk yard as a parts locator. At eighteen he got into trouble and was sent to Mountaineer Challenge Academy in Kingwood, West Virginia. After six months there, he came to Kanawha County, where he met and married the sister of a man whom he had met at the Kingwood facility. The marriage lasted only a year. He then worked as a forklift operator in Nitro for four years, but during that time he suffered a back injury that led to increased medication use. He remarried and had a daughter, now age ten, whom he saw only about once a year, because that marriage ended after five years. Then he met and married his third wife, Heather. During their marriage, which lasted another five years, he used drugs more heavily. He worked in a couple of truck driver jobs for more than a year until he again ran afoul of the law.

Shawn Plumley's history was sprinkled with legal diffi-

culties. In 2001 he pled guilty to burning a truck and report-
ing to police it had been stolen, in order to get the insurance money. He served twenty months in jail. In 2004 he was
charged with stealing tools, and in 2005 he was charged with
third offense drunken driving, a felony. He eventually served
out his sentences and was released from prison in November
2008, about three months before the robbery of James Topping.

During one of the periods he was not in prison, he met and
married Tiffany. He soon was using cocaine, crack, pills and
"you name it." Often he got pills from Dr. Dawson, he said.
Sometimes he bought them from James Topping, he added. The
baby whom he did not want to end up in foster care, a son, was
now eleven months old and getting along well enough, he said.

As we talked it became clear that, in the months that had passed
since his confession, Plumley had given thought to whether he
wished to shoulder all the blame for the death of James Topping.
Now he was telling a different story, one that diverged significantly
from his recorded confession. He said that on the evening of the
robbery, he and his wife had gone to his sister's apartment around
six o'clock. They were playing video games when someone, whom
he did not see, came to the door and delivered Xanax pills to his
sister. After the three of them snorted the Xanax, his sister Shelly
said, indicating upstairs, "I know where we can get some money."
Shelly added that she knew Topping had cash because he had
closed out an account on which she had written one or more checks
she had stolen from him. Plumley told me that he stood lookout
while Shelly climbed in the window. A few minutes later, his sister
came out with three or four hundred dollars, Plumley now claimed.
Then he and Tiffany got in their truck and went home. Interestingly,
he still made no effort to implicate Tiffany, nor did he attempt
to account for her activity while the robbery and assault were
taking place. He added that he felt that neighbor Gary Price was
involved somehow, but gave no explanation as to how this was so.

We came to the key question. What, if anything, had been
said by the troopers about the state taking his baby? Plumley
told me that, while in Dr. Dawson's parking lot, Trooper Ellis

said, in essence, "Tell me what I want to know or the State will take your baby." At that point, he was ready to confess. There was no recording of either the parking lot conversation or what might have been said on the ride to the state police detachment.

* * * * * * * * *

I shared the conclusions of my examination with Long and Navy. Aware it was a long shot, the lawyers petitioned the court to suppress Shawn Plumley's confession on the basis that Plumley had feared for the well-being and future of both his pregnant wife and unborn child to such an extent that his alleged confession "was not the product of a rational intellect and free will." The inducement "overcame Shawn's mental freedom of choice."

At the suppression hearing on October 25, 2010, I testified to two issues. First, I discussed what people will do to protect their children, and how that might relate to Shawn Plumley's confession. The answer to the first of these, of course, is "almost anything." Parents will risk, and even sacrifice, their lives for their children. They will rush into a burning building or jump into a raging river. It certainly doesn't take a forensic psychologist to understand any of that, but the attorneys needed a qualified expert to put it into the record. Thus, I testified that a parent might well suffer prison, if he thought it was in the best interest of his child. But the more central question of my testimony related to what might have led Shawn Plumley to talk to the police at all, or even to confess falsely that he alone did the crime.

I testified that there were several factors to consider. First was the likelihood that, like most individuals, Plumley did not understand the legal concept of felony murder. If a person dies during, or as a result of, another crime such as robbery, the concept of felony murder applies, and the sentencing consequences are the same as if the crime had been premeditated murder. For example, if a bank robber's getaway car runs over and kills an uninvolved pedestrian who happened to be crossing the street in front of the bank, the robber may be charged with felony murder. If convicted, he may suffer the same penalty as if he had premeditated the pedestrian's death. I added that it was likely that Plumley believed his confession would lead to several years in prison, but not to a life sentence. Because, as Plumley told me, he didn't believe he had killed James Topping.

Beyond those reasons, I told the judge that Plumley might have confessed because he believed the trooper's alleged assertion that the state could take his baby and place it in less than optimal circumstances. Moreover, it was likely that Plumley overestimated the power of the state to do so. Actually, the state generally is reluctant to place children outside the family. Grandparents and other relatives typically are the state's first choice of placement, which Plumley probably hadn't known. Added to these possible motivations for his confession was that Shawn Plumley's relatively low general intellectual functioning rendered him more vulnerable than the average person to coercion, pressure and promises.

Three troopers also testified at the suppression hearing. Trooper Greg Ellis described his meeting with Shelly Plumley in which she implicated her brother and advised Ellis that he might find Shawn at Dr. Dawson's office. Ellis testified that, while in the doctor's parking lot, he told the defendant of James Topping's death. The trooper added that Shawn Plumley immediately said that his "wife had nothing to do with it." Trooper Dean Brinegar testified that, while being driven to the state police detachment, Plumley once or twice reiterated that his wife had nothing to do with the robbery and assault, but made no other comments during the drive. Trooper N. W. Samples, the lead investigator on the case, told the judge that he wasn't at Dr. Dawson's office when the arrest was made. He said he remembered Shelly Plumley telling him that putting pressure on her brother, relative to the baby, would bring about a quick confession. And the trooper admitted that it would not have been the first time that one family member attempted to cover up for another, although he was unable to say how, or whether, he had ruled out such a possibility in the present case. Finally, Shawn Plumley testified that, upon being told the case now involved murder, he immediately asked for a lawyer and that Trooper Ellis had said, "…I know your wife is pregnant…and the state will take your baby…" He had confessed, he said, because he had feared his wife would go to jail and the state would take his son. None of the troopers testified to any circumstances that would indicate that Plumley's confession had been coerced by references to the state taking his baby.

Judge Jay M. Hoke considered the testimony. He then denied the motion to suppress Shawn Plumley's confession. At trial, the confession would be allowed. However, attorneys Long and Navy negotiated a plea bargain and a trial was avoided. The felony murder charge was dropped. Shawn Plumley pled guilty to first degree robbery and attempted robbery. He was sentenced to twenty-eight years in prison which, with good behavior, meant he could be released in fourteen years.

* * * * * * * * *

There was a final chapter to the case. Because Plumley had implicated his sister Shelly, charges of felony murder were brought against her. Like her brother, Shelly reached a plea arrangement and, thus, avoided trial. Also like her brother, she was sentenced to prison, where she remains.

In preparation of this book, I spoke with attorney Robby Long. He told me that, because Shawn Plumley had been cooperative in his sister's case, he might be released prior to his projected release date of 2023.

Tiffany Plumley was never charged in the case. Today she is raising the couple's son.

* * * * * * * * *

Note: Upon learning of James Topping's death, police caught up with Shawn and Tiffany Plumley at the office of Dr. Anita Dawson in Milton, West Virginia. The couple probably was unaware that authorities were investigating Dawson for overprescribing addictive painkillers. Another of Dr. Dawson's patients was local resident Erma Brown.

Early on April 2, 2009, five weeks and one day following James Topping's death, Erma Brown, under the influence of drugs prescribed by Dr. Dawson, was driving along alternate Rt. 10 near Barboursville. Coming the other direction was Carole Crawford, forty-seven, who was driving her sixteen-year-old daughter Meaghan and fifteen-year-old Kelsey Kuhn, to school. As Erma Brown's and Carol Crawford's vehicles approached each other, Erma Brown crossed the center line, killing Crawford and the two girls. Brown later pleaded guilty to three counts of DUI causing death and was sentenced to the maximum of three sentences, two to ten years each.

In July 2013, Dr. Anita Dawson admitted that between 2006 and 2009, she had written prescriptions for nearly 6,000 pills containing oxycodone for patient Erma Brown, at a time when she was aware that Brown also was seeking pain medication for an addiction and for other inappropriate reasons, according to a report by local station, WSAZ-TV. Dr. Dawson, fifty-five, pleaded guilty to "aiding and abetting in obtaining controlled substances by misrepresentation, fraud, forgery and subterfuge." She was sentenced to two years in prison, four times the recommended federal guidelines of zero to six months.

According to the West Virginia Board of Osteopathy, Dr. Dawson had caused or contributed to eight drug overdose deaths, as well as to the car crash that killed Crawford and the two teens.

At Dr. Dawson's sentencing, U. S. District Judge Robert C. Chambers said, "Doctors are doing nothing different than the drug dealers from Detroit on the streets and if we're going to deal with this horrible problem, doctors have to be held responsible."

Thirteen

More About Forensic Psychology

IN THE COURT SYSTEM there are two kinds of witnesses, fact witnesses and expert witnesses. A forensic psychologist is an expert witness. The designation of one as an expert witness, whether one is a psychologist, physician, engineer, historian, economist, geologist, or an individual in another specialty, is done by the judge in a given case and is based on the witness's training, experience and/or scholarly works. The judge makes his or her decision during a process termed "qualifying." The qualifying process usually takes only a few minutes and begins when the expert is called to the stand and is asked to describe his or her credentials. Then the attorney who has called the expert will ask the judge to rule that the individual is qualified as an expert in a given discipline or area. The judge has the final say.

Assuming the judge finds that the witness is an expert in his or her field, the expert witness then is able to do something that most other witnesses may not – the expert may offer opinions. In contrast, a "fact witness" may testify only about things he or she has seen or heard. Thus, the judicial permission to state opinions is the primary difference between an expert witness and a fact witness.

When giving an opinion regarding clinical psychology, such as whether the accused is competent to stand trial, a forensic psychologist must be ready to describe the basis for that opinion. The basis typically includes the forensic psychologist's interview with the client, any interviews with others who provided information about the client, documents such as police reports that relate to the case at hand, direct observation of the client (how he conducts himself during the examination), any standardized testing that was done and background documents such as an examinee's school records, mental health records or other records. More on the court process later.

Frequent Activities of Forensic Psychologists

The defendant's competence to stand trial and criminal responsibility are the two most frequent issues addressed by a forensic psychologist. "Competence" means that the defendant is psychologically able to stand trial and that he can assist his attorney in his defense and generally knows what is going on at trial. Determination of "criminal responsibility" answers the question of whether or not the defendant suffered a mental illness or disorder that prevented him from obeying the law at the time of the alleged crime.

Other activities, each with its own set of issues and demands, also frequently are addressed by a forensic psychologist. These include matters as diverse as determination of child custody, assessment of a convict's likelihood of re-offending, assistance in jury selection, determination of whether an individual has pedophiliac tendencies, assessment of child sexual abuse and more. In my view, it is unwise for a forensic psychologist to hold himself out as an expert in more than three or four of these areas. The bodies of research in these fields are vast and growing, too numerous and detailed for one individual to claim to be a credible expert in all of them, in my view.

Another frequent activity of forensic psychologists is background consultation. In this case, the psychologist works with the attorney in case preparation. At times this may not result in testimony in court. Rather, the forensic psychologist works to bring greater understanding of mental health issues to the attorney. This may range from helping the attorney understand the diagnostic terminology and process, to providing information about psychometric testing, to suggesting methods and directions for questioning various witnesses. In essence, the forensic psychologist's role is one of educating the attorney with whom he consults.

Criminal profiling is another area of expertise, one of high interest to the public, primarily due to its depiction in the movies and on television. However, contrary to media versions of profiling, there is very low demand for this service. I do not do criminal profiling, and have never been asked to do so. Anyone who envisions a career as a criminal profiler is facing very long odds simply because the services of a profiler are requested so infrequently.

The Forensic Examination Process

Leading up to a court appearance often there is an examination of an individual who has been accused of a crime. Before proceeding with a forensic examination, however, it is important that the examinee understand that anything he or she says or does during the examination may be repeated in court by the forensic psychologist, or may find its way into the written report which then may be seen by the examinee's attorney and perhaps by the opposing attorney, the judge and the jury. Thus, it is necessary that the examinee be advised of each of these possibilities, and agree to the examination, prior to the start of the formal assessment. For purposes of documentation, the examinee must sign a form that indicates he understands the warnings and that he agrees to proceed.

Most states require forensic examinations in criminal cases to be video recorded. Recording is advisable, as it protects everyone from later misunderstandings and misrepresentations as to what occurred during the assessment.

Competence to stand trial. Determination of whether a defendant is competent to stand trial usually boils down to assessing whether the defendant may be characterized as a person with either intellectual disability (retardation) or psychosis. However, these disorders, even if present, do not rule out competence. For example, some individuals who function in the upper range of intellectual disability may be competent. However, in such a case the forensic psychologist should recommend to the court that the individual be allowed more time for his attorney to explain to him what is happening during a court appearance.

In the case of an individual who is actively out of touch with reality – psychotic — it is unlikely he will be found competent. Typically, a judge will order such an individual to be placed in a secure mental health facility until such time as he is competent to stand trial. That may take weeks or months, and on occasion may take years.

The forensic psychologist who wishes to make a determination about competence must assess a number of dimensions of the examinee's functioning, such as whether he understands the charges against him, is able to assist his attorney in his defense, understands the roles of the judge, the jury, the prosecutor, and his defense attorney; understands what will happen if he is found guilty, or not guilty, and other basic facets of the process.

The first and most useful procedure in determination of competence is a well-conducted forensic interview. The interview should include the components of any clinical interview including establishment of rapport, taking a history and direct observation of the client's behavior. During the interview, the examiner will assess the examinee's understanding of the role of the principal players as I have described them above. For example, when an examinee is asked the role of the judge, an acceptable answer would be that the judge is the one who runs the trial, or is the "boss of the courtroom." An unacceptable answer is that the judge is the one "who lets you go home" or who decides guilt or innocence. An exception to the latter is a bench trial, in which there is no jury and a judge alone hears the evidence and renders a verdict.

Also in determination of competence, it may be helpful to interview other individuals. For example, in the case of suspected retardation, interviews with one or more former teachers and with family members may shed light on an individual's history of functioning.

A review of documents also may be useful in determination of competence. For example, a review of school records may shed light on an individual's general intellectual functioning. A history of special education placement due to subpar cognitive functioning, as well as the absence of such a history, is useful information. Similarly, if the examinee has received disability benefits based on behavioral or psychological difficulties, a review of related documents may be helpful. For individuals who may be psychotic, any history of mental hospital treatment or outpatient mental health treatment often is germane. Referring attorneys are generally able to gather such documents and forward them to the forensic psychologist.

A formal assessment of intellectual functioning, such as the Wechsler test and/or a standardized assessment of adaptive behavioral functioning, should be accomplished for the individual who is suspected of having poor cognitive or adaptive functioning. I recommend against use of projective personality tests because their validity is known to be subpar. In contrast, an objective personality test such as the Minnesota Multiphasic Personality Inventory-2 (Hathaway & McKinley, 1989) may be useful. But there is a warning regarding use of such tests. Unfortunately, objective assessment devices too often are misinterpreted to be measures of the amounts of various traits or mental illnesses that are said to exist within the person. This is an erroneous interpretation of the results. That is, the examiner must not illegitimately elevate what is merely a descriptive label (major depressive disorder, bi-polar disorder, ADHD, etc.) that is suggested by a personality test to the status of an entity, a thing within the person that exactly and conveniently is said to have caused the very behaviors that the label only describes. As an example of what can go wrong, consider the patient who is found to have an elevation on the scale of the MMPI-2 that measures depression. While it is accurate to say that the individual feels depressed, it is inaccurate and a misuse of the test to also conclude that the test has revealed that he is overloaded with depression, which then causes his sadness. In short, the test tells you that he is depressed, not how he got that way. A forensic psychologist must avoid circular interpretations such as, "The examinee has a lot of depression, which causes him to feel sad, have crying spells and engage in suicidal talk." Although that sounds professional and cogent, the circularity is made clear when the forensic psychologist next is asked how he knows the individual has excess depression, and he answers, "Because he feels sad, has crying spells and engages in suicidal talk."

Assessment of malingering. Throughout the chapters of this book, I have described instances of suspected malingering. At times an individual who is faced with potential criminal penalties may malinger by feigning psychological illness or retardation. There are several ways of assessment for malingering. Fortunately, most individuals who malinger have relatively little understanding of behavior from a behavioral sciences perspective. Dissociative disorders as presented in popular media often serve as role models for the malingerer. I have described one such case in Chapter Three.

As another, high-profile example, in the 1970s a man named Kenneth Bianchi, who became known as the Hollywood Hillside Strangler, successfully feigned multiple personality disorder (now termed dissociative identity disorder). With his cousin, Bianchi savagely murdered a number of women, then dumped their bodies in the Hollywood hills. He was caught, but successfully pretended to be suffering from the disorder. Bianchi concocted two "alters" who, in Hollywood style, alternatively came to the surface or remained hidden in the unconscious mind, as he repeatedly was examined by several experts. The alters wrangled with each other for dominance, and one claimed to be responsible for Bianchi's crimes. Bianchi's ruse ultimately was exposed by Dr. Martin Orne, whose methods involved careful observation and behavioral testing (Woorduff & Barnes, 1984). Bianchi ultimately admitted to having malingered and subsequently reached a plea agreement in which he avoided the death penalty in exchange for his testimony against his cousin. Bianchi remains in prison.

The forensic examiners who were duped by Bianchi's malingering all had made a critical mistake. They were convinced that a descriptive label (multiple personality) actually referred to entities within Bianchi's body that could cause him to behave in deadly ways. In contrast, Dr. Orne observed Bianchi's actions without assuming that he might be possessed by demon-like entities or personalities.

For forensic psychologists, the lesson learned is this: One must not interpret diagnostic labels as causal. Rather, such labels merely describe the individual. Factors that caused an examinee to commit a crime lie elsewhere, typically in the person's environmental history.

There are several formal devices that may be useful to assess malingering. One of these is the Miller Forensic Assessment of Symptoms Test. This twenty-five item, well-validated instrument contains descriptions of behaviors that never are reported by those diagnosed as psychotic. For example, one question asks the examinee whether, when people are talking to him, he sees the words spelled out. If an individual answers "yes" to several such questions, it is likely he is faking a mental illness.

One also may assess for malingering using the "window test." Once the formal assessment has ended and the examinee has been excused, the forensic psychologist may observe through the window as the individual exits the building. If the examinee has said that he is illiterate, and then he is observed purchasing a newspaper or reading his phone messages, it is likely that he was malingering. Similarly, if he has feigned severe depression, complete with crying, and then is observed to drop the sad demeanor as he walks to the parking lot, he probably was malingering. In contrast, the examiner may observe behavior that is consistent with the symptoms presented, an indication that the examinee was not pretending to suffer from a mental disorder.

Criminal Responsibility

In most states the question of criminal responsibility is posed in terms similar to the following: At the time of the event (crime), did the defendant suffer a mental disorder or defect that prevented him from knowing right from wrong or prevented him from conforming his actions to the requirements of the law?

To answer the question, the forensic examiner must learn about the examinee's history of life experiences. Thus, the forensic examiner will search for records of, or witnesses to, histories of childhood abuse, extreme job stress, financial stress, combat trauma or other elements of the individual's background that are documented and relevant. The examiner is searching for variables in the individual's life circumstances, rather than in the unconscious parts of the mind. The pitfalls of references to hypothetical, unverifiable causes such as egos, unresolved complexes, libidos, fixations, traits, moods, needs, neuroses and the like should be clear. What may provoke an uncomfortable feeling for the forensic psychologist, on the witness stand, is being asked on cross-examination how he knows that an unverifiable entity such as an id, ego, or sadistic impulse prompted a crime that the defendant otherwise would not have committed. Thus, it is much more credible to reference causal variables such as a violent father role model or a history of intractable childhood abuse, or the like as causes of both the individual's mental disorder and his criminal act.

Theoretical aspects. To best understand criminal behavior, I advise that the forensic psychologist consider what the defendant's actions accomplished for him. That is, if the individual committed a crime, what was his anticipated payoff? In slightly more technical terms, how did the unlawful activity "function" for him? The case of John Hinckley is an example. When he shot President Ronald Reagan, Hinckley was convinced that his action would cause actress Jodie Foster to love him. One may ask what convinced Hinckley that this was a way to impress anyone, let alone an actress whom he had never met. Yet, in his thinking, shooting the president would function as a way to accomplish his goal, which clearly was delusional.

As another example of how searching out the functions, or anticipated functions, of behavior may be useful in understanding criminal activity, consider a low-end crime such as shoplifting an item that one easily could have paid for, for instance a CD. A frequent initial cause is a dare presented to a young person. Once the dare has been taken up and the item has been shoplifted successfully, both peer acceptance and possession of the CD itself tend to make the crime more likely to be repeated, as the fruits of the criminal behavior are enjoyed. Moreover, it is easy to overlook the causal power of what psychologists term negative reinforcement which, like positive reinforcement, increases the likelihood of a repeat of the behavior. In the case of shoplifting, there is a buildup of tension as the thief approaches the exit. He experiences anxious thoughts and feelings. He may ask himself whether he has been spotted and whether he hears pursuing footsteps. He may worry that police have been called already. His heart races, his blood pressure skyrockets, his muscles become tense and he begins to perspire. Then, upon exiting the shop and finding himself several blocks distant, he experiences great relief from his anxious thoughts and feelings. Such a feeling of relief is quite rewarding and actually adds to the likelihood that he will shoplift again in the future. Thus, phenomena such as dares, merchandise obtained, peer approval and relief from anxiety (even self-imposed anxiety that arises from the act of shoplifting) are variables that maintain a pattern of shoplifting. In contrast, a diagnostic label such as kleptomania tells us only that an individual steals, not why he steals. Unfortunately, too often labels such as kleptomania are employed illogically, in circular fashion, to explain what they only describe. Consider the embarrassment to the expert witness of the following hypothetical exchange, as his circular reasoning is exposed:

Question: Doctor, you have already testified that a mental disorder known as "kleptomania" causes him to steal compulsively. But how do you know he has kleptomania?
Answer: Because he steals compulsively.

As another example of the usefulness of searching out the functions of a defendant's actions, the chronic fire setter is rightly described as a pyromaniac. But it is circular to say that we know he is a pyromaniac because he sets fires, and he sets fires because he has a lot of the trait (disorder, etc.) called pyromania. A forensic psychologist must avoid such circularity, also termed explaining-by-labeling or mentalism. Instead, the expert witness is advised to consider how fire setting has functioned in the individual's life. Perhaps in his childhood he received little attention from his busy parents. Then, when he was caught playing with matches, his parents provided a great deal of attention, even if the attention mainly was negative. Fire setting then may have acquired rewarding power. Then, in his adulthood, he continues to set fires as a means of arousing attention from the community, whose rules and standards have by then replaced those of the parents. Also, the behavior has the special appeal of doing what is taboo.

He would be even more at risk to revert to fire setting in adulthood if he had poor communication skills, particularly the skill set I will term "requesting support." Such an individual may have little control over his environment, including the people in it. Thus, as an adult, others' reactions to his fire may reinforce the act. Fire trucks, police and onlookers flock to the scene. There probably will be breaking news and follow-up reports in the media. Thus is a relatively feckless individual able to exert massive control over others, which tends to be powerfully rewarding, though in a highly maladaptive way. Thus, the fire setter commits his crime because of a particular set of identifiable variables — historic, current or both, that are causal. He does not set fires because he somehow acquired too large a dose of a mystical trait called pyromania, which "explains" his behavior.

One additional example, the obscene phone caller, will further illustrate the importance of avoiding the trap of providing the court with testimony that is circular. Such a person likely has poor social skills and poor stress-coping skills. As with most of us, having some sense of influence within his world is rewarding, gaining social support from others because he, in turn, provides the same to them.

However, if he lacks the people skills to achieve that goal, he may find that his anonymous obscene call is rewarding because he knows he is controlling the feelings of the person he has dialed. If the person he has called becomes visibly angry, humorous or tearful, the caller's activity is likely to be repeated because he perceives that he controls that person's feelings. If the annoyed caller wisely hangs up quickly without talking, the caller's effort has not worked for him, and he is less likely to re-dial that number.

In summary, when searching out a defendant's criminal responsibility, or lack of it, it is wise to avoid the trap of circularity, the trap of explaining-by-labeling, by considering the examinee's behavior in functional terms. How did his act function, or work, for him? If, like John Hinckley, the action worked in ways compatible with a delusional system, the individual likely was not criminally responsible.

Coping with Courtroom Tactics

It is useful to consider a number of courtroom tactics with which the expert may be confronted on cross-examination. The cross-examiner's goal is nothing more than to discredit the expert forensic psychologist. There are several means by which that may be attempted. One of these, simply put, is to show that the expert's opinion is only weakly supported by the data. The solution for that problem is to do a better job of documenting one's findings next time.

However, often the cross-examiner will attempt to discredit the expert by attacking elements that are not substantive to the case at hand, such as the expert's training, experience, scholarly activities or other areas that do not relate directly to the facts of the case that is being litigated. Any expert's credentials are fair game for courtroom scrutiny. However, in my opinion, the greater the effort to undermine one's credentials, the greater is the crossexaminer's avoidance of the substance of the opinions and basis for them. If, on cross-examination, a lawyer attacks me with numerous questions designed to undermine my credentials, I generally feel that he or she considers my opinions about the individual I have examined to be on fairly solid ground and hard to assail. Thus, my credentials are attacked for purposes of distraction.

On direct examination the expert witness will be treated well. The expert will be asked to describe his credentials, his methods and conclusions in the present case. The mood changes with cross-examination. As the opposing attorney attempts to discredit the expert's credentials, methods and conclusions, it must be kept in mind that the court system is adversarial and, although these attacks may create some discomfort for the expert, the system generally works well.

When one's credentials are questioned, it is unwise to become defensive. Many times I have been confronted with the fact that I am not a psychiatrist. I have resisted an urge to respond with "Thank goodness, I am not a psychiatrist." Rather, I always reply, "No, I am a psychologist." The questioner's gambit is an effort to play to the public's perception of greater esteem for those who are medically trained.

That gambit may be followed by asking me to explain the difference between the two professions. I usually respond by asking whether the attorney wishes that I explain to the jury the differences in training, or practice, or both. Often I am asked to talk about both. I respond by pointing out that, during four years of medical school, the future psychiatrist typically has completed only two graduate courses in mental health plus about three hundred hours of on-the-job experience. That minimal mental health training is due to the fact that medical school also includes coursework and on-the-job training in pediatrics, family medicine, oncology, urology, nephrology, and other specialties. Upon graduation from medical school, the psychiatrist-to-be undertakes an internship of several years. This is on-the-job training, most of it in psychiatry. In contrast, a clinical psychologist completes four years of graduate coursework, about eight hundred hours of on-the-job training, along with research, all of which are in the behavioral sciences and mental health field, rather than in other specialties. Those years are followed by a one-year, full-time internship in clinical psychology. Often, that description of the differences in training of psychologists and psychiatrists blunts the cross-examining attorney 's effort to play the psychology-is-not-medicine card.

However, should the attorney ask about differences in practice, it is wise to point out that today most psychiatrists seldom do therapy. Rather, they spend their days conducting fifteen-minute medication reviews. In contrast, psychologists conduct therapy and assessments including psychological testing, which psychiatrists are not trained and qualified to do, except in the most minimal terms. These explanations are brief and non-defensive, and I have found that most jurors are ready for the cross-examiner to move on.

Another frequent cross-examination ploy involves a question about the number of times one has testified "for the defense" (question from a prosecutor) or "for the prosecution" (from a defense attorney). In fact, most expert witnesses have testified significantly more often for one side or the other, and for an understandable reason: Prosecutors generally use the same local experts, which leaves defense attorneys to repeatedly request the aid of other experts. A sophisticated reply is important because one does not wish to be seen as one-sided. Ideally, one should work "both sides of the street," taking cases referred by both prosecutors and defense attorneys, as well as from judges. When I am asked this question I explain that most of my forensic consulting has been with defense attorneys. I like to add that often following my initial consultation, many defense attorneys do not then ask me to give courtroom testimony because my findings were not favorable to their cases. This tends to neutralize the suggestion that my testimony is unfair, or that I have a bias in favor of one side or the other.

Another question that attempts to cast the expert in a difficult light involves his fees. If asked, one must accurately report the per-hour amount he or she charges, which may sound exorbitant to members of a jury. By asking the question, the cross-examiner is suggesting that the expert is a person who will say anything for money, a "gunslinger" whose opinions should not be trusted. Unfortunately, there are such money-grubbing individuals among the population of forensic experts. To neutralize the suggestion that I am one of them, I tend to state my hourly fee, and add that my full-time employment (until my recent retirement) is as a university professor, and that the cases on which I consult require a great deal of time and expertise. Thus, I must charge a relatively significant rate. I believe that most jurors will not discount an expert on the basis of his or her fees, if the expert generally is perceived as competent.

In conclusion, when challenged regarding one's credentials, fees or in other ways that are not germane to the substantive issues, it is important to remember that the greater the focus on such challenges, the less the cross-examiner is inclined to focus on one's methods and conclusions in the case at hand.

Substantive Challenges

Conclusions based on direct observation, testing, verified elements of the client's history, and reliable reports from third parties are difficult to attack, and serve the pursuit of justice well. Nevertheless, it is important to be alert to a variety of ploys that may be used on cross-examination. For example, the expert may be asked whether an unknown (to the expert) factor might change his or her opinion. For example, assume that you are the forensic psychologist and the case involves auto theft by a gang that includes your client who suffers subpar general intellectual functioning. On direct examination you have testified that his low IQ renders him more likely than the average person to be led into illegal activity by sharper members of the gang. Then, on cross examination, you are asked, "If you knew that the defendant had previously been arrested six times for auto theft completely by himself, would that change your opinion?"

Such surprises are not welcomed by expert witnesses (and show the importance of taking a thorough history and reviewing all case documents carefully). However, there are two possible explanations for the question. First, it is possible that this question is a complete red herring. That is, it is possible the defendant has no such history of previous arrests. If so, the defendant's attorney should object immediately and ask that the question be withdrawn. Alternatively, it is possible that this information is accurate, but has been withheld from (or not known to) the defense attorney. If so, you as the expert are left to deal with the question as best you can. A suitable response is to assert that such new information could change your opinion, but that you would need to talk to the defendant about it in order to render an opinion relative to the new data. This tells the jury that you are reasonable, but does not involve an immediate change in your opinion

A similar cross-examination ploy occurs when the attorney produces a new document and asks whether the expert has seen it. For example, suppose the cross-examiner produces a report by a qualified professional that reaches a conclusion opposite of your own. It is wise to answer that if the judge will take a thirty-minute recess to review the document, you will provide a reaction. Since judges are reluctant to take such breaks, the report may quickly become a non-issue for the expert on the stand. On occasion, however, a judge will grant the expert's request for time to read the document. When that happens, the expert must review the report and respond as appropriate, once his or her testimony resumes.

For greater breadth and depth on the courtroom process, several books authored by Stanley L. Brodsky contain a number of practical suggestions (Brodsky, 1999; Brodsky, 2004; Brodsky 2013).

Training of a Forensic Psychologist.

To become a forensic psychologist, following undergraduate school one must undergo training as a clinical psychologist in a Ph.D. or PsyD program, in a university department of psychology. This takes five years, including a one-year internship, beyond undergraduate school. During those five years, most universities train their students for general practice, for a good reason – it is unlikely that a newly graduated doctor of clinical psychology will be able to make a living doing only forensic work. Rather, one must be able to work with a variety of patients, doing therapy and assessments.

For the student who is interested in forensic psychology, once admitted to a doctoral program it is vital to become connected with the faculty members in the department of psychology who work with attorneys and the courts, who conduct forensic examinations and who give expert testimony. Helping those faculty members work on their cases is an excellent way to learn how to become a forensic psychologist. This may be accomplished in almost any fairly large university department of psychology. Also, many such departments of psychology offer at least one didactic course devoted to forensic psychology. As well, it may be possible to be assigned to work in a forensic setting for one year of required practical experience, prior to internship. The full-time internship may offer additional opportunities to learn how to practice forensically.

A few universities have tracks that involve several courses and several faculty members who are forensic psychologists. Admittance to these, like all clinical psychology training programs, is highly competitive. One-page descriptions of each clinical psychology program, including those that specialize in forensic psychology, may be found in a book that is published by the American Psychological Association. To order the APA's "Guide to Graduate Study" you may call 202-336-5500.

It is relevant that a number of psychologists who are trained in specialties other than clinical psychology also provide the courts with expert testimony. For example, an experimental psychologist whose expertise lies in the area of memory may help jurors understand more about the fluidity of memory, how memories change over time and are imperfect. A prime example is the work of psychologist Elizabeth Loftus, who provided testimony about her research into the ways that false memories of child abuse were implanted in the minds of thousands of therapy patients by well-intentioned but misguided therapists, in the 1980s and 1990s. Her work, and that of similar researchers who are not clinically trained, brought about much needed changes in the practice of therapy and in how the law and the courts view claims of recovered memories of childhood abuse. Loftus was trained in experimental psychology, rather than in clinical psychology. Nevertheless, her influence has been wide-reaching and dramatic where the courts are concerned.

REFERENCES

Brodsky, S. L. (1999). *The Expert Witness: More Maxims and Guide Lines for Testifying in Court.* Washington DC: American Psychological Association.

Brodsky, S. L. (2004). *Coping with Cross-Examination and Other Pathways to Effective Testimony.* Washington DC: American Psychological Association.

Brodsky, S. L. (2013). *Testifying in Court: Guidelines and Maxims for the Expert Witness* (2nd Ed.).

Washington DC: American Psychological Association. *Diagnostic and Statistical Manual of Mental Disorders (4th ed.).* (1994). Washington DC: American Psychiatric Association.

Hathaway, S. R. & McKinley, J.C. (1989). MMPI-2. Minnesota Multiphasic Personality Inventory-2.

New York: National Computer Systems, Inc: Miller, H. A. (2001). M-FAST: Miller Forensic Assessment of Symptoms Test. New York: PAR Psychological Assessment Resources, Inc:

Woodruff, J. (Reporter) & Barnes, M. (Director). (1984). "The mind of a murderer," part II (Television series episode). In D. Fanning (Executive producer), *Frontline.* Boston: WGBH Educational Foundation.

INDEX

References are selective.

Abbingdon, VA, 109

Accoville, WV, 106

Adamski, Dr. Thomas, 57

Adkins, Charlotte, 107-19

Adkins, Ernest, 107-19

APA Guide to Graduate Study, 216

APA's Guidelines in Child Protection Matters, 183

Arnold, Lee, 17

Asperger's disorder, 129-33

Athens, WV, 21

Austin, Carrie, 45

Autism spectrum disorder, 129

Bailey, Brian, 80

Barboursville, WV, 82, 186, 200

Bateman Hospital, 92

Battered woman syndrome, 97-104

Beasley, Lt. A. D., 32, 41

Beck Anxiety Inventory, 13, 38

Beck Depression Inventory, 38, 141

Beckett, Herman, *Acknowledgements*

Beckley,WV, 55, 139

Behavior and Social Issues, 73

Behavior, functions of, 208-10

Behavior, situational control of, 123, 175

Behavioral Medicine and Psychiatry, WVU, 47, 125

Bexar County, Texas, 137

Bianchi, Kenneth, 206

Big Bang Theory, 133

Blaine, Mr., 79

Blake, Kenneth W., 136

Bleattler, Karen L., 131

Bluefield Daily Telegraph, 24

Bouchillon, Neil, 150, 152-53, 168-70

Branchland, WV, 5

Braxton County, 127

Bridgeport, WV, 44

Brinegar, Trooper Dean, 198

Brooks, Emmett, 1-19

Brougham, Pat, 143-59

Brown, Erma, 199-200

Brown, Jack, 89-104

Buckey, Ray, 174

Buckeye Village, 64

Betts, Grace, 65

Buffalo Creek, 105

Burris, Mrs., 79

Cabell Huntington Hospital, 186

Cabral, Deborah, 61

Cabral, Misty, 60-73

Cabral, Rhuann, 43-44
Capitol High School, 123
Carver Vocational School, 125
Cary, Dep. C. J., 41
Castelle, George, 139
Century 21 Four Seasons, 21,
    27, 35, 37
Challenges, substantive, 214
Chambers, Judge Robert, C.,
    200
Chambers, Trooper J. C., 109
Charleston Gazette, 72
Charleston, WV, 59, 60, 64,
    68-69, 72, 81, 121-22,
    131-32, 134, 138-40
Charnock, Bill, 71
Child Sexual Abuse
    Accommodation, 180
Chiles, Chris, 78, 82, 84
Cole, Dr. Jacqueline, 33
Competence to stand trial,
    202-07
Concord College, 21
Congleton, William Claude,
    88
Constantino, Frank, 25
Constantino, James, 20-42
Constantino, Nellie, 25-26
Conway, Crista, 77-86
Cook, Alijah, 120-22
Cook, Dreama, 121-33
Cook, Greg, 77
Cook, Stephen Arlo, 120-33
Cook, Thomas, 91
Cooper, Sheldon, 133
Copenhaver, Judge John T.,
131
Crawford, Carole, 200
Crawford, Meaghan, 200
Criminal profiling, 203
Cross Lanes, WV, 134, 140
Cross-examination, 15, 85, 99,
    101, 117, 132, 165, 208-16
Crown, WV, 105-06
Cruz, Dr. S. B., 110
Cummings, Judge John J., 101
Curry, Arden II, 140-47
Danville, WV, 186
Davis, Gerald Wayne, 139-40,
    146
Dawson, Dr. Anita, 190, 193,
    196, 198, 200
Dean, Terry, 11
Department of Psychology,
    WVU, 57, 215
Direct examination, 211-14
Dodd, Dr. Jack, 94-99, 110
Donald . Kuhn Juvenile Center,
    81
DSM -5, 97, 111, 129
DSM-IV, 130-31
Dunbar, WV, 78
EconoLodge Motel, 44-46, 49,
    53
Edenton, North Carolina, 173
Eighth Amendment, 144
Electroconvulsive shock
    therapy, 92
Ellis, Trooper Greg. H., 185-99
Experimental psychology, 216
Expert Witness, 11, 138, 140,
    201, 209-14

Explaining-by-labeling, 211
F Scale, MMPI, 100, 112
Fact witness, 201
Fairmont, WV, 43, 49, 51-52,
    54
Family Services of the
    Kanawha Valley, 163
Farrell, Judge Paul T.
    86, 150, 168
Felician College, 23
Ferguson, Judge Alfred, 81,
    150
Finding Words, 152, 157-58,
    161-64, 175
First Community Bank
    Princeton, 22-24,
Flatwoods, WV, 61
Forbes, Bill, 138
Forensic psychologist,
    activities, 12, 34, 201-16
Forensic psychology,
    training, 215-16
Foster, Jodie, 40, 208
Fremouw, Dr. William, 57
Gelido, Rev. Father Manuel,
    24
Gershman, Andrew P., 93
Gibson, Michael, 24-41
Gibson, Trooper W. R., 109
Gilfilin, Kelli, 134-47
Gillispie, Eva, 94
Good, Hope, 60, 67
Greenbrier County, 109
Greer, James, 136
Greiner, Cathy, 86
Hagen, Brent, 16

Hamlin, WV, 9-10, 185, 187,
    189-90
Harris, William O'Dell,
    139-40, 146, 148
Harts Creek, WV, 186
Harvey, Perry, 108
Hasan, Dr. Nusrath, 25-28
Hawkins, Barbara, 24
Hearst, James, 56, 58
Henry, Walter Lee, 74-86, 90
Herold, Larry L., 136
Hinckley, John, 40, 57, 208, 211
Hiriani, Dr. B. M., 112
Hobbs, Linda, 87
Hobbs, Mark, 115
Hoke, Judge Jay, M., 11, 16-19,
    199
Holliday, Judge James. O.,
    138-39
Hollywood Hillside Strangler
    case, 206
Houdyschel, Charles, 90, 97,
    101
Huntington Herald-Dispatch, 81
Huntington Mall, 137
Huntington State Hospital, 92,
    110
Ibara, Dr. Maria, 109
Internal Revenue Service, 47
Jackson, Neil, 25
James H. "Tiger" Morton
    Center, 78, 81
JB's Club, 60, 69
Jefferson, WV, 60, 69
Job Corps, 114
Johnson, Curtis, 81

Julian, WV, 81

Kanawha County, 36, 138-40, 147, 195

Kelly, Bob, 173

Kingwood, WV, 44, 195

Kiser-Griffith, Dr. Sandra, 194

Kleptomania, 209

K-Mart, 46

Kornbrath, Brian J., 122, 124, 130-32

Kubow, James, 108

Kuhn, Kelsey, 200

Laishley, Jack, 77-86, 151-68

Lambert, Scott, 184-94

Lees, Jim, 139

Lincon County, 9-10, 16-17, 184-86, 192

Lincoln County Journal, 17

Little Rascals Day Care Center, 173

Lodi, New Jersey, 22

Loftus, Dr. Elizabeth, 216

Logan County, 105-17

Logan General Hospital, 186

Long, Robby, 193, 199

Louisa, KY, 60-61, 69

Love, St. Sen. Shirley, 23

Lowe, Keith "Bobby", 60-73

Lowe, Michael, 65-67

Loyd, Roy, 60-73

Lupardus, Timothy P., 118-19

Luria Nebraska Test Battery, 126

Malingering, assessment of, 206-07

Man Appalachian Regional Hospital, 105, 109

Manhattan Beach, California, 174

Maplewood, NJ, 172

Marion County, 48

Marshall University, 79, 103, 114, 122, 126, 141

Martin, Minnie, 85

Martinsburg, WV, 83

Mauro, Bertha, 58

Mauro, Frances, 43-59

Mauro, James II, 43-59

Mauro, James, 43-59

Mauro, Jeff, 43-59

Mauro, Nicholas, 43-59

Mauro, Sandy, 43-59

Mayberry, Tony, 7, 16

McCalla, Rev. Mark, 72

McComas, Jessie, Jr., 89

McCoy, Earl Sr., 1-19

McCoy, Earl, 1-19, 192

McCoy, Julia, 3

McCoy, Kristie, 1-19

McCoy, Luther, 7

McDowell County, 20

McGowan, Steve, 140

McMartin Preschool, 174

McMillan, Harold, 126

Mentalism, 209

Mercer County, 36

Messina, Lawrence, 72

Michaelson, Gail I., 63

Michales, Kelly, 172-73

Midkiff, Dr. Donna, 73

Midkiff, Sabrina Gayle, 136, 138, 141

Miller Assessment of Symptoms Test, 38, 207

Mills, Gary R., 24

Milton, WV, 191, 199

Minnesota Multiphasic Personality Inventory, 12, 38, 98, 111, 205

Montgomery, WV, 142,

Moreland, Lynn Inman, 136, 138, 141

Moundsville, WV, 49-50, 138, 141-46

Mountaineer Challenge Academy, 195

Mt. Olive, WV, 41-42, 59, 71, 84, 142, 146

Napier, Bobby, 8

Navy, Vic, 10-19, 192-99

New Jersey Supreme Court, 173

New York Times, The, 139

Nitro, WV, 185

North Carolina Supreme Court, 173

O'Briant, Judge Eric, H., 111, 117-18

O'Hanlon, Judge Dan, 84-85, 137

O'Keefe, Dr. Stephen, 126

Obscene phone calls, 210

"Ochese", David, 22

Offutt, Ted, 44

Ojeda, Stephanie, 23

One flew Over the Cuckoo's Nest, 92

Orne, Dr. Martin, 206

Oswego, NY, 65

Parkersburg, WV, 91, 93, 96

Parkwest, 6

Parsons, Jim, 133

Pearse, Ronald, 125

Phelps, William, 126

Plumley, Corbet Shawn, 184-98

Plumley, Shelly, 184-98

Plumley, Tiffany, 184-98

Poe, Charles, 23

Poffenberger, Donald, 144-46

Poindexter, Barbara Mays, 87

Point Pleasant, WV, 74, 79

Porter, Doug, 5

Powers, Tina, 32

Prestera Behavioral Health Center, 6

Price, Gary, 184-89, 193-94, 196

Projective tests, 205

Pyromania, 209-10

Qualifying an expert, 201

Quarrick, Dr. Eugene, 125

Ramey, April, 11

Ramey, Teresa, 7-8, 16

Rappaport, Dr. Jonas, 57

Reagan, President Ronald, 40, 57, 208

Responsibility, criminal, 77, 112-13, 116, 131, 202, 207

Rey Sixteen Items Test, 128

Richardson, James, 134-49

Riffle, Andrew, 11-15

Riley, Betty, 87-104

Riley, Donna, 91-95

Riley, Harold, 91, 94

River Park Hospital, 30-33, 36, 39

Robertson, Dr. Philip B., 28-29, 38

Rubenstein, Jim, 72

Rush, Dr. Robert J., 111

Rustic Motel, 60, 61, 69

Sablay, Dr. Teodoro, 11-13

Salt Rock, WV, 188-89

Samples, Trooper N. W., 185-88, 190, 192, 200

San Antonio, TX, 137

Save-A-Lot, 6

Saywitz, Dr. Karen, 176

Sexual abuse, assessment of, 151, 171-83

Shavers, Zoe, 62-63, 65

Shawnee Regional Park, 78

Sheets, Ronnie, 71

Shields, James, 48-52, 56, 58

Shoplifting, 208-09

Skeens, Kim, 79-80

Skeens, Timothy "Scott", 74-86, 90, 152

Smith, Daniel, 72

Smith, Dr. Ralph, 98, 99, 131

Smith, Dr. Rosemary, 98, 99, 131

South Central Regional Jail, 64, 68-69

South African Ministry of Energy Minerals, 20

South Charleston, WV, 60

Spangler, Trooper M. D., 109

Sperry, Det. Chris, 86

Spurlock, James, 10-19

St. Albans, WV, *Dedication,* 60, 139, 189

St. Joseph's Hospital, 93

St. Mary's Hospital, 3, 6, 77, 87, 94-95, 110, 151

Stack, Charles, 58

Stallo, Maria, 89, 94-94, 101

Stanford University, 148

State v. Constantino, James, 20-42

State v. Lowe, Keith "Bobby", 60-73

State v. Mauro, Nicholas, 43-59

State v. McCoy, Earl Ray, 1-19

State v. Plumley, Corbet Shawn, 184-98

State v. Richardson, James, 134-49

State v. Riley, Betty, 87-104

State v. Skeens, Timothy "Scott", 74-86

State v. Walls, Charles, 102-19

Steptoe and Johnson, 140

Stevens, Jack, 15-19

Strosser, Kathleen Klaus, 25

Stroupe, Trooper W. E., 109

Stump, Trooper C. E., 187

Swango, Roger, 94, 99

Sweat, Linwood, 91

Swimm, Bobby, 9

Takubo, Tom, 108

Taylor, Judge Harry C. II, 127

Three Rivers Hospital, 69

Topping, James, 184-99

U. S. Secret Service, 120-21, 132

U.S. Congress, 73

UCLA, 176
"Umbezie", Oliver, 21-23
Upward Bound, 21
Vance, Diana Lynn, 106-08
Vance, Trooper M. L, 185
Veith, Victor, 150, 162, 175
Vidal, Dr. Andrea, 33
Virginia State Police, 109
Walls, Ballard, 119
Walls, Charles, 102-19
Walls, David, 106-09
Wal-Mart, 5-6, 11, 16-17, 35
Wandling, Donald C., 113-14,
    117
Wayne County, 1-19
Wechsler Adult Intelligence
    Scale, 111, 127-28, 194, 205
Wee Care Nursery, 172
West Virginia State College,
    136
West Virginia University, 44,
    47-48, 56-57, 125
Western Regional Jail, 82, 186,
    190, 192
Weston State Hospital, 110-13
Westover, WV, 44
Wilkinson, Robert "Bob",
    Foreword, 90, 101-03, 150,
    153
William R. Sharp Hospital, 57
Williams, Sue, 35-39
Williams, Dr. Patricia, 113
Wilson, Dawn, 173
Wilson, Stephen, 72
Winfrey, Oprah, 21
Wise, Gov. Robert, 23

Woodall, Glen Dale, 137-38,
    140, 146
Woodcock-Johnson Achieve-
    ment Test, 129
WSAZ-TV, 200
WV Board of Osteopathy, 200
WV Supreme Court of
    Appeals, 17-18, 20, 86, 101,
    103, 118, 138, 144, 173
Yeager, Brig. Gen, Charles, 9
Yost, Tina, 45
Zain, Fred, 135-48
Zimbardo, Philip, 148

Acknowledgements

I thank the following individuals who aided in preparation of this book: Publishers Place executive director Patrick Grace, who also served as editor; artist Deborah Richardson, who did the cover and interior art; typesetter and index editor Erika Bias, and proofreader Chris Washington. Many others also deserve thanks. They include *The Charleston Gazette* and its Opinion Page Editor, Dawn Miller, its photographer, Chris Dorst, its photo librarian Ron Miller, Tammie Toler of *The Princeton Times*, Misty Poe of *The Fairmont Times West Virginian*, Investigators Greg Cook and Herman Beckett, Jenny Holderby and Michelle Alford of the Marshall University Library, Dr. Sandra Kiser-Griffith for her assistance on the Corbet Shawn Plumley case, and therapist Maria Stallo for her assistance on the Betty Riley case.

I have consulted with dozens of attorneys throughout my career, and have found that virtually all of them represented their clients zealously. Those whose cases are described in this book are: James Spurlock, Vic Navy, Michael Gibson, James Shields, Patrick Wilson, Ronnie Sheets, Gail Michaelson, Zoe Shavers, Jack Laishley, Crista Conway, Charles Houdyschel, Robert Wilkinson, Donald Wandling, Tim Lupardus, Brian Kornbrath, Arden Curry III, Neil Bouchillon and Robby Long.

Last, I greatly appreciate those who read the manuscript version of this book and provided valued feedback on it. They are Dr. Dwight Harshbarger, Dr. Jennifer Tiano, Dr. Sarah Jarvis, and especially Cabell Public Defender Services Director Robert Wilkinson, who wrote the Foreword.

To contact the author regarding speaking engagements or other consulting: wyatt@marshall.edu